BRUISER
The World's Most Dangerous Wrestler

Other publications from Crowbar Press

Inside Out
by Ole Anderson, with Scott Teal
Wrestlers Are Like Seagulls
by James J. Dillon, with Scott Teal
Assassin: The Man Behind the Mask
by Joe Hamilton, with Scott Teal
"Is That Wrestling Fake?"
by Ivan Koloff, with Scott Teal
Bruiser Brody
by Emerson Murray, edited by Scott Teal
Wrestling with the Truth
by Bruno Lauer, edited by Scott Teal
The Solie Chronicles
by Bob Allyn, with Pamela S Allyn/Scott Teal
Wrestling in the Canadian West
by Vance Nevada
Long Days and Short Pays
by Hal West, edited by Scott Teal
Drawing Heat
by Jim Freedman
ATLAS: Too Much, Too Soon
by Tony Atlas, with Scott Teal
The Last Laugh
by Bill De Mott, with Scott Teal
HOOKER
by Lou Thesz, with Kit Bauman
The Last Outlaw
by Stan Hansen, with Scott Teal
NIKITA
by Nikita Koloff, as told to Bill Murdock
The Strap
by Roger Deem
BRISCO
by Jack Brisco, as told to Bill Murdock
The Mighty Milo
by Phillips Rogers
"I Ain't No Pig Farmer!"
by Dean Silverstone, with Scott Teal
The Hard Way
by Don Fargo, with Scott Teal
Whatever Happened to Gorgeous George?
by Joe Jares
"It's Wrestling, Not Rasslin'!"
by Mark Fleming, edited by Scott Teal
**BRUISER
The World's Most Dangerous Wrestler**
by Richard Vicek, edited by Scott Teal
The Mat, the Mob & Music
by Tom Hankins, edited by Scott Teal
**BREAKING KAYFABE
THEY CALL ME BOOKER**
by Jeff Bowdren, edited by Scott Teal
BATTLEGROUND VALHALA
by Michael Majalahti, edited by Scott Teal

Florida Mat Wars: 1977
by Robert D. VanKavelaar, with Scott Teal
When It Was Real
by Nikita Breznikov, with Scott Teal
The Annotated Fall Guys
by Marcus Griffin,
annotated by Steve Yohe & Scott Teal
Pain Torture Agony
by Ron Hutchison, with Scott Teal
Raising Cain: From Jimmy Ault to Kid McCoy
by Frankie Cain & Scott Teal
Master of the Ring
by Tim Hornbaker
Tonight! Tonight! Tonight!
by Bert Prentice & Scott Teal

— Wrestling Archive Project —
by Scott Teal
Volume #1 • Volume #2

– Through the Lens ... Through the Ropes –
Compiled by Scott Teal
— Volume #1 —
Southeastern Championship Wrestling
— Volume #2 —
Championship Wrestling from Florida
— Volume #3 —
All South Wrestling Alliance

— The Great Pro Wrestling Venues —
Volume #1 — Madison Square Garden
by Scott Teal & J Michael Kenyon
Volume #2 — Nashville, volume 1
by Scott Teal & Don Luce
Volume #3 — Alabama: 1931-1935
by Jason Presley
Volume #4 — Japan
by Haruo Yamaguchi,
with Koji Miyamoto & Scott Teal
Volume #5 — Knoxville: 1905-1960
Volume #6 — Knoxville: 1961-1991
by Tim Dills & Scott Teal
Volume #7 — Amarillo: 1911-1960
Volume #8 — Amarillo: 1961-1997
by Kriss Knights & Scott Teal

— Classic Arena Programs —
Volumes #1-2 — SLAM-O-GRAM
Volumes #3-4 — Florida
Volume #5 — Knoxville
Volumes #6-8 — St. Louis

BRUISER

The World's Most Dangerous Wrestler

by Richard Vicek

Edited by Scott Teal

CROWBAR PRESS

Gallatin, Tennessee

BRUISER

The World's Most Dangerous Wrestler

Copyright © 2016 by Richard Vicek

All rights reserved. No part of this book may be reproduced or transmitted in any form or by any means, electronic or mechanical, including photocopying, recording, or by any information storage and retrieval system, without permission in writing from the publisher.

Published by Crowbar Press
106 Tattnal Court
Gallatin, Tennessee 37066

http://www.crowbarpress.com

Book layout and cover design by Scott Teal

Library of Congress Cataloging-in-Publication Data

Vicek, Richard
    BRUISER: The World's Most Dangerous Wrestler / by Richard Vicek

1. Vicek, Richard.   2. Sports—United States—Biography.   3. Wrestling—United States—Biography.   I. Title.

Printed in the United States of America
ISBN 978-1-940391-07-6

First Edition / March 2016
Second printing / May 2016
Third printing / March 2017
Fourth printing / September 2018
Fifth printing / August 2020
Sixth printing / September 2021

Table of Contents

Dedication	8
Acknowledgements	9
Introduction	13
Foreword by Chuck Marlowe	16

PART I - The Evolution of the Bruiser (1929-1954)

1. Not So Humble Beginnings (1929-46)	18
2. Hard Knocks at Purdue (1947-48)	28
3. Hard Knocks Continue at Nevada (1950-51)	33
4. As Wide As He Was Tall (1951-54)	38

PART II - Quick Rise to Main Events (1955-1963)

5. I Just Acted Naturally (1955)	44
6. A Voice Like A Ruptured Foghorn (1956)	54
7. A Night to Remember (1957-58)	60
8. No Lilacs, Bobby Pins, or Peroxide (1958)	64
9. I Created A Monster (1959-63)	68
10. I Got In A Fight (1963)	82
11. Spreading The Mayhem (1959-63)	90

PART III - Co-Executive Producer and Co-Star (1964-1974)

12. Build A Better Mousetrap (1964)	97
13. Championship Wrestling Inc. (1964-65)	102
14. The Pfefer Experiment (1963-65)	120
15. Chicago Wrestling Club, Inc. (1966-68)	128
16. Yippies, Dippies, Hippies (1969)	136
17. Comiskey Cage Contest (1970-71)	142
18. Making Money ... and Lots of It (1972)	150
19. The Sheik vs. The Bruiser (1973-74)	158

PART IV - Slow Fall from Grace (1975-1991)

20. Ten Year Decline Begins (1975-76)	170
21. Another Bruiser Arrives (1977-79)	178
22. Continued Lethargy (1980-83)	183
23. Bruiser's Last Stand (1984-90)	194
24. The Final Fall (1991)	203
25. Epilogue	205
Photo Gallery	209
Index	228

CHAPTER CONTENTS

PART I
The Evolution of the Bruiser (1929-1954)

1. Not So Humble Beginnings (1929-46)
Born June 27, 1929 ... Childhood in Delphi ... Biggest House in Town ... Family Moves to Indianapolis ... Shortridge High School ... Varsity Football at Shortridge ... Lives in YMCA in Lafayette ... Death of Walter William Afflis ... All-State Football ... Amateur Wrestling

2. Hard Knocks at Purdue (1947-48)
Beta Theta Pi ... Freshman Football ... Sophomore Football ... 1948 Opener at Notre Dame ... Disappointing Season ... Post-Purdue Activities ... First Marriage

3. Hard Knocks Continue at Nevada (1950-51)
Scholarship Offer ... Practice Squad ... NFL Draft ... First Wrestling Exhibition ... Bruiser's Mother Remarries ... Nevada Cancels Football Program ... Second Marriage

4. As Wide As He Was Tall (1951-54)
After Lambeau, Before Lombardi ... 1951 NFL Season ... 1952 NFL Season ... 1953 NFL Season ... March of Dimes Telethon ... Professional Wrestling Initiation ... 1954 NFL Season

PART II
Quick Rise to Main Events (1955-1963)

5. I Just Acted Naturally (1955)
Debuts in Minnesota ... Bronko Nagurski in Winnipeg ... Impresses Jack Lanza ... Kohler's Chicago Territory ... Marigold Debut ... International Amphitheatre Debut ... Midwest Expansion ... Faces Major Wrestling Stars ... Returns to Indianapolis ... National Publicity

6. A Voice Like A Ruptured Foghorn (1956)
Amphitheatre Main Event ... Wilbur Snyder, Opponent ... Publicity in *Life* Magazine ... Milwaukee County Stadium ... Feud with Antonino Rocca

7. A Night To Remember (1957-58)
Madison Square Garden Debut ... Fundraiser in Boston ... Riot in New York City ... State Athletic Commission

8. No Lilacs, Bobby Pins, or Peroxide (1958)
Faces Gorgeous George ... One-Man Parade ... Bruiser Defeats George ... Fort Wayne Sequel

9. I Created A Monster (1959-63)
Doyle and Barnett Launch Promotion ... Opening Night at the Olympia ... A Who's Who of Wrestling ... University of Detroit ... Cowboy Bob Ellis ... Leaping Larry Chene ... Antonino Rocca Returns ... Ongoing Feud with Bobo Brazil ... Tiger Stadium

10. I Got In A Fight (1963)
Feud with Lord Athol Layton ... Detroit Sports, 1963 ... Karras Suspended by NFL ... Lindell Athletic Club ... The Morning After ... Grudge Match at the Olympia ... Legal Headaches ... JFK

11. Spreading The Mayhem (1959-63)
Bruiser as a Heel ... Indianapolis ... Atlanta ... Los Angeles ... Cincinnati ... Louisville ... San Francisco ... St. Louis, The One-Town Territory ... Debut in St. Louis ... Feud With Fritz Von Erich ... Warning From Sam Muchnick ... Minneapolis ... At Home in Indianapolis

PART III
Co-Executive Producer and Co-Star (1964-1974)

12. Build A Better Mousetrap (1964)
Indianapolis Wrestling ... Bruiser and Snyder Become Partners ...Bruiser Goes to Los Angeles ... Bruiser Wins WWA Title ... Debut of WWA in Indianapolis

13. Championship Wrestling Inc. (1964-65)
Bruiser and Snyder Go Into Business ... Booking Calendar ... Harem Lounge ... Television Interviews ... Ballpark Spectacular ... Wrestling Business in Indianapolis ... Reliable Employees

Chapter Contents • 7

... Expanding the Territory ... Supporting Cast ... Finishing Up in Los Angeles ... The Fate of Barnett and Estes ... Back to Detroit ... First Card at Fairgrounds Coliseum ... Feud with the Funks ... Wrestling Giant Baba in Japan ... Raymond Louis Heenan

14. The Pfefer Experiment (1963-65)
The Jack Pfefer Era ... A New Partner for Kohler ... Bruiser Returns to the Amphitheatre ... Tag Team Titles in Minneapolis ... Action in Chicago ... Chicago Wrestling Club, Inc.

15. Chicago Wrestling Club, Inc. (1966-68)
The Three Amigos ... AWA vs. WWA Titles ... Successful Momentum ... Bruiser's Mother Dies ... Regular TV and Arena Work ... Kansas City Chaos ... Arrival of Dick Beyer ... New Talent in Chicago and Indianapolis

16. Yippies, Dippies, Hippies (1969)
The Chain Gang ... Tag Team Champions in Japan ... AWA Invasion in Los Angeles

17. Comiskey Cage Contest (1970-71)
Return to Comiskey Ballpark ... Mad Dog and Butcher Vachon ... Baron Von Raschke ... Business Story From Louisville ... Bob Luce Wrestling ... Feud with Harley Race ... Return to Detroit ... Sam Menacker Arrives

18. Making Money ... and Lots of It (1972)
Blackjacks Lanza and Mulligan ... Talented Roster ... WRTV-TV, Channel 6 ... First Expo Center Card ... TV Taping from the Expo Center ... Soldier Field Spectacular ... Blackjacks Depart WWA

19. The Sheik vs. The Bruiser (1973-74)
Wrestling War in Detroit ... Banned from St. Louis ... Peace Treaty Between Bruiser and The Sheik ... Handsome Jimmy Valiant ... The Texas Outlaws ... Ernie Ladd ... The Valiant Brothers ... Bruno Sammartino ... Bruiser and Sheik Make Peace, Outside the Ring ... Charity Softball Game ... Bobby Heenan Leaves ... The Business of Professional Wrestling ... Private Finances ... Cutting up the Pie ... Payoff Formula

PART IV
Slow Fall from Grace (1975-1991)

20. Ten Years of Decline Begins (1975-76)
Sgt. Jacques Goulet and the Legionnaires ... Ox Baker ... Handsome Johnny Starr ... Challenger to Jack Brisco ... Gunshots at the Amphitheatre ... More New Faces ... Last AWA Tag Title Reign ... Challenger to Terry Funk ... Muhammad Ali vs. Antonio Inoki

21. Another Bruiser Arrives (1977-79)
The Masked Strangler ... Ivan Koloff ... Angelo Mosca ... Pepper Gomez ... Missouri State Title ... Lawsuit by International Championship Wrestling ... King Kong Brody ... Another "Bruiser" Contender

22. Continued Lethargy (1980-83)
Decline in Business ... David Letterman Connection ... Sam Muchnick Farewell ... *"Curiouser and curiouser!"* ... Challenger to Ric Flair ... The Escapist ... Memphis Experiment ... Menacker Leaves ... David McLane Arrives ... Divorce in Chicago ... Wilbur Snyder Retires ... State Tax Lawsuit ... The WWF Invades St. Louis ... There's Only One Bruiser

23. Bruiser's Last Stand (1984-90)
The Road Warriors ... Final Run for the WWA ... Wrestlers Remember ... Lean Times for the WWA ... The Vogue ... Super Clash I ... Bruiser Bedlam ... Final Twin Cities Visit ... Leon Spinks ... Starrcade 1990 ... High School Benefit Card

24. The Final Fall (1991)
Pays Respects to Dr. Holladay ... Events of 1991 ... November 9, 1991 ... November 10, 1991 ...Congressional Tribute ... Distinguished Service to Veterans

25. Epilogue
Remarkable 62 Years ... Wrestling Magazine Ratings ... Associates Speak Out ... Farewell

Dedication

To my loving wife, Arlene Vicek — for providing ceaseless encouragement for this project.

To my dad, Richard Vicek, my mom, Marion Vicek, and my sister, Rosemarie Gould — for patiently tolerating my obsession with pro wrestling since childhood.

To my cousins, Raymond J. Best and John J. O'Keeffe — for attending countless "Bruiser" wrestling cards with me in the 1970s.

Acknowledgements

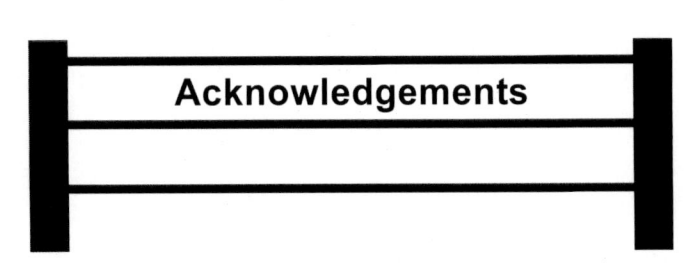

The successful completion of this project would not have been possible without the assistance of more than 240 people who shared their experiences, observations, and collectibles concerning Dick the Bruiser. Whether through an interview or written correspondence, they provided the little pieces necessary to create the big story of Bruiser. There was a small group of individuals who were true standouts and are listed here in the order they got involved with the project.

• **Ted Kundrat**, my college classmate and valedictorian from St. Joseph's College of Indiana, spent many hours doing library research and reviewing the transcript drafts for the Bruiser's pre-wrestling years.

• **The late Chuck Marlowe**, the Bruiser's Shortridge High School classmate and long-time voice of professional wrestling in Indianapolis, provided multiple interviews, written responses, and the foreword to this book.

• **Chris Parsons**, who wrestled as Mike DuPree and was the former webmaster of www.rasslinrelics.com, gave multiple interview sessions, reviewed the transcript drafts during the Bruiser's wrestling years, and shared his wrestling collection. Nobody else spent more time helping the author with the project than Chris.

• **Dorothy Mills Newman**, Bruiser's grammar school classmate in Delphi, Indiana, spent considerable time on the telephone locating other interview candidates and searching old newspaper archives in Delphi.

• The late **Les Wilson**, Bruiser's high-school classmate from Jefferson High School and alumni newsletter editor, put me in touch with all Bruiser's still-living classmates.

• The late **Norman Willey**, who passed away at age 95 in 2012, served as football coach and the first wrestling coach at Jefferson High School during the Bruiser's years, and met with the author no less than three separate times.

• **Robert Hall**, from Beta Theta Pi of Indiana, put me in touch with Bruiser's still-living fraternity brothers from Purdue University.

• The late **Jerry Wyness**, Bruiser's football teammate at the University of Nevada, answered multiple questionnaires and put me in contact with other teammates.

• **Rick Johnson**, antique dealer from Indianapolis, provided access to his unpublished photographs of the Indianapolis wrestling scene in the mid-1960s.

• The late **James Mandl** gave full access to his Detroit 1960s wrestling archives.

- **George "the Authority" Schire**, the foremost expert on the AWA, provided several interviews and rare photographs.
- **Tom Lynch**, 13-year veteran of the Bruiser's promotion and long-time gym owner in South Bend, Indiana, provided countless hours reminiscing on Bruiser's territory during its heyday.
- The late **James C. Zordani**, long-time wrestling webmaster known as "the Clawmaster," performed countless hours doing research compilations of Dick the Bruiser's wrestling record from the 1950s through the 1980s.
- Throughout this project, two Chicago area friends, **Richard Tito** and **Glen Rylko**, have been there for me for regular discussions and generous sharing of their wrestling collections.
- Another Chicagoan, **Allan Fujara,** provided me with access to his vast audio tape and printed wrestling collections, as well as his never-ending enthusiasm for the project.
- **Rob Bauer**, who has observed and written about the Detroit professional wrestling scene for seven decades, granted multiple interviews and provided many illustrations.
- **Dennis** and **Tom Holladay,** associated with the Fire Department in Lafayette, Indiana, provided profound insights into their former guardian (Bruiser) and shared rare photographs.
- **William Ondecko** provided numerous photos he took during the early 1970s.
- **Greg Oliver,** producer of *SLAM! Wrestling* website and co-author of many wrestling books, provided interview assistance and gave the author his first online publication opportunities.
- **Scott Romer**, outstanding wrestling photographer and former son-in-law of Bruiser, furnished many photographs and granted countless discussion sessions.
- **Maureen Power**, graduate of the University of Dayton, provided steady assistance with records management.
- **Tim Replogle**, formerly known as the Golden Lion and former son-in-law to Dick the Bruiser, provided multiple interview sessions and access to his archives. Replogle has wrestled as Dick the Bruiser Jr. since the year 2000.
- **David Chestnut**, long-time Bruiser fan from Indiana, spent many long hours helping the author locate interview sources using social media.
- **Tim Tassler,** wrestling researcher from Fort Wayne, Indiana, provided abundant material from Bruiser's long career in that city and helped the author with a variety of assignments.
- My longtime co-worker from my real life job, **Corey Gabel**, has provided longtime encouragement for the project and reviewed the entire draft transcripts.
- Another longtime co-worker, **James Schweitzer**, should be thanked for long-time pop culture dialogues with the author.
- The author sincerely wants to thank **Sharon Luce** and **Robin Luce** for allowing the inclusion of photographs of legendary Chicago wrestling promoter, **Robert A. Luce**.
- Finally, **Scott Teal**, the editor, layout artist, and publisher of this biography, provided countless suggestions and additions to the manuscript.

Acknowledgements • 11

The following provided assistance to the author:
- Phyllis Moore Davis, Carroll County Museum, Delphi, Indiana
- Phyllis Porter, Carroll County Museum, Delphi, Indiana
- Mary Bewley, Indianapolis Public Schools, Indianapolis, Indiana
- Les Huddle, Lafayette School Corporation, Lafayette, Indiana
- Kelly Coleman, Lafayette School Corporation, Lafayette, Indiana
- Thomas Miller, Jefferson High School, Lafayette, Indiana
- Mark Vopelak, Indiana State Library, Indianapolis, Indiana
- Brett Abercrombie, Indiana State Library, Indianapolis, Indiana
- Marcia Iles, Purdue University, West Lafayette, Indiana
- Stephanie Schmitz, Purdue University, West Lafayette, Indiana
- Chad Hartley, Sports Information, University of Nevada, Reno, Nevada
- George Rugg, University of Notre Dame, South Bend, Indiana
- Rose Hoshaw, Delphi Public Library, Delphi, Indiana
- Lee Brumbaugh, Nevada Historical Society, Reno, Nevada
- Robert Blankenship, *Rensselaer Republican*, Rensselaer, Indiana
- Heather Johnson, Lake County Discovery Museum, Wauconda, Illinois
- Anne Wells, Chicago Film Archives, Chicago, Illinois
- Gretchen Snelling, Indianapolis Motor Speedway, Indianapolis, Indiana
- Jacob Sorensen, University of Utah, Salt Lake City, Utah
- Heather Greenburg, The Topps Company, New York, New York
- Angela Jun, The Topps Company, New York, New York
- Karen Grau, Calamari Productions, Indianapolis, Indiana
- Mike Roupas, Beta Theta Pi Fraternity, Oxford, Ohio
- Vicki Underhill, Dickinson County Library, Iron Mountain, Michigan
- Jason Schlafer, University of Kentucky, Lexington, Kentucky
- Aries Tabique, National Football League, New York, New York
- Laura Weston-Elchert, The *News-Sentinel*, Fort Wayne, Indiana
- Alan King, *Milwaukee News-Sentinel*, Milwaukee, Wisconsin
- Edward Policy, The Green Bay Packers, Green Bay, Wisconsin
- Mark Vopelak, University of Indianapolis, Indianapolis, Indiana
- Greg Perrotto, *Rensselaer Republican*, Rensselaer, Indiana

Several individuals conducted interviews on behalf of the author.
- **Lanny Poffo**, ex-WWF performer, conducted an interview with his dad, Angelo Poffo, about six months prior to Angelo's death.
- Veteran wrestling photographer, **Dr. Mike Lano**, interviewed wrestling legend Bruno Sammartino.
- Wrestling journalist, **Greg Oliver** did rare interviews with Cowboy Bob Ellis and the late Hans Schmidt.
- **Tim Tassler** conducted several other interviews, including Fred Curry.

The author would also like to thank these professional wrestling historians and authors for their insights during the production. These individuals were generous with this first-time biographer: Tim Hornbaker, George Lentz, Don Luce, Larry Matysik, Jeff Walton, J Michael Kenyon, and the late Fred Hornby.

Many individuals did research of newspaper microfilm to find material on the career of the Bruiser. The author thanks Len Lupo, Jessica Lupo, Julie Lupo, Nick Strok, Martha Carranza, Ramona Carter, Jean Scigliano, Beverly Lawrence, Jennifer Thomason, Kristin Hylek, Eric Akiwumi, Elizabeth Ewing, and Anne Rosen.

The author wants to thank Indiana attorneys Victor Indiano of Indianapolis and Jeremy Gayed of Fort Wayne for their guidance in the production of this biography.

Finally, the author salutes these people who have passed away since their initial contact with the author.

- From Bruiser's grammar and high school years: Arthur Bradshaw, J. Dan Hull, James Allerdice, and Donald Ambler.
- From his college years: Patrick Brady, William "Moose" Skowran, Angelo Brucato, John Gonda, William Feldkircher, Bob Meeker, and Gwen Baxter.
- From the Green Bay Packer years: Arthur Daley.
- From the wrestling world: Sir Oliver Humperdink, Joe Blanchard, Ed Chuman, Jackie Fargo, Dutch Savage, Dennis Hall, Doug Gilbert, Edward Gersh, Mad Dog Vachon, Bob Geigel, Don Manoukian, Ox Baker, Percival A. Friend, Don Fargo, Stan Lisowski, and Nick Bockwinkel.
- From the business world: Douglass Shortridge, Johnny Lattner, Roy Powers, and John Anderson.

Introduction

Our story is based on the grand entertainment spectacle known as professional wrestling. Professional wrestling debuted on network television on the defunct DuMont network from Chicago in 1949. Colorful early performers such as Gorgeous George, Lou Thesz, Verne Gagne, Antonino Rocca, Buddy Rogers, Killer Kowalski, Gypsy Joe, and Yukon Eric captured the imagination of the American public. In the 1950s, people may have been exposed to professional wrestling because their grandmother was screaming at the small figures on a small black-and-white TV set. Or they may have become aware of professional wrestling in the '60s and '70s when it was telecast in various timeslots on the newly introduced UHF TV frequency (although, usually not during prime time). Later, professional wrestling heightened TV exposure on the new phenomenon of cable TV beginning in the late 1970s on Atlanta's WTBS-TV, and WOR-TV out of Secaucus, New Jersey.

Professional wrestling would evolve into many local and/or regional business structures with about 30 wrestling geographical territories in Mexico, Canada, and the United States. The territorial promoters would hire wrestling talent, stage live wrestling events within that territory, and utilize television or newspapers to promote their talent and events. As a rule, the owners/promoters would confine their operations to that particular geographic area. Their employees, the wrestlers, would travel from territory to territory, selling their services and performing until it was time to move on to the next territory.

By 1985, the professional wrestling business in North America witnessed several ups and downs in business cycles. Many of the territorial promoters organized themselves under the banner of "Pro Wrestling USA" to fend off the largest and most rapidly growing of all the territories — The World Wrestling Federation (WWF), now known as World Wrestling Entertainment (WWE). In 1985, the WWF was led by its controlling owner, chief executive, and principal broadcast personality, Vincent Kennedy McMahon. For many years, McMahon confined his operations to the northeastern seaboard of the United States. However, in late 1983, he embarked on his first successful attempt at a coast-to-coast professional wrestling promotion. He hired star talent from other territories, most notably Hulk Hogan, Randy (Macho Man) Savage, Bobby (The Brain) Heenan, Paul (Mr. Wonderful) Orndorff, The Junkyard Dog, "Rowdy" Roddy Piper and countless other personalities. The WWF purchased time slots on television stations once controlled by the other wrestling promoters and began showing a nationally syndicated wrestling program that appealed to fans from coast-to-coast. The WWF staged wrestling events in many of the same venues and arenas the local territorial promoters previously rented.

In response to the WWF momentum, the newly formed "Pro Wrestling USA" members staged *Super Clash I* on September 28, 1985, at Chicago's Comiskey Park. Comiskey Park had a distinguished history; not only as the home of baseball's Chicago White Sox, but as the location for several legendary wrestling matches. On September 5, 1911, George Hackenschmidt defeated Frank Gotch there, while on June 30, 1961, Buddy Rogers won the National Wrestling Alliance (NWA) heavyweight championship from Pat O'Connor in what was the largest box office gate in professional wrestling history at that point. Now, more than 24 years later, 13 wrestling matches were scheduled that night.

Ten of the matches on the card entailed championship wrestling titles associated with the various territories. In the eighth match of the night, a 56-year-old veteran workhorse of a wrestler, Dick the Bruiser, was a participant in the NWA six-man tag team title match. He teamed with Crusher (Reggie Lisowski) and Baron Von Raschke (Jim Raschke) to challenge the champions, Ivan Koloff, Nikita Koloff and Krusher Khruschev.

Bruiser's real name was William Franklin Afflis. He became a full-time professional wrestler in January 1955 — some 30 years earlier. During his years in the squared circle, Bruiser headlined professional wrestling events in New York, Boston, Chicago, Detroit, St. Louis, Indianapolis, Cincinnati, Los Angeles, Milwaukee, Atlanta, and many other cities (including Japan), and held many singles and tag team titles during his illustrious career. He also co-owned successful wrestling promotions, beginning in the mid-1960s in Chicago and Indianapolis, which enabled him to serve both as the producer and the leading performer in the show. This made him one of the higher-paid individuals in the professional wrestling business.

However, on that cool autumn night in 1985, things had changed considerably.

Bruiser no longer was the big draw and top performer he had been from the '50s through the early '70s. He and his regular tag team partners were not in the main event that night and there were five higher-profile bouts scheduled after their match. His team didn't hold the title, either, and they ultimately lost the title challenge. Taking all that into account, he didn't receive a large

Replica poster of the SuperClash '85 card
Created by Scott Teal

share of the talent payoffs since most of the money went to the main-event wrestlers.

There was a new generation of wrestling superstars at *SuperClash I* that night, namely Ric Flair, Stan Hansen, Magnum T.A., Rick Martel, The Road Warriors, Sgt. Slaughter, and the Fabulous Freebirds. While there were respectable cheers when Bruiser was introduced to the 20,347 fans in attendance (reported as 25,000), it was a far cry from the thunderous hysteria and passion of prior decades. Longtime fans and observers of Dick the Bruiser realized the proverbial show was over and his best days were memories.

Bruiser was no longer an owner of a meaningful territorial promotion, either, as his limited promotional activities were usually confined to small-town fairs or high-school gyms. That night in 1985 would be Dick the Bruiser's final appearance as a professional wrestler on a significant wrestling card. The last hurrah would be at the same old ballpark where Bruiser had once been one of the headline attractions.

What happened to the professional wrestling business in the 30 years since Dick the Bruiser became a full time wrestler in the northern Midwest states?

How did this native of Indiana develop his athletic potential and personality during his youth?

How did this budding athlete utilize the sport of football to distinguish himself at the two high schools he attended?

What happened after he won football scholarships to both Purdue University and then University of Nevada?

What was it like being drafted by the Green Bay Packers and playing on losing teams during the dark days of the National Football League, prior to large TV audiences and big money?

How did Afflis break into professional wrestling and make a reputation for himself as Dick the Bruiser?

How did he apply his primary asset, namely his physical strength and appearance, into a lucrative career for so many decades?

What did Bruiser do to expand his professional wrestling career into becoming a controlling partner in the ownership of companies promoting the sport?

Who were some of the professional wrestling personalities Bruiser employed and developed over the years?

What skills did Bruiser utilize to develop his cast of characters and create the story lines of his wrestling promotions?

What do members of the professional wrestling fraternity recall and remember about this monster of the mat?

How did Bruiser and his business partners react when business models for the professional wrestling industry changed in the 1980s?

These are just a few of the subjects we will explore in the pages that follow.

Foreword
by Chuck Marlowe

I first met Bill Afflis in the fall 1943 when we both enrolled as freshmen at Shortridge High School in Indianapolis after graduating from Indianapolis public grade schools. It was football season, and freshman football coach Roy Aberson quickly recognized that Bill was more talented and had a greater passion for the game than other 14-year-olds. In the early 1940s, most high schools did not have a weight room, and that held true at Shortridge. So, in order to build his body, Bill worked out regularly at Hoffmeister's gym in downtown Indianapolis, and could be seen walking the halls at school, between classes, doing the Charles Atlas Dynamic Tension exercise — bicep against tricep, one arm against the other. Bill, as a young man, was tough and rugged, and rumor had it he used to stand outside a local bar and antagonize the patrons into a fight. However, at school, I never witnessed him involved in any fights.

Bill left Shortridge after his sophomore year and enrolled at Jefferson High School in Lafayette. I didn't see him again until after his high-school years when he was a lifeguard at Riviera Swim Club in Indianapolis. By that time, Bill had grown to about 260 lbs. of solid muscle. When kids at the pool teased him by splashing him with water, he would respond by reaching into the pool and pulling them out with one arm. Those actions created quite a show. Around that time, it also was reported that he would frequent a local drive-in restaurant and, while seated in his car, would insult people. When they approached his car, ready for a fight, he would step out and flex his muscles, and that would end any idea of taking him on.

I pretty much lost contact with Bill during his college years. He was kicked out of Purdue University after a confrontation with line coach Jack Mollenkopf, had a brief stay at the University of Notre Dame, and ended up at the University of Nevada. He played four years with the Green Bay Packers. The next thing I knew, William Franklin Afflis was known as Dick the Bruiser — "The World's Most Dangerous Wrestler."

By 1957, Dick was one of the headliners in pro wrestling, and I began my career as a wrestling announcer. I was tutored by Sam Menacker, former wrestler and star of the movie *Mighty Joe Young*. *Big Time Wrestling* was promoted by Jim Barnett, Johnny Doyle and Balk Estes and featured all the top names: Gorgeous George Wagner, Lou Thesz, Cowboy Bob Ellis, Verne Gagne, Wilbur Snyder, and Dick the Bruiser.

As a football player, Afflis was recognized as an athlete with a high "pain threshold." His ability to rebound from physical trauma was demonstrated on many occasions. While a Green Bay Packer, Afflis lost one of his biceps while tackling an opponent. Dick said later this was probably the worst pain he had ever endured. Yet later, as Dick the Bruiser, while appearing on a wrestling card in Cincinnati, he was jumped by an angry fan who slashed him savagely with a knife or straight-edged razor. Dick protected his face and neck, but suffered a deep gash to his arm, which required several stitches to repair. Dick refused to go to the hospital. Instead, he instructed the commission doctor to bring him two six-packs of beer and to sew him up there in the locker room. All of this was to the amazement of the wrestlers who had witnessed the attack.

Bruiser was hated and despised by the fans in those days, but in subsequent years, when Bruiser and Wilbur Snyder became promoters, Bruiser was considered a hero, rather than a heel. And yet, Dick didn't change his style of wrestling one bit. Fans seemed to accept that he no longer was the bad guy he had been perceived to be for such a long time. Bruiser and Snyder ran their business, "Championship Wrestling, Inc.," with a professional attitude, and during their tenure, Championship Wrestling, Inc., drew big crowds at every venue.

By 1970-71, my other professional commitments made it difficult to continue with *Championship Wrestling*, and I relinquished my role as wrestling announcer to Sam Menacker, my mentor. During my 14-year sojourn with *Big Time* and *Championship Wrestling*, I became good friends with Dick and Wilbur and enjoyed many personal experiences with them.

Richard Vicek, the author of this work, has to be complimented for the thoroughness of his research in the writing of this book. I am amazed by the number of contacts and personal interviews — former classmates (high school and college), personal friends, and teammates. Also amazing is the number of photographs and illustrations he has compiled. This book is for the fans of professional wrestling who grew up during the "Dick the Bruiser" era, and I believe Dick would have felt honored to have been profiled in such a complete and professional manner.

Charles W. Marlowe, Indianapolis, Indiana
July 2014

Author's note:
Chuck Marlowe had a long and distinguished career broadcasting sports in Indianapolis, for which he was elected to the Indiana Broadcast Pioneer Hall of Fame in 2008. For 29 years, Chuck was the host of *The Bobby Knight Show*, which featured the head coach of the three-time NCAA Division I men's basketball championship teams from Indiana University, of which Chuck also was the play-by-play broadcaster for 25 years. Chuck also covered the "Greatest Spectacle in Racing" for 40 years as part of the Indianapolis Motor Speedway Radio Network broadcast team. During part of that time, he also was sports director and sports anchor on WTTV-TV Channel 4 in Indianapolis. His broadcasting career crossed paths with many show business legends, such as Elvis Presley, John Wayne, Kirk Douglas, and Liberace. Chuck passed away on February 11, 2016.

Photo by Scott Romer

PART I
THE EVOLUTION OF THE BRUISER

Chapter 1
Not So Humble Beginnings — 1929-1954

— **Born June 27, 1929**

William Franklin Afflis was born Thursday, June 27, 1929, to Walter William and Margaret Louise Afflis (nee Atkison) at Home Hospital in Lafayette, Indiana. It was the exception in those days for a baby to be born in a hospital, as most babies during that era were born at home.

Walter William was born January 21, 1896, in Reed City, Michigan, to Julius and Amelia Afflis, German immigrants from Hamburg who had three other children — Karl, Gwendolyn, and Alma. Walter's background included affiliation with Duke University, the Pennsylvania Railroad, and the U.S. Army during World War I.

Margaret Afflis was born June 11, 1898, in Delphi, Indiana to Frank (1854-1928) and Harriet Atkison (1872-1926), who also had another daughter named Ethel. Frank was a partner in the prominent local bank, the A.T. Bowen Bank, where Margaret would later rise to a management role. She graduated from Delphi High School in 1916 and attended the University of Illinois. Records indicate Margaret had previously been married to a Charles H. Kirkpatrick on November 1, 1916, in Delphi.

Walter William Afflis and Margaret Louise Atkison, married on September 22, 1928, at the home of an Indiana-born dentist in Chicago's Hyde Park neighborhood, honeymooned in northern Michigan. At the time of the wedding, Mr. Afflis was professionally associated with Burton and Seal Laboratories in Chicago. The couple first lived at 217 E. Franklin Street in Delphi, which actually had been the Atkison family home for many years. Margaret bought out her sister's ownership interest.

Margaret Louise & William Franklin Afflis
1929
Source: Indiana State Museum

Herbert Hoover was the president of the United States at the time, having been elected the previous year. While campaigning for president in 1928, Hoover proclaimed, *"We in America today are nearer to the final triumph over poverty than ever before in the history of any land."* Unfortunately, the economy headed in the wrong direction and the Great Depression evolved.

Author's note: Local newspapers — The *Logansport Press*, *Logansport Pharos-Tribune*, and The *Delphi Citizen* — all provided wide coverage of the prominent Afflis family in the 1930s.

The 1930 U.S census for Delphi, taken on April 11, 1930, listed Walter's occupation as a drug store owner. The drug store included a Western Union telegraph office and soda fountain where young students would gather after school. By 1934, mother Margaret (right) would switch jobs after the closing of her bank employer by bank regulators due to the death of the primary owner. Margaret then scored a political appointment by the governor of Indiana as the manager of the Carroll County driver license bureau. Margaret also was active in political, civic, and social organizations in her native Carroll County.

Margaret Louise Afflis
Source: Indiana State Museum

— **Childhood in Delphi**

Young William, affectionately known as "Sonny," would eventually enroll in the Monroe School in Delphi and learn alongside students from both first and second grades. In 1935, young William celebrated his sixth birthday with a party attended by 26 boys and girls. Sonny's classmates, many of whom are still living, provided memories of their classmate.

Youth Bible school group at Methodist Church • Delphi, 1933
Courtesy of Arthur Bradshaw

Richard Smith of Cincinnati remembers wrestling Sonny on the sidewalk ... and winning. When Smith was first asked about Sonny, he asked the author why he was researching Afflis. Smith had no idea Sonny had wrestled professionally.

Rosella McCain Gushwa of Delphi remembers receiving a box of candy from Sonny on Valentine's Day when she was seven.

Dorothy Newell Mills of Delphi vividly remembers a young Afflis who had a keen interest in physical fitness. Dorothy visited her best friend, the late Joann Bradshaw (who lived across from the Afflis' home), and watched young Afflis doing physical exercises in the yard — pushups, head-stands, jumping jacks. Dorothy never knew if Bill realized the girls were both watching him.

Herbert Clawson of Colfax kept his school autograph book from the 1930s and shared a slice of Afflis' sense of humor with messages such as, "*Why didn't you* give me a piece of candy, you little skunk?" Clawson also said Afflis would squirt water near the zipper on Clawson's pants to give the impression that Clawson had "an accident." Young Sonny also would take piano lessons and participate in school recitals, playing a piano solo for the standard piece, "The Dirigible." (Yes, in the year after the horrific Hindenburg Disaster in Lakehurst, New Jersey)

Almost all classmates explicitly remembered that early in his school career, Afflis was sometimes dressed like the 19th century fictional character, Little Lord Fauntleroy, from the children's fiction book by the same name authored by Frances Hodgson Burnett and illustrated by Reginald Birch. Little Lord Fauntleroy wore an outfit with knee high stockings, a velvet tunic, short knickers pants, a wide lace collar, and extra-long frilly sleeves.

Young William Afflis
From room 2 class picture
October 1936
Source: Rosella M. Gushwa

— **Biggest House in Town**

In 1938, the Afflis family began renting out their home at 217 E. Franklin and purchased the biggest and most expensive house in town, which was located at 404 E. Main Street in Delphi. The home had previously been owned by the Bowen family, the same Bowens of the banking institution where Margaret and her father worked for so many years. In the 1930 U.S. census for Delphi, no residence had a higher market value. The three-story brick Victorian mansion had a large brick carriage house in the rear; so large, in fact, that it would later become a single family residence. Two of Afflis' classmates, Richard Smith and Della Herr Craig, would say there wasn't any class envy or division at that time and that kids just treated each other as kids. In 1939, mother Margaret organized and became the first president of the local chapter of the sorority Psi Iota Xi (pronounced "see eye oh tah see"). Margaret served in the organization in a leadership position for decades. The sorority continues to this day, providing college scholarships for graduates of her hometown Delphi High School.

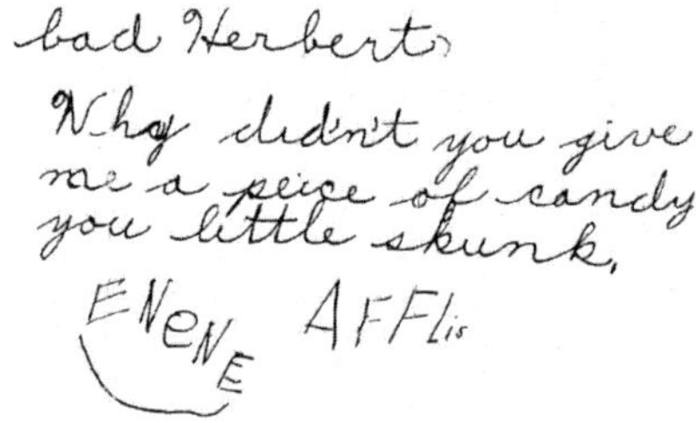

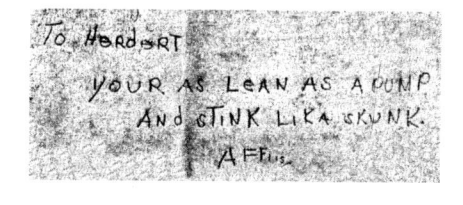

Pages from grammar school autograph book of classmate Herbert Clawson
(above) READS: Bad Herbert, Why didn't you give me a peice of candy you little skunk.
AFFLIS

(above right) READS: To Herbert - Your as lean as a pump and stink lik a skunk.
AFFLIS

Source: Herbert Clawson, Colfax IN

```
                        RECITAL

    Pupils of Lois & Kathryn McCain

    Wed. Sept 6, 1938 -7:30


    Donny Day . . . . . . . .Yankee Doodle
    Violin Trio. . . . . . Lightly Row
                          Melody . . . . . . . . . . . Haydn
         Jimmy Trent, Glenn Brown, Wilbur Lane
    Herbert Parks. . . . . . . Home on the Range. . . . . . . .
    Douglas Patton. . . . .Moccasin Dance. . . . . . .Long
    Wilbur Lane. . . . . . . The Shower. . . . . . . . .Blake
    Florence Graham. . . . What They Love. . . . . .Cramm
    Glenn Brown. . . . . . . The Little Patriot. . . .Krogman
    Dorothy and June Newell. The Cradle Song. . . . .Merrill
    Jimmy Trent. . . . . . . Russian Dance. . . . . . .Berul
    Norma Lee Nagele. . . .Ding Dong Bell. . . . . . .Cramm
    June Brookshire. . . . Familiar Tunes. . . . . . .Farris
    Normalee Ward. . . . . In the Boat. . . . . . . . Norris
    Louise Nagele. . . . . Gladys Waltz. . . . . . . .Fearis
    June Newell. . . . . . Dream Time Song. . . . . . Munn
    Sonny Afflis. . . . . .The Dirigible. . . . . . . Thompson
    Dorothy Newell. . . . .Birds Bath. . . . . . . . .Blake
    Dora Wagoner. . . . . .Evening Thoughts. . . . . .Wecker
    Gene Barnhart. . . . . .Dixie. . . . . . . . . . .Emnett
    Dorothy Clifford. . . .Little Girl Dancing. . . .O'Hara
    Bonnie Jean McCarty. . Arpeggio. . . . . . . . . .Carter
    Jean Myers. . . . . . .Theme and Variations. . . .Papini
    Rosella McCain. . . . .Minuet In G. . . . . . . . Beethoven
    Doris Landes. . . . . .Gypsy Life. . . . . . . . .Engelman
    Mary Louise Reppert. . Air Varie No. 6. . . . . . Dancla
    Dora Wagoner. . . . . .Rhapsody Espana. . . . . . Chabrier
    Mary C. Clauser. . . . Solfeggietto. . . . . . . .Bach
    Jane Brookshire. . . . Silver Sleigh Bells. . . .
    Anadel Craig. . . . . .Perpetual Motion. . . . . .Bohm
    Glenn Fisher. . . . . .The Skaters. . . . . . . . Waldteufel
    Carolyn Pearson. . . . Polish Dance. . . . . . . .Severn
    Evelyn Barnhart. . . . Gavotte. . . . . . . . . . Popper
    Violin Quartet. . . . .Annie Laurie
                           The Red Sarafan. . . . . .arr. Rissland
    Mary Louise Reppert, Anadel Craig, Joan Griffith, Carolyn Pearson
```

(above) Piano recital program, Sept. 6, 1938
Sonny Afflis played The Dirigible
Source: Rosella McCain Gushwa

(below) Family home on East Main in Delphi
Source: Carroll Country Museum

(above) From the Monroe School
Grade 5-6 class photo • 1940
Source: Carroll Country Museum

— Family Moves to Indianapolis

In 1940, statewide political developments had a profound effect on the Afflis family. On Tuesday, November 5, 1940, the same day U.S. president Franklin Delano Roosevelt was elected to his third term, sitting Lieutenant Governor of Indiana, Democrat Henry F. Schricker, was elected governor of Indiana. By early 1941, Schricker offered Margaret Afflis an appointment as director of the probation department in Indianapolis. The probation department was responsible for almost 11,000 adult and juvenile individuals on probation. Their goal was to save taxpayer money since, according to the *State of Indiana Yearbook - 1942*, probation cost less than incarceration and 80 percent of the "clients" would then go on to become useful citizens. The Afflis family kept their home in Delphi, but moved to an apartment at 1 East 28th Street at Meridian Street in Indianapolis, a few miles north of downtown where Margaret worked. With the move, father Walter became associated with a retail jeweler named Adolph Blickman at 1 North Illinois Street in downtown.

— Shortridge High School

Young William attended Public School 60 on nearby Pennsylvania Street during seventh and eighth grade. One of his report cards, which survives to this day in his mother's archives in the Indiana State Library, indicates he was a very good student. William earned a grade of B in English, math, and science, an A in social studies, industrial arts, and music, and, of course, an A+ in physical education. In spite of the exemplary grades, a teacher wrote to his parents, *"We do not feel that Bill has been doing his best work."*

After graduating from Public School 60, William was enrolled at Shortridge High School at 34th and Meridian Streets, only six blocks away from the apartment he shared with his parents, an apartment building that still operates today. Originally named Indianapolis High School, Shortridge opened in 1864 and was the state's first free, public high school. The name was changed to Shortridge in 1897 in honor of an educator named Abraham C. Shortridge. Famous alumni of Shortridge High School in Indianapolis included author Kurt Vonnegut and jazz drummer Benny Barth, but in a 1964 article in *Sport* magazine, Afflis would claim *"the only one who really made it big was Bill Afflis."* The building in which William attended classes was built in 1927 and is still in use today.

William Afflis
Shortridge High School • 1944
Source: Indianapolis Public Schools

— Varsity Football at Shortridge

By the fall of 1944, William would become one of only two sophomores to earn a spot on Shortridge's varsity football team, the other student being J.B. King, who later would become a prominent corporate attorney in Indianapolis. William also participated outside of high school in the February 1945 Golden Gloves Boxing tournament as a heavyweight.

Teammate J. Dan Hull, a senior at Shortridge that year and also a member of that same football team, remembers that *"Afflis wore number eighty-nine ... seldom played, but had great hands."* James Allerdice, who played football for Shortridge in the mid '40s, recalls that *"equipment was poor with no face guards."* Teammate Ray Schakel said, *"Afflis was so muscular that he had to cut the arm holes on his T-shirt"* and that he *"was the most muscular high school athlete I have ever seen."*

While none of William's report cards from Shortridge survive, a short school essay from February 1945 does survive as William wrote *"my ambitions, from the very day I could remember to now, are to become a great athlete, be a chemist, and join the Navy."*

During the 1940s, many high schools in the USA were segregated by race, which reflected the residential neighborhoods at the time. That was the case with Shortridge High School, as a review of the Class of 1945 yearbook (Bill's sophomore year) showed no African American students.

Political developments in Indiana once again brought on another major change for the Afflis family. In the fall 1944, Governor Schricker did not run for re-election. During that time, Indiana governors were not allowed to serve consecutive terms. As a result, mother Margaret lost her job when a Republican governor was elected. The upcoming move back to Delphi posed a problem for the young budding athlete. William would be unable to continue his football ambitions because Delphi High School did not have a football team. The situation called for a creative solution near the start of William's junior year in the fall 1945.

— Lives in YMCA in Lafayette

In the fall 1983, a grown-up Dick the Bruiser told the story to radio sports reporter, Lanny Sigo of WASK-AM in Lafayette, Indiana:

> *"My folks moved back to Delphi and there was no football team. I played two years at Shortridge. To have been able to have eligibility and play at Lafayette Jefferson [High School], I moved to the YMCA in Lafayette. I lived my junior and senior year at the old YMCA on Seventh Street. I lived here, ate here, and slept the nights here, so I was a resident of Lafayette."*

The YMCA in Lafayette was located in downtown at 107 N. 7th Street, a relatively short walk from Jefferson High School, located between 9th, 10th, Elizabeth, and Cincinnati Streets. William Afflis occupied one of 32 single-occupancy rooms at the YMCA, which also housed students from nearby Purdue University.

Classmate Harry Leader remembered, *"In 1945-47, I spent most afternoons at the YMCA, playing basketball, and most of the time, William was there pumping iron."*

William enrolled as a junior at Jefferson High School in the fall 1945. His junior-class photo shows him wearing a plain t-shirt, a "look" that several of his classmates later recalled. Classmate Robert Lennon remembered a small automobile parked in front of the YMCA each night. William would lift and bounce the automobile onto the entrance, perplexing the owner the following

(above) Jefferson High School, Lafayette, Indiana • circa 1947
(above right) Jefferson High School logo
Source: Lafayette School Corporation

morning. Occasionally, William would have dinner at the home of one of his fellow classmates. Gale Schnaible, older brother of classmate Dick Schnaible, recalls that when William was expected for dinner, his mother cooked a second chicken, just to be sure there was enough to go around.

Classmate Barbara Condra Baer also had memories of William at Jefferson High School:

"He was very polite, and the teachers seemed to like him. As far as I know, he was a good student — nothing outstanding. But then, athletes don't seem to have much time for study. Never in my recollection was [he] in any trouble with teachers, guidance counselors, or principals. ... He rarely missed school and was an extraordinary good high-school athlete. He was an excellent role model for younger athletes and was looked up to by all."

— Death of Walter William Afflis

Later in Bill's junior year, he would be faced with a personal blow that would devastate any 16-year-old. Bill's father, Walter William Afflis, then worked as regional sales supervisor for the National Optical Company, a company headquartered in downtown Chicago. On Friday night, December 14, 1945, Bill's dad was stricken with an appendicitis attack at his Chicago apartment and was taken to St. Luke's Hospital on South Wabash Avenue. Newspaper accounts indicate the hospital was not successful in attempts to notify Margaret Afflis by telephone that night. After an emergency appendectomy on Saturday, December 15, 1945, Walter William Afflis died at age 48. Military funeral rites were held on Tuesday afternoon, December 18, 1945, at the Grimm Funeral Home in Delphi. Attendees included the deceased's wife, son, mother, brother, and sisters. A military color guard and a firing squad, in addition to pallbearers consisting of local business and political leaders, all participated in the ceremony. He was buried at nearby Masonic Cemetery in Delphi in the plot next to Margaret's deceased mother and father.

Grave of Walter William Afflis
Masonic Cemetary, Delphi
Source: Richard Vicek

If Bill spent much time grieving over his father's death, it wasn't visible at high school. Several of Bill's classmates couldn't recall even knowing Bill's father had died.

— All-State Football

The primary claim to fame for Bill Afflis at Jefferson High School was when he wore jersey number 23 on the school football team during his senior year. His widowed mother, Margaret, took out an insurance policy on Bill with the Illinois Mutual Casualty Company, a policy that would pay out benefits based on the severity of a potential sports injury, such as up to $250 for the loss of sight in one eye. The head football coach at Jefferson was Marion Crawley, who later would win four Indiana high school basketball championships; two with Jefferson High School and two with Washington (IN) High School. A new assistant football coach that year was Norman Willey, a Purdue graduate who would also be the first wrestling coach when the school started a wrestling program that year.

William Afflis
Jefferson High School
1947
Source: Lafayette School Corporation

Bill's teammate, Gordon L. Manis, wrote extensively about Bill's football days at Jefferson:

"He [Afflis] was the strongest player I played with in high school and college. One time, he picked me up (210 lbs.) with one hand and threw me at the quarterback in practice. He was good — very good. He just couldn't stand being told what to do. He was a loner. I couldn't tell you anyone he socialized with."

Teammate Max Morehouse added some other comments:

"He [Afflis] was a bodybuilder and liked to show off his physique. We played on the football team together; he played guard and I played center. He was good on the football field, and he liked to hit people. I remember one time, I was hit with a cheap shot with an elbow after I was down. Bill saw it and said to me, 'Don't worry.' A few plays later, they carried that fellow [opponent] off the field. You wanted Bill as your friend, not an enemy."

Teammate Bob Field remembers another story that revealed young Bill's character:

"One time, our team traveled to Richmond [IN] for an overnight game and we had a black player, Charlie Simmes, on our team. A local hotel would not allow Charlie to register. Bill stepped up and said, 'If Charlie can't stay, we all can't stay.' And we didn't! I don't know where we went, but Coach Marion Crawley took care of us."

The Jefferson High School Broncos had an outstanding season during Bill's senior year in the fall 1946. They compiled a record of 8-0 and defeated opponents from Frankfort, Richmond, Marion, Crawfordsville, and others. The biggest game of the year was against the West Side Red Devils, rivals from adjoining West Lafayette. After a Friday night postponement due to heavy rain, Lafayette Jefferson won by a score of 20-6 in the home game played on Saturday, November 2, 1946. Afflis started at left guard that game for the final outing of his high-school football career.

> Bill Afflis, Lafayette guard, repeatedly broke through Indianapolis Tech's line ...
> *Evansville* (IN) *Courier and Press*, September 24, 1946

> Although the Bronco first line of defense was stout from end to end, at no spot was it stronger than at left guard, where Bill Afflis was a tower of power.
> *Kokomo* (IN) *Tribune*, September 28, 1946

> One big reason why the Kokomo Kats found the going rough at Lafayette was big Bill Afflis, Bronco left guard, who played a whale of a game. After the shouting had subsided, old Heze Clark, who has seen 'em all come and go, and who annually picks the Indianapolis Times' all-state football team, said, *"Boy, he [Afflis] was hotter'n a bon fire."*
> *Kokomo* (IN) *Tribune*, September 30, 1946

The following week at the sports award banquet, Afflis was awarded his official letter in football, which is now housed in his mother's special collection at the Indiana State Museum. On December 3, 1946, United Press International reported from Indianapolis that Bill Afflis had been selected as first-team left guard on the All-State high school team by a poll of coaches and sportswriters.

In fall 1946, Bill's mother ran unsuccessfully as a Democrat against Republican incumbent Charles Abraham Halleck for Congress in the second district of Indiana. Only fourteen women were running for a seat in the House of Representatives in that election. During the campaign, she was a guest of U.S. President Harry Truman in the Oval Office. In 1947, she moved to Indianapolis and, in 1949, began her second stint as Director of Probation for the State of Indiana.

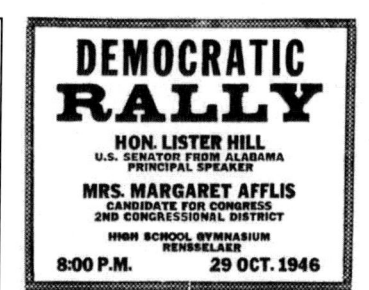

Afflis for Congress ads • 1946
Source:
(left) Kankakee Valley News, Demotte, Indiana
(above) Rensselaer Republican
Rensselaer, Indiana

— Amateur Wrestling

Bill's senior year also was the first year the high school had a sanctioned wrestling team. Afflis' senior portrait photo includes credits for being a member of the team. Purdue heavyweight wrestler Ray Gunkel (1924-1972), who later would become a top professional wrestler and promotion owner in Georgia, occasionally provided guidance to the Jefferson wrestling team. None of the few surviving newspaper clips from that year indicates Afflis participating in contests against other schools. Teammate Max Morehouse, whose name appears in some newspaper clipping, specifically remembers defeating Bill during an internal scrimmage that was needed to decide who would represent Jefferson High School in an upcoming meet against other schools. Jefferson wrestler Gordy Buck, who would become an Indiana state champion during the 1947-48 school year, does not remember Afflis ever wrestling against another school. Another Jefferson wrestler, who requested anonymity, remembers an instance where Afflis stormed out of a practice session after being solidly defeated by a teammate. While he wasn't a big star in amateur wrestling, as he was in football, Afflis was on the track team. Teammate Donald Ambler specifically credited Afflis with being a distinct leader.

Source: Indiana State Museum

Chapter 2
Hard Knocks at Purdue — 1947-1948
— Beta Theta Pi

Bill's next stop, Purdue University in West Lafayette, was only a few miles away from Jefferson High. The enrollment at Purdue was 15,784 for the 1947-48 school year. Of those, only 2,496, or 15.8 percent, were women. Bill became of a member of Beta Theta Pi and moved into the fraternity house located at 150 Littleton, which still houses fraternities today, more than 60 years later. The four-story Tudor dormitory sits atop a hill on the east side of Purdue's campus. Dick's roommate was fellow football player, Herbert Campfield, from Niles, Ohio. Fraternity brother John Merrell remembers that Afflis and Campfield were both recipients of football scholarship and were assigned to the fraternity, not recruited by existing members. The fraternity assigned Bill roll number #714. Other famous Purdue frat alumni over the years include actor George W. Peppard Jr. (#746) and legendary basketball coach John Wooden (#303).

Fraternity brother Tom Witter shared his memories about Bill and the fraternity. *"Bill Afflis was a waiter in the* [fraternity] *kitchen when I was house treasurer ... he was so barrel-chested* [in both directions] *that his arms curved over his sides."* Fraternity brother Robert Meeker recollects that Afflis was stubborn about learning the chants and songs required during the initiation into Beta Theta Pi. A photo Meeker took of the bare-chested, muscular Afflis standing on the top of the fraternity house survives to this day. (below left)

West Lafayette City Directory • 1948
Source: Tippecanoe County Library

Fraternity brother Jackson H. Teetor remembers this story:

"Someone in the group challenged Bill to a push-up duel if he [Bill] *would just use one arm. Bill agreed to the handicap and we started the count. When the count went over fifty, Bill looked over and found the competition had given up, so he stopped. We never learned how many one-arm push-ups Bill could do. Certainly, the challenger hoped to be able to brag about beating Bill."*

Fraternity brother Jack Longstreth, the president at the house at one time, recalled this about Bill:

"I had a large, heavy oak desk that I asked ... no, told Bill to carry up the three flights to my room. 'No problem, Jack,'

[Bill said] *as he grabbed the desk by the underside with the legs pointed behind him and carried that huge desk up three flights of stairs — face first — without stopping and seemingly without much effort.* [He was] *unbelievably strong."*

Bill did not appear in the fraternity group photos in the Purdue "DEBRIS" yearbooks for 1948 and 1949. Classmates believe he likely just missed the photo sessions.

— **Freshman Football**

Logo for William's fraternity
Source: Beta Theta Pi

While Bill had the benefits of a football scholarship, he was not on the varsity football team his freshman year at Purdue. A printed football program in his mother's archives indicated Bill was a starting guard and wore #70 on the freshman team during an intersquad game against the junior varsity "B" team on November 8, 1947. Afflis would later be awarded with a freshman numeral at the annual Kiwanis Club football banquet on Monday, November 25, 1947. The head coach for Purdue varsity football, also starting in 1947, was Stuart K. (Stu) Holcomb, who had a standout collegiate career as a Ohio State fullback and as an assistant football coach at Army prior to joining Purdue. Holcomb would later serve as general manager of baseball's Chicago White Sox from 1971 to 1973.

At the time, there were several individuals in the Purdue football program who would go on to become notable contributors in professional and college football. An assistant football coach for the junior varsity "B" team was Henry "Hank" Stram. Stram would later head coach the Kansas City Chiefs to a victory in the 1970 Super Bowl IV. One of the starting offensive guards at Purdue, Abraham (Abe) Gibron, would be head coach of the Chicago Bears from 1972 to 1974, while Bob DeMoss, starting quarterback from 1945 to 1948, served as head football coach at Purdue from 1970 to 1972.

— **Sophomore Football**

Bill earned his spot on the roster of the varsity football team for the 1948 season, wearing #99. Bill's teammates on the varsity included some players from his high-school years at Jefferson and Shortridge high schools. The football conference for Purdue was then called the Western Conference, or the Big Nine, not yet called "Big Ten." There were nine teams in that conference — Ohio State, Michigan, Minnesota, Purdue, Northwestern, Illinois, Indiana, Wisconsin, and Iowa, with Michigan State becoming the tenth team years later. For Purdue varsity football in 1948, there were six conference games (Northwestern, Michigan, Iowa, Illinois, Minnesota, and Indiana) and three non-conference games (Notre Dame, Marquette, and Pittsburgh).

Purdue varsity football • 1948
Source: Purdue University

Quarterback Bill Feldkircher remembers Afflis as a *"rough and tough kid who knew no fear."* In 2009, he also noted that playbooks in 1948 were simple with only 25 to 30 plays and that there were no organized weight-lifting programs because coaches believed players would get muscle-bound. Feldkircher also knew Afflis was not a starter. Another individual, who preferred to remain anonymous, said Afflis did not get a lot of playing time at Purdue. Jack Fredericks said, *"I remember he used to do handstand push-ups on the benches between our lockers ... he was very strong."* Fullback Harry Szulborski recalls Afflis being there for only a brief time during Szulborski's junior year, and that Afflis didn't last long. Several players either did not remember or did not know Afflis.

Student manager Angelo Brucato wrote to the author:

> *"Too much of what I remember is negative ... as I recall, he was not regarded favorably by the coaches. Once, while I was at the field house, he asked me for a ride home on my motorcycle. Then, as now, motorcycling tended to be somewhat dangerous. Just before Dick and I rode away, one of the varsity coaches saw us and scolded me. 'Don't you ever take any of our players for a ride on your motorcycle — except Afflis!'"*

— 1948 Opener at Notre Dame

The season opener was a big event in the fall 1948 as Purdue traveled to South Bend (IN) to face the Fighting Irish of Notre Dame, who were unbeaten in 1947 under legendary quarterback Johnny Lujack. The game for 1948 was previewed in the September 20, 1948, issue of *Time* magazine, in which Notre Dame's legendary coach, Frank Leahy, said, *"I think Purdue will beat us."* The author of the article added, *"Purdue looks like the strongest team on Notre Dame's ten-game schedule."* The game was broadcast on radio and television throughout the Midwest with Notre Dame favored by a spread of 7 to 13 points. Purdue coach Stu Holcomb only took a squad of 36 Boilermaker football players on the trip to South Bend and it does not appear that Afflis made the trip since his name was missing from team rosters in post-game summaries. Before 59,343 fans on Saturday, September 25, 1948, the Fighting Irish won the game 28 to 27. Afterwards, a reporter wrote, *"Purdue will never lose a greater football game than the one the gallant Boilermakers dropped in bulging Notre Dame stadium."*

The second game of the season was scheduled for October 2, once again on the road, against the Northwestern Wildcats. In a pre-game interview, Coach Holcomb talked about utilizing some inexperienced linemen for the Northwestern game, but Afflis was not among the players mentioned. He did, however, make the trip to Evanston and appeared in post-game summaries. Northwestern rolled over the Boilermakers by a score of 21 to 0, about which a columnist wrote afterwards, *"The Boilermaker performance at Evanston Saturday was just as bad as it sounded."*

The third game of the season was booked for October 9 at Ross-Ade Stadium in West Lafayette against the Michigan Wolverines. It was homecoming weekend at Purdue with Indiana-born music legend Hoagy Carmichael as the main entertainment attraction. In addition, the largest all-time home attendance at the game was anticipated. Afflis was dressed for the game, but whatever contribution he made couldn't help the Boilermakers. Purdue was spanked 40 to 0 by a Michigan squad led by All-American quarterback Pete Elliott. Michigan would go on to win the national championship that year.

The fourth game of the season found the Boilermakers traveling to Iowa City (IA) on October 16 to face the Hawkeyes. Purdue scored their first win of the year, defeating Iowa 20 to 13, and Afflis again appeared to have made the trip. The fifth game of the season found the team traveling to Champaign-Urbana (IL) to face the Illini of the University of Illinois on October 23, a game in which Illinois edged out Purdue by a score of 10 to 6. Afflis did not appear on the post-game roster and would never appear on any other post-game rosters for the remainder of the season.

The game against the Minnesota Gophers on November 6 (lost, 34-7), had an interesting side story as two players from Minnesota, tackle Leo Nomellini and end Verne Gagne, would later have successful professional wrestling careers with Afflis. For the full season, the Purdue varsity ended up with a losing record of 3-6, winning over Marquette (Oct. 30, 14-9) and Indiana (Nov. 20, 39-0) but losing to Pittsburgh (Nov. 13, 13-20).

— Disappointing Season

It was a disappointing season for the Boilermakers. Running back Harry Szulborski remembers team morale being "terrible" and that *"we should have won against Notre Dame."* Lineman Louis Karras, older brother of Alex Karras of Detroit Lions fame, remembered, *"We were depressed and demoralized."*

In spite of the losing season, the annual post-season Kiwanis Club awards banquet was held on Monday, November 22, 1948. 118 football players received awards from various levels, but Afflis' name was not listed in either the *Lafayette Journal and Courier* or the *Purdue Exponent*. Several of Afflis' fraternity brothers and football teammates became aware that something happened resulting in Afflis losing his football scholarship. Later, in 1983, at halftime during a Jefferson Bronco football game broadcast, Bruiser told Lanny Sigo of WASK-AM:

> *"I was at Purdue for two years before I got in a fight ... well, I got in an argument and hit him in the head. Bless his heart. He's gone now — Coach Mollenkopf. I felt that I wouldn't be treated fairly and I shouldn't have been treated fairly. I had a hot temper, and I left there to go to the University of Alabama for six weeks, and from there, to the University of Miami in Florida for six weeks."*

— Post-Purdue Activities

In December 1948, Afflis went to Miami Beach, Florida, for a vacation and stayed at the Stephen Foster Motel at 61st and Collins Avenue. There were postcards and letters from the motel in his mother's archives, including a letter from a Purdue student threatening to sue Afflis, claiming Afflis damaged his car. In addition, a letter from Purdue University's registrar noted that Afflis was no longer considered a student at Purdue since he left in the middle of his sophomore year and never returned. While at Purdue, Afflis' transcript card showed passing grades for sociology, physical education, German, biology, and speech, by no means a free ride with easy courses.

After Bill left Purdue, some Purdue students remembered him working as a bill collector for an Indianapolis department store. Jackson Teetor also remembers seeing Bill's photograph in the *Indianapolis News* as Bill was walking on his hands atop the Indianapolis Athletic Club building (corner of Meridian and Vermont Streets) in downtown Indianapolis. The photo is likely buried in rolls and rolls of unindexed newspaper microfilm archives and could not be located by the author or his associates.

— First Marriage

Sometime in late 1948 or early 1949, Bill likely courted Indianapolis-born Patricia Ann Cave. In the 1930 U.S. census for Indianapolis, her family was listed as living on Winthrop Avenue. Cave also attended Shortridge High School and is pictured in the Class of 1947 yearbook, the same class from which Afflis would have graduated if he had remained at Shortridge. Cave could have been acquainted with Afflis during their freshman and sophomore years.

Marriage license archives from Florida confirm that William F. Afflis and Patricia Ann Cave were married in Dade County, Florida in 1949. On August 7, 1949, the *Logansport* (IN) *Pharos* reported that a daughter, Judith, was born to William and Patricia Afflis at St. Vincent's Hospital on Fall Creek Road in Indianapolis. By mid-year 1950, Afflis lived with his mother in apartment #420 at the Marott Hotel at 2625 North Meridian Street in Indianapolis. The Marott is now listed in the National Register of Historic Places. At the same time, wife Patricia Afflis was living with young Judith in Florida based on documents in the Indiana state archives. Margaret Afflis stayed in contact with Patricia and occasionally sent gifts to Judith, her only granddaughter. Presumably, the marriage ended in divorce. Florida records show Patricia remarried in Dade County in 1953. Patricia had one daughter and one son with her second husband. Her last-known residence was in Seminole, Florida, where she passed away on August 15, 2002.

Purdue University, West Lafayette, Indiana
Source: Lake County Discovery Museum, Waukonda, IL; Teich postcard collection

Chapter 3
Hard Knocks Continue at Nevada — 1950-1951

— Scholarship Offer

In late July 1950, Afflis received a letter that would drastically change his life. The letter was written by Joseph Sheeketski, director of athletics and head football coach at the University of Nevada at Reno. Sheeketski played college football at the University of Notre Dame under the legendary coach Knute Rockne in the early 1930s, and later was assistant football coach at Holy Cross, Notre Dame, and Iowa. The assistant football coach at Nevada during that time was Glenn (Jake) Lawlor, who also was the varsity basketball coach. Lawlor would achieve legendary status as a Nevada basketball coach as the modern-day basketball venue is named after him — the Lawlor Events Center.

Joseph Sheeketski • 1950
Source: University of Nevada

Sheeketski offered a football scholarship to Afflis that included "room, board, tuition, fees, books, and round-trip transportation once a year." According to teammate Buddy Brooks, while at Nevada, Afflis lived in a room at the University Fieldhouse.

Afflis' resume, found in his mother's archives, listed his weight as 257 lbs., chest at 58 inches, neck at 22 inches, waist at 35 inches, biceps at 21 inches, and height at 5-foot-11 inches.

— Practice Squad

While Afflis did have the football scholarship, it should be noted that, according to modern day University of Nevada spokesman, Chad Hartley, Afflis "*never actually played at Nevada,*" as he sat out the 1950 season as a transfer. This was confirmed by Afflis' absence from the 1950 *Nevada Press and Radio Guide* and a September 23, 1950, sampled game program for Nevada vs. Texas A&M. Nonetheless, Afflis practiced with the Nevada Wolf Pack and earned accolades from his teammates. The late teammate, Patrick Brady, remembered that Afflis practiced at any position in which they put him and was well-positioned to make the varsity team the following year. Late teammate Jerry Wyness remembered these incidents:

> "*The first time I tried to block him, he shortened my height [by] about four inches, or so it felt. The second time I decided to use a cross body block, and Afflis picked me up by my head and crotch, and ran me like a horizontal beam into the fullback.*"

Teammate and lineman, the late John Gonda noted:

> "*Dick [Afflis] was a super specimen of a man. He had a body that all men love to have. He was very agile and had great quickness. He could*

do hand stands very easily and accurately — a man that you do not see too often. A very unusual thing that Dick would do occasionally when we were in the gym was to get a medicine ball [probably 10-20 lbs. in weight] and he would ask me to throw it as high as I could, and then he would let it hit [him] in the face on the way down. We all just shook our heads."

Teammate and running back Buddy Brooks reminisced:

"He [Afflis] practiced with us in 1950. His speed and quickness was impressive for a down lineman. He was so quick; he covered the field from sideline to sideline. I know this because I was in the backfield trying to run the ball against him."

Local sports columnist Ty Cobb of the *Nevada State Journal* took notice of the "massive lineman from Indianapolis" in a preview article for the 1950 season. A columnist for the rival *Reno Evening Sun* would label Afflis as *"260 lbs. of former Purdue heft."* However, the 1950 football season was something the team would like to forget as the final record was only one win and nine losses. Nevada allowed 363 points and only scored 117.

— NFL Draft

An event in January 1951 changed Afflis' life. The National Football League entry draft commenced on Thursday, January 18. In the early rounds, several players who would later become legendary names in pro football were drafted, such as Kyle Rote, Y.A. Tittle, Bill George, Andy Robustelli, and Art Donovan. William Afflis, drafted in the 16th round in position #186 by the Green Bay Packers as an offensive tackle, was now listed with the first name "Dick." Being selected was an incredible accomplishment considering Afflis never played in a game for Nevada during the 1950 season and didn't play any college football in fall 1949. For the record, the Green Bay Packers later drafted Ohio State offensive tackle Bill Miller (1929-1997) in the 26th round in position #305. Bill Miller didn't play professional football against him, but would later cross paths with Afflis in the professional wrestling world when he wrestled as Dr. Bill Miller.

Editor's note: Despite exhaustive research, we could not determine exactly why "William Franklin Afflis" began calling himself "Dick."

One pro wrestler who did play football with Bruiser was Hard Boiled Haggerty (Donald Stansauk), who played for Green Bay during the 1950 and 1951 seasons. In November 1995, Haggerty shared his memories of Bruiser with Scott Teal:

"Dick the Bruiser and I had played together for Green Bay. When I was in Los Angeles, I saw him on the field one day. He has that bulky uniform on and does a dropkick, right there on the field. He was an agile SOB."

Afflis frequently worked out with a young high school athlete named Don Manoukian, who would later play college football at Stanford and then wrestle professionally. Don recalled his weightlifting buddy years later:

"It was 1951 in the basement of the old Reno downtown YMCA. Though dusty and dank, it housed a weight room the size of a bedroom with antiquated weights. A filthy boxing ring not intended for wrestling was where I met Afflis. Bill was a legendary character by any standard, both in his physical presence and aloof arrogance that effectively hid his sense of humor. I emulated his work ethic. He was intense and silent, except for grunts and heavy breathing. We would work out by the hour with not a lot

more than body language guiding me through the paces. Bill was a fierce squatter and bench presser. These two exercises, along with the dead lift, are the cornerstones of raw power. He comically would be a rude jerk and we made sport of it when others were not around. I looked forward to our encounters at the gym. They are memorable to this day."

Big Campus Heavyweights Clash In Half-Time Wrestling Tonight

— First Wrestling Exhibition

On Saturday, January 27, 1951, Afflis "performed" at half-time of the college basketball contest between the University of Nevada Wolf Pack and the California Aggies in what would undoubtedly change the course of his life. The headline in the sports section of the *Nevada State Journal* that day stated, "*Big Campus Heavyweights Clash in Half-Time Wrestling Tonight.*" The article said, "*The match was announced by athletic director Joe Sheeketski, who says the big fellows will tangle at professional rules, which permit speed and slam-bang action, rather than the less colorful collegiate style.*" Those "big fellows" were Bill Afflis and football teammate Buddy Brooks, who were scheduled to wrestle for twelve minutes. Afflis' late football teammate, Jerry Wyness, who played basketball for the Wolf Pack that same night, remembered:

> "*I managed to sneak out of coach's half-time talk so I could see the Afflis and Brooks Show. Bill was the bad guy and Buddy [was] the handsome youngster, whom it was arranged would defeat the mean Afflis at the end of the presentation.*"

Afflis' opponent that fateful night, Buddy Brooks, recalled:

> "*We would practice pro wrestling holds and moves with each other. We thought it would be fun to execute what we were practicing. We practiced what we watched in the pro matches.*"

Football teammate John Gonda reported:

> "*The wrestling matches with Buddy were very nice to watch ... and since Dick was so strong, and also such a good wrestler, he could really make it look like it really was a live match. I was involved with him once as he put the show on and I did what he told me to do.*"

Afflis also had a side job during his Nevada days in the gaming industry. Teammate Buddy Brooks said, "*We both worked as bouncers ... he [Afflis] at Harold's Club and I worked at Harrah's ... they were the premier casinos in Reno.*" Both Afflis and Brooks worked the graveyard shift so they could attend school after their shifts. Roy Powers, former public relations man with Harold's Club, recalled that Harold's was the largest casino in the world during its heyday in the 1950s with as many as 5,000 visitors a day.

Afflis also was enrolled in the Reserve Officers Training Corp (ROTC). One of his ROTC classmates was football teammate George (Mert) Baxter, who would later become a Brigadier General in the U.S. Army. Baxter remembers the ROTC being unable to find a military uniform that fit Afflis. Baxter added, "*Afflis wore a short-sleeve shirt that fit him like a glove, but he looked out of place.*"

Afflis also participated in inter-frat track-and-field competition and won the shot put event at the April 1951 meet. During spring football sessions that same month, Afflis was listed at 255 lbs., the heaviest player on the team.

— Bruiser's Mother Remarries

On June 16, 1951, Margaret married Leroy O. Johnston Sr., at a wedding ceremony held at the 4th Presbyterian Church in downtown Chicago. Mr. Johnston was an executive at the Allison Division of General Motors Corporation and also resided at the Marott Hotel. After the election of Republican Governor George Craig, Margaret submitted her resignation as Director of Probation on January 20, 1953. Within a few months, Governor Craig appointed Margaret to the Women's Prison Board for a four-year term. Margaret would serve a total of thirteen years on this board. Other boards served on over the years included the State Teachers Retirement Board and the Indiana State Tuberculosis Association.

With all his sports activities and his anticipated debut for the 1951 football season at Nevada, things were looking up for Afflis ... but nothing could be further from the truth.

— Nevada Cancels Football Program

On Monday, July 23, 1951, the Board of Regents of the University of Nevada met in the office of President Malcomb A. Love. Also present were representatives of the press, alumni, and chamber of commerce. The board adopted a resolution that would drastically change Afflis' life. Those provisions of the resolution included (1) canceling the football program and upcoming games; (2) terminating the head coach's employment; and (3) revoking all football scholarships. The board cited a shortage of money from Nevada lawmakers and alumni, as well as the "present national emergency" (i.e. the Korean War) as justification. Within days, Afflis received an official letter from President Love at the Marott Hotel in Indianapolis. The letter said:

> "The University is very proud of the contribution you have made to the athletic department program of the University. We want to say again how sorry we are that it has been necessary to discontinue the program in which all are so vitally interested. We will do everything possible to find a job for you when you return in the fall."

The letter could not have arrived at a worse time in light of another event scheduled that same week.

The Marott Apartments
Source: Lake County (IL) Discovery Museum, Teich postcard archives

— Second Marriage

On Saturday, July 27, 1951, Bill Afflis reportedly was married to a University of Nevada co-ed named Elizabeth Darrah at the First Presbyterian Church in Chicago. The story ran in early September in both major newspapers in Reno and was featured on the front page of the Nevada State Journal. During Afflis' Nevada tenure, teammate Jerry Wyness remembers Afflis having two unwavering companions — a

German Shepherd and his girlfriend. A photo of Elizabeth with an association of women students from Artemisia Hall was found in the 1949-50 University of Nevada yearbook. Newspaper stories indicated she was the daughter of Mr. and Mrs. C.T. Darrah, formerly from Las Vegas. University of Nevada archives also indicate Elizabeth was employed by the agricultural extension. The Reno newspapers published identical word-for-word accounts about the Chicago wedding, saying the bride wore a "ballerina-length organza dress in pale blue with a bouffant skirt." After the wedding, the couple reportedly honeymooned in the Chicago and around the Great Lakes Region, followed by Bill reporting to the Green Bay Packers for training camp.

In spite of the detailed account in two newspapers of the wedding, there are problems with the story. Neither the First Presbyterian Church of Chicago, nor the prestigious Fourth Presbyterian Church of Chicago, have any record of an Afflis/Darrah wedding taking place. The Fourth Presbyterian Church of Chicago did have a record of the second marriage of Afflis' mother, Margaret, on Saturday June 16, 1951. The Nevada State Archives, however, does have a record of a marriage license being issued to William Afflis and Elizabeth Darrah in Carson City, Nevada ... with a marriage on June 14, 1952, almost a year after the public newspaper announcements.

The young couple had one daughter Karen, whose photo was published the following year in the baby section of the *Reno Evening Gazette*. The author was unable to find any information on what became of Elizabeth and Karen.

Chapter 4
As Wide As He Was Tall — 1951-1954

— After Lambeau and Before Lombardi

Bill, now going by the name Dick Afflis, played four seasons (1951 to 1954) with the Green Bay Packers. His time with the team was sandwiched between the two biggest legends in the history of the Green Bay Packers — Earl (Curly) Lambeau (who left the Packers in 1950) and Vincent T. Lombardi (who joined the Packers in 1959). At the time Afflis reported to football camp, it was reported in a Milwaukee newspaper that he was still being recruited for university and college football teams.

The Green Bay Packers were a unique team in the NFL as they were publicly owned and nonprofit since 1923. The head coach at the time was Gene Ronzani, who had been hired for the 1950 season. Ronzani had spent time with the Chicago Bears, first as a player and then as an assistant coach to George S. Halas. The Packers' record was 3-9 during Ronzani's first season at the helm (1950).

Gene Ronzani
1952 Bowman football card
Source: The Topps Company

The Packers played most of their home games at old City Stadium on the east side of town, plus some home games in Milwaukee. Due to Green Bay being known as the "Siberia of the NFL," the final two games of regular season were frequently played on the road against the San Francisco 49ers and the Los Angeles Rams. The Packers would travel by train, taking three days to reach the west coast, staying there for both games, and returning again by train. During Afflis' four years with the Packers, the team didn't win a single game on those west coast trips. At the time, the NFL was not the dominant sports entity in the United States that it would become at the end of the 1950s. The NFL had two conferences of six teams each, with many teams surviving to this day. During all four years of Afflis' service with the Packers, the Packers would be featured in the Thanksgiving Day game against the Detroit Lions at Tiger Stadium. The Packers lost all four contests.

The lore surrounding Afflis as a Green Bay Packer is legendary. In the book *Packers by the Numbers*, author John Maxymuk discussed various incidents involving Afflis, such as smashing beer cans into his forehead, or using a broken beer bottle to scare off a rowdy fan. Long-time reporter Art Daley retold

Rookie year • 1951
Source: Green Bay Packers

an incident whereby African-American teammate Bob Mann was refused a taxi ride in Baltimore because of his skin color. Afflis intervened and told the taxi driver in no uncertain terms to "*take him wherever he wants to go,*" and the driver obeyed. Teammate Dick Logan, who played with Afflis during the 1952-53 seasons, recalls, "*Dick was a mean fellow and a little whacky.*" Vito (Babe) Parilli remembers Afflis drinking milk shakes loaded with a half-dozen to a dozen eggs and eating his dessert first at dinner. On a multi-day train trip to the west coast, Parilli remembers Afflis eating two 20-ounce slabs of prime rib in a single sitting. Teammate Veryl Switzer said, "*He was about 5-foot-11, was almost as wide as he was tall, and loved showing off his biceps.*" Packer teammate Dan Orlich, who remembered Afflis from his own days at Nevada, recalled:

> "*Dick was a body builder, which back in those days was kind of frowned upon, as opposed to today when it is part of every pro's regimen. Once, when asked how he acquired his gigantic neck, he replied, 'I go to the gym and toss a medicine ball as high as I can, and then catch it on the side of my head.' Medicine balls are rarely seen today, but they are huge, leather-encased balls weighing at least twelve to fifteen pounds. To toss one of those in the air and catch it like Dick did would break any ordinary man's neck.*"

— 1951 NFL Season

On Sunday, September 30, 1951, the Green Bay Packers opened the 1951 season at home before a crowd of 24,666 fans, only to be defeated by the Chicago Bears with a score of 31 to 20. The game program included a photo and profile of young Dick Afflis. Afflis was one of only four draftees to make the team that year. The post-game summary in the *Chicago Tribune* the next day indicated he was on the roster, but wasn't considered an offensive starter. The website www.pro-football-reference.com listed Afflis as a tackle, guard, and defensive guard, and the team photo showed him wearing jersey #15.

The 1951 season was something the team would have liked to forget as the record was three wins and nine losses, with the Packers placing fifth out of six teams in the National Conference of the NFL. The Packers scored 254 points, but allowed 375 points that season. Only the now-defunct New York Yanks had a worse record in the league.

— 1952 NFL Season

For the 1952 season, the Green Bay Packers' record improved to six wins and six losses for a fourth place finish in the National Conference. The Packers improved the point differential by scoring 295 points and allowing 312 points. Afflis wore jersey #62 this second season and was listed as a starting offensive tackle, and sometimes as an offensive guard.

During the off-season, back in Reno in February 1953, advertisements announced that Afflis was the "new host and special officer" at Harold's Club.

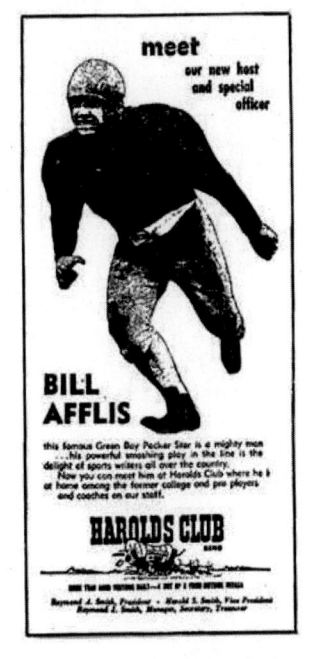

GREEN BAY PACKERS

No.	Name	Pos.	Ht.	Wt.	Age	School	Yrs. In Pro Ball
3	Canadeo, Tony	B	6:0	190	30	Gonzaga	11
8	Forte, Bob	B	6:0	205	30	Arkansas	6
15	Parilli, Vito	B	6:1	190	23	Kentucky	1
18	Rote, Tobin	B	6:3	200	24	Rice Institute	3
20	Sandifer, Dan	B	6:2	190	23	Louisiana State	4
22	Grimes, Billy	B	6:1	195	25	Oklahoma A & M	4
24	Reid, Floyd	B	5:10	185	25	Georgia	3
28	Self, Clarence	B	5:9	180	27	Wisconsin	3
26	Pelfrey, Ray	E	6:0	190	24	Eastern Kentucky State	2
31	Cone, Fred	B	5:11	200	26	Clemson	2
33	Floyd, Bobby Jack	B	6:0	210	23	Texas Christian	1
37	Reichardt, Bill	B	5:11	205	22	Iowa	1
47	Moselle, Dom	B	6:0	193	26	Superior State	3
44	Dillon, Bobby	B	6:1	185	22	Texas	1
50	Rhodemyre, Jay	C	6:1	215	28	Kentucky	4
54	Schmidt, George	C	6:3	225	25	Lewis College	1
61	Ruzick, Steve	T	6:2	225	24	Ohio State	1
62	Afflis, Dick	G	5:11	250	23	Nevada	2
63	Bray, Ray	G	6:0	235	35	Western Michigan	11
65	Boerio, Chuck	G	5:11	205	22	Illinois	1
66	Teteak, Deral	G	5:10	210	23	Wisconsin	1
69	Stephenson, Dave	G	6:1	235	26	West Virginia	3
70	Dowden, Steve	T	6:3	235	23	Baylor	1
72	Johnson, Tom	T	6:2	230	21	Michigan	1
75	Ruetz, Howard	T	6:3	270	25	Loras College	2
76	Logan, Dick	T	6:2	235	22	Ohio State	1
77	Hanner, Dave	T	6:2	245	22	Arkansas	1
80	Elliott, Carleton	E	6:4	220	25	Virginia	2
81	Barrang, Ed	E	6:2	215	28	Villanova	4
83	Martinkovic, John	E	6:3	240	25	Xavier	2
85	Wimberly, Abner	E	6:1	215	26	Louisiana State	4
86	Howton, Bill	E	6:2	185	22	Rice Institute	1
87	Mann, Bob	E	5:11	173	28	Michigan	5

On March 17, 1953, Afflis and his NFL colleagues participated in a local YMCA sports banquet held on the University of Nevada campus. The theme of the evening's festivities was "Me and My Dad Are Pals." In attendance that night were four hundred fathers and sons, wrestling promoter Andy Rockne, and nationally known entertainer Rudy Vallee, who sang his hit tune "Whiffenpoof Song." Also there was local high school star athlete Don Manoukian, Afflis' old workout buddy, who remembered that evening:

> "I had the opportunity to be in the presence of five of the best athletes ever, and in more than one sport. Bill Afflis was a unique football player with Green Bay and [later] the ultimate pro wrestling villain. Leo (The Lion) Nomellini was consensus All-American football player at Minnesota and a fine amateur wrestler, and is in Canton, Ohio, in the Football Hall of Fame. Buster McClure was a football pioneer with the Boston Yanks. Dan Orlich was a former Green Bay Packer and, in later years, became the skilled and most famous trap shooter in the world. Pat Brady was selected to the 75th Anniversary All-Time Pittsburgh Steeler team as a punter. He holds a punting record that can be tied, but not broken. He punted from his own one-yard line and into the opponents' end zone."

Youth athletic banquet • Reno, Nevada • 1953
(left to right) Dick Afflis, Leo Nomellini, Buster McGuire, Dan Orlich, Pat Brady
Courtesy Don Manoukian

A group photo of these men survives to this day. That night, Leo Nomellini addressed the crowd, first about professional football as he was then a standout player with the San Francisco 49ers. He later changed the subject to professional wrestling. When somebody in the audience asked if he had *"been offered a bribe and if any of his matches were fixed,"* Nomellini retorted, *"I've been wrestling professionally for a year and a half, and no one has ever told me anything."*

— **1953 NFL Season**

For the 1953 NFL season, Afflis wore jersey #72 and was again listed as a tackle, guard, and defensive guard, but he wasn't listed as a starter. Rookie teammate Roger Zatkoff recalled an incident that took place during the 1953 training camp with Afflis and fellow rookie Jim Ringo (who would later make the Football Hall of Fame). Zatkoff recalls that a "big ass" Cadillac pulled up with a "broad-shouldered" guy (Afflis) who stepped out and yelled, *"Hey, rookies! Come here and get my bags."* Zatkoff and Ringo brought Afflis' bags up to the room, whereby Afflis removed two handguns from his shoulder holsters and placed them on the tabletop. Zatkoff thought, *"This guy is really crazy."*

The 1953 season didn't go well at all for the Packers, who posted a record of 2-9-1, good for last place in the newly renamed Western Conference. Coach Gene Ronzani was released from his head coaching position after the Thanksgiving Day loss to the Detroit Lions. The only positive events included a new national TV contract for the NFL and some Packers' home games played at the new County Stadium in Milwaukee.

— March of Dimes Telethon

On Friday, January 29, 1954, Dick Afflis participated in a telethon for the March of Dimes broadcast on KZTV-TV in Reno. The telethon, which aired simultaneously on five radio stations in Reno, raised tens of thousands of dollars for the National Foundation for Infantile Paralysis. Afflis and his old college friend, Buddy Brooks, put on a "mock tag team wrestling match" with actor Joe E. Brown and local broadcaster Lee Giroux. Afflis also put on a weight-lifting demonstration for the audience. That event was the beginning of a life-long tradition of Afflis lending his name and services in the name of charity.

Later, during the off-season in spring 1954, Afflis met up with Louis Dickey, one of his Purdue fraternity brothers. Dickey had been a varsity wrestler at Purdue during the 1948-49 years and was already wrestling professionally in the upper Midwest. Dickey had been trained for his pro wrestling debut by Joe Pazandak, the legendary, and tough, wrestling trainer from Minnesota. Pazandak would later be linked to Afflis when Dick got into the wrestling business. Dickey recalls:

> "I was wrestling in Green Bay myself. I was there early and must have called the Packers. He was there for spring training, so I got ahold of him at his hotel. I went up to see him and must have spent an hour talking to him. He was pretty beat up from football and said, 'I'm going to get out of this thing.' I told him that he ought to get into professional wrestling, with your body. The next thing I know, he [Afflis] was in the wrestling game."

Nomellini Will Take on Pletchas Thursday; Bill Afflis Schedules Pro Wrestling Debut

— Professional Wrestling Initiation

On Thursday June 24, 1954, a posed photo of a bare-chested Dick Afflis appeared on page 11 of the *Nevada State Journal*.

> Making His Pro Debut
> Tonight in the wrestling card at Moana Ball Park will be burly Bill Afflis of Reno, already noted as a professional football player, the Green Bay tackle, who is prominent as a weight-lifter, will face a rough customer in the more experienced Ramon Cernandes of Argentina in the semi-windup.
>
> *Nevada State Journal* (Reno), Thursday, June 24, 1954

In the main event of the evening, Leo Nomellini was scheduled to face Bulldog Danny Plechas in a two-out-of-three fall main event. Wrestling ticket prices at the Moana Ballpark in those days were $2.30 for ringside, $1.10 general admission, and 50 cents for servicemen in uniform. The next day, the sports headline in the *Reno Evening Gazette* read "Afflis Debut Successful" as "Afflis ended the match at the 23-minute mark with an elbow smash and drop kick."

The following week, on July 2, 1954, a full-length photo of Afflis vs. Cernandes appeared in the newspaper, showing Afflis breaking the full Nelson hold applied by Cernandes. Afflis would later be victorious at Moana Ball Park on July 8th over Juan Humberto and on the July 22nd main event against Bulldog Danny Plechas. Plechas was required to win two consecutive falls against Bruiser to win. In those days, it was rare for a debuting professional wrestler to win his first three matches, evidence of the confidence the promoter bestowed on this rookie and a reflection of Afflis' credibility as an in-ring performer.

— 1954 NFL Season

Afflis signed again with the Green Packers for the 1954 season and attended training camp held in Stevens Point, Wisconsin. The new head coach was Lisle Blackbourn, who had no experience in professional football, but who had previously been the head coach at the University of Marquette in Milwaukee. Blackbourn later got attention for, reportedly, expressing interest in recruiting Harvard gridiron player Edward M. Kennedy, of the famous political Kennedy family. Blackbourn had a long list of 20 rules for his players; rules he expected to be followed. They included "hard liquor prohibited," "poker playing and dice games will not be tolerated," and "no wives on road trips."

Afflis wore jersey #75 in the role of utility player on both sides of the line. In the opening game of the season against the Pittsburgh Steelers, played at home, Afflis actually intercepted a pass thrown by quarterback Jim Finks. A future member of the Pro Football Hall of Fame, Finks would later become the general manager of the Minnesota Vikings, the Chicago Bears, and the New Orleans Saints.

During the same season, offensive guard Al Barry joined the team and would later write about Afflis in the book *The Unknown Lineman / the lighter side of the NFL*. Barry remembers Afflis pointing out a particular player just prior to a kickoff, delivering a forearm blow, and literally knocking that unlucky opponent unconscious. That opposing team was the number-one nemesis of the Packers, the Chicago Bears.

Offensive end Gary Knafelc, newly drafted from the University of Colorado, joined the Green Bay Packers that season and remembers Dick Afflis well:

> "*He* [Afflis] *was a character; I'll tell you that. His last year with the Packers (1954) was my rookie year. We lived in the same hotel* [The Astor]. *For some reason, he took a liking to me and was very nice to me. He would call me and take me out to have dinner with him. I would go up to his room, and he would be sitting there with 80-pound barbells, doing lifts like it was nothing.*"

The Packers continued their losing ways and posted a record of 4-8, good for fifth place out of six teams in the Western Conference. That would be Dick Afflis' final season with the Green Bay Packers. Afflis had been steadily employed for four seasons with the Packers in an NFL which had only twelve teams with 33 roster spots on each team. This made Afflis a part of a very select group of professional athletes in the United States. In other words, there were spots in the NFL for about 400 players in a country with a population, at the time, of 130 million. Afflis' days in the NFL were over, but new opportunities loomed on the horizon — the professional wrestling business.

PART II
QUICK RISE TO MAIN EVENTS

Chapter 5
I Just Acted Naturally — 1955

In January 1955, the professional wrestling business in North America was largely organized under the banner of the National Wrestling Alliance (NWA), a confederation of dozens of wrestling promoters from coast-to-coast. All the promoters within the NWA recognized an undisputed heavyweight champion of the world, a cherished role selected by the board of directors of the organization. At the time, the throne was occupied by a 38-year-old legendary scientific, but tough, wrestler named Lou Thesz. Thesz defended his championship title hundreds of times every year in the various cities controlled by the NWA promoters. The most prominent NWA promoter and its president was a 50-year-old wrestling impresario named Sam Muchnick, who regularly promoted wrestling events at the Kiel Auditorium in St. Louis, Missouri.

— **Debuts in Minnesota**

At this time, Dick Aflis embarked on his professional wrestling career in Minnesota with several early influences. In a 1981 feature story by Dick Mittman of the *Indianapolis News*, interview transcripts reveal the early influence of Leo Nomellini, who both wrestled and played professional football with the San Francisco 49ers. The Bruiser told Mittman how he was impressed with the kind of money wrestlers were making and said, "*That's for me.*"

Nomellini attained rapid success in professional wrestling and challenged Lou Thesz for the NWA heavyweight title on June 16, 1953, at the Cow Palace in San Francisco. Another influence was Verne Gagne, a former Minnesota Gopher college football player and U.S. Olympic wrestler. Verne's son, Greg Gagne, who himself became a professional wrestler, remembers Verne being instrumental in recruiting Afflis to join the professional wrestling ranks.

Leo Nomellini, SF 49ers
1952 Bowman football card
Source: Topps Company

Wrestling historian and author George Lentz has researched and documented the influence of Wisconsin-born professional wrestler Mike Blazer, who was wrestling all over the state of Wisconsin during Afflis' days at Green Bay. Mike was quoted saying: "*When Bruiser was playing for the Packers, he walked into St. Norbert's* [College in De Pere, Wisconsin] *where we were working out. I invited him to join us.*"

Another Afflis influence would reside right in Minnesota, one of the toughest legitimate wrestlers of that era, named Joe Pazandak. Wrestling historian and author George Schire recalls Pazandak being *"the type who would break your finger off your hand and then hand it back to you."* Veteran wrestler Stan Kowalski (who also wrestled as the Big K) would later confirm that Pazandak was legendary in Minnesota and was affiliated with the University of Minnesota. Afflis and Pazandak appeared together on several wrestling cards during the Bruiser's initial run.

Former Green Bay Packer teammate, Hardboiled Haggerty recalled his exchange with Afflis:

> *"I said, 'Have you ever thought of wrestling?'"*
>
> *"He says, 'Yeah, but I don't know what to do.'"*
>
> *"I called Wally Karbo and bought Bruiser his first wrestling trunks. He went into Minneapolis, and did so well there, he went down to Chicago. He got in with Fred Kohler and was on his way."*

At that time, professional wrestling in Minnesota was operated under the auspices of NWA promoters Dennis Stecher and Wally Karbo in a wrestling territory headquartered in Minneapolis, Minnesota. That territory had previously been run by a former wrestler and long-time promoter named Tony Stecher, who died in late 1954. Dennis was Tony's son and his wrestling territory included the Minnesota cities of St. Paul, Minneapolis, and Duluth. In addition to the bigger towns in Minnesota, wrestling events were staged in countless small towns. In those days, the wrestlers who appeared in the major cities were expected to wrestle in the smaller venues, as well. In addition, to Minnesota, Stecher and Karbo promoted wrestling in Winnipeg, Manitoba, Canada.

— **Bronko Nagurski in Winnipeg**

Dick Afflis' first professional match in the Stecher territory appears to have taken place at Municipal Auditorium in Winnipeg. *The Winnipeg Free Press* published a dressing room photograph of Afflis on Saturday, January 8, 1955, and talked up Afflis' experience in the NFL with the Green Bay Packers. Afflis' football reputation enabled him to get early publicity, whereas other rookies were confined to preliminary matches without any hype. In fact, the story was circulated that Afflis had been kicked out of the NFL for being too rough. While technically not true, it made a good story and solidified his reputation as a roughhouser.

In the photograph with Afflis was one of the most legendary former-NFL stars who also wrestled professionally — Bronko Nagurski. Nagurski played for the

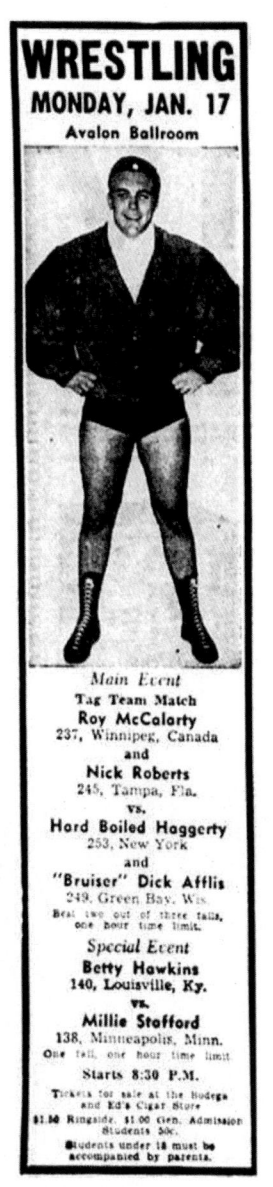

La Crosse, Wisconsin
January 10, 1955

First article we could find of Afflis being referred to as "Bruiser."

One of Bruiser's first publicity shots • 1955
Source: Robert Luce family

Chicago Bears in the 1930s and would later be inducted into the Pro Football Hall of Fame in the charter class of 1963. As a pro wrestler, Nagurski held the world heavyweight title on three different occasions.

Afflis won his opening match in Winnipeg against Stan Mayslack, while Nagurski was victorious in his tag-team main event with Johnny Kostas as his partner against Sir Alan Garfield and Fred Atkins. Afflis would return to Winnipeg many times over the next 20 years.

— **Impresses Jack Lanza**

During Afflis' introduction to full-time professional wrestling in the Stecher/Karbo territory, many newspaper ads spelled his last name as "Affles," with some 1950s broadcasts pronouncing his last name "apples." Also during this time, Bruiser Afflis caught the attention of a teenager who lived in the Twin Cities named John R. Lanzo. Lanzo would later have an outstanding pro wrestling career as Blackjack Lanza.

During a 2012 interview, while reminiscing about Afflis' entry into the pro wrestling ranks, Lanza said, "*That's when I first heard of him, as I went to high school around Minneapolis, and he got a lot of publicity after Hard Boiled Haggerty.*" Haggerty, whose real name was Don Stansauk, played in the NFL before Afflis and also wrestled in Stecher's territory. Lanza added, "*Haggerty was one of the first who was media-friendly ... he wasn't that great of a worker, but he sure could talk. What was interesting about Bruiser was, he wasn't that tall, but he was wide and athletic — sort of a beer-drinking Bozo ... Bruiser could move and talk and he looked the part.*"

Bruiser wore long tights during the early days of his career, was introduced as being from Green Bay, and, in contrast to later days when he was a huge star, he actually lost matches. He appeared on wrestling cards with an interesting cast of characters, many of whom would go on to become prominent and notable personalities, both inside and outside the ring. Those people included the aforementioned Verne Gagne (who later would own his own promotion and train countless wrestlers in the business), Arnold Skaaland (who later became part-owner and manager in the WWF), and Wladek Kowalski (who became more famous using the name Killer Kowalski). All three became members of the WWE Hall of Fame. In addition, Kinji Shibuya (who achieved fame as one of the villainous Japanese wrestlers of the time) wrestled with Afflis, along with stalwarts Ilio DePaolo and Jack Pesek. Afflis wrestled in all the Minnesota territory towns, both big and small.

— **Kohler's Chicago Territory**

After wrestling around the Minnesota circuit for almost six months, Afflis thought it was time to move on to potentially bigger and better things in the wrestling business. He caught the attention of the legendary Chicago wrestling promoter, Fred Kohler, who brought Afflis to wrestle in Chicago and other Midwest towns. That certainly turned out to be a giant step forward in Afflis' career development. Afflis recalled his early wrestling days in the 1981 Dick Mittman interview:

> "*When I started wrestling, everyone like Gorgeous George had on capes. I just acted naturally, and that's why I made it in the big time so fast. I didn't try to put on anything; just anything that came to mind. In that era, almost everybody had big robes: really gaudy and everything. Then I came*

along and all I had was pair of trunks and my shoes. I had no gimmick. It was the absence of gimmicks that made me different."

— Marigold Debut

Chicago was one of the most prominent professional wrestling cities in the United States at that time. The early television program, *Wrestling from the Marigold*, was broadcast nationwide on Saturday evenings from September 1949 until March 1955 on the now defunct DuMont television network. The show originated at the Marigold Gardens, a 2,000 seat venue located at 817 W. Grace Street, on Chicago's north side, very close to baseball's Wrigley Field. The show continued on local WGN-TV after the network run ended with Baseball Hall of Fame broadcaster Jack Brickhouse doing play-by-play. Later, in the 1980s, Brickhouse would recall Afflis' debut, saying *"he was better known as a villain, and villains are the most precious commodity in wrestling. They're the ones that sell the tickets."*

It is believed that Bruiser Afflis' first appearance at the Marigold Gardens was on Saturday, June 4, 1955, where he lost to the scientific master, Pat O'Connor. Fred Kohler's primary showcase was the International Amphitheatre located at 43rd and Halsted Streets, just east of the famous Union Stockyards. Kohler first promoted a wrestling card at the 12,000 seat Amphitheatre on January 14, 1949, with a card headlined by Lou Thesz. By 1955, Kohler would promote cards at the Amphitheatre every few weeks, as well as the weekly Marigold show. Kohler also would be involved in promoting and/or supplying talent to Milwaukee and many other Midwest towns.

Also recently arriving in Chicago around this time was a young wrestler and New York State native named Len Rossi. Rossi was hired after writing a personal letter offering his services to Fred Kohler. Rossi remembered that he just missed appearing on the nationally televised Marigold programs. Rossi recollected about Afflis during those early days in Chicago:

"He was very outgoing and was not a bashful person. He was a pretty nice guy and very boisterous. He had a heck of a body on him — very strong and powerful looking. I think when Kohler and Barnett saw him, they saw a lot of potential in that man, and they started pushing him real big. And then he became a big hit."

Chicago's International Amphitheatre
Source: Lake County Discovery Museum

— International Amphitheatre Debut

Rossi posed with Afflis in a 1955 publicity still that sat for decades in photo files at the *Chicago Tribune*. In that photo, Afflis pressed a horizontal Rossi high into the air like a large barbell. Rossi doesn't remember where or when that photo was taken, but they both made their Amphitheatre debuts on the night of Friday, June 10, 1955.

It was a stroke of luck that Afflis was booked that night. A big card was scheduled at the Amphitheatre, which included a bout between Yukon Eric and Ivan Rasputin. A few days before the match, the Illinois State Athletic Commission suspended Yukon Eric for disobeying a referee's instructions during a match at Marigold Gardens in May 1955. On Thursday, June 9th, a small headline in the *Chicago Tribune* announced "State Revokes Mat License of Yukon Eric; Dick Afflis to substitute." Wrestling cards are traditionally subject to change in the line-up without notice, and that was the case here as Yukon Eric appeared in the ad (below) in the *Chicago American* even on the day of the show.

Russ Davis called the play-by-play that night in Chicago and mistakenly announced Dick's name as Dick "Barlett," but corrected himself later. Davis also announced that promoter Fred Kohler was present at ringside, no doubt to watch Bruiser and determine his potential.

Wrestling webmaster Chris Parsons commented on Bruiser's first appearance at the Amphitheatre:

"Dick Afflis made his debut against roughhouse artist Ivan Rasputin. Entering the ring in long tights and a lighter jacket, and sporting a black eye, he was cheered by the throng, who were equally taken by his impressive build. Dick was roughed-up and pushed around quite a bit by the more experienced Rasputin, who threw several very heavy shots to Afflis' iron midsection. At near the five-minute mark, Dick had enough, rebounding from the ropes and hitting Rasputin with several football tackles before pinning Ivan with a body press."

The crowd loudly cheered the decision when the referee awarded the match to Bruiser.

That card drew 4,523 fans and grossed $9,850. In the main event that night, Antonino (Argentina) Rocca and Roy McClarity defeated Don Leo Jonathan and Hans Schnabel. Don Leo, now in his eighties and living in Langley, British Columbia, Canada, remembers newcomer Dick Afflis during that period. Jonathan recalled Afflis *"was pretty meek at first and realized he had a lot to learn."* Don Leo added, *"He developed pretty fast and*

learned quickly and eventually became a star." After this Amphitheatre debut, Afflis returned to the Minneapolis territory to close out his engagement.

— **Midwest Expansion**

Beginning in July 1955, Afflis would spend most of the next seventeen months wrestling in Illinois, Indiana, Michigan, and Wisconsin, with a few matches in Toledo and Denver. The Wisconsin towns included Milwaukee, Madison, Fond du Lac, Elkhorn, Sheboygan, and Beloit, while the Illinois cities included Rockford and Chicago (Amphitheatre, Marigold, and sometimes The Trianon Ballroom). Angola, Indianapolis, Gary, and Fort Wayne were regular stops in Indiana, and he also made regular appearances in Benton Harbor, Michigan.

WRESTLING - FRIDAY 9 PM
DOUBLE MAIN EVENT
Hans SCHMIDT
vs
Reggie LISOWSKI
The SHEIK
vs
Dick (Bruiser) AFFLIS
TAG TEAM MATCH
Louis MARTINEZ and Mitsu ARAKAWA
vs
Roy URBANO and Zack MALKOV
BUCK LAKE 2 MILES WEST ANGOLA

Angola, Indiana • August 12, 1955

On Monday, August 1, 1955, he appeared at the Porter County Fairgrounds in Valparaiso, Indiana, in the main event against Angelo Poffo. The *Vidette-Messenger* (local newspaper) would report about this match the next day by saying Bruiser's bout, "... *ended with an old-fashioned alley brawl, outside the ring.*" It took "several members of the city and county police," "a dozen Jaycees" (who sponsored the event), and promoter John Zawadzki to separate Poffo and Afflis after the match. Poffo would father two sons who would achieve fame in professional wrestling in the 1970s — Randy (Macho Man) Savage and "Leaping" Lanny Poffo.

The following month, on September 1, 1955, Bruiser defeated Hans Schmidt in the main event at the Sports Arena in Toledo, Ohio. Schmidt wrestled earlier with Afflis that same year in the Minneapolis territory under his real name of Guy LaRose. In 2012, wrestling author and webmaster Greg Oliver would ask the aging Schmidt about Bruiser's early career. "*I didn't show him too much; he always said he knew everything.*" On that same card, in Toledo, a former Pittsburgh bodybuilder named Don Kalt appeared and remembers the first time he saw Bruiser. Kalt, who wrestled for decades under countless ring names, such as Don Stevens, Don Fargo, Jack Dalton, and Jack Dillinger, said, "*I met Dick the Bruiser for the first time in Toledo, Ohio.*" Kalt also recalled the legend that Afflis played football without a helmet and Kalt added, "*I kind of believed it.*"

As the 1955 NFL season started up, Afflis was given an option to attend Green Bay Packers training camp and continue his football career, but he opted to stay on the professional wrestling circuit. Afflis would sometimes visit his old football coach from Jefferson High School in Lafayette, Norm Willey, and told the coach he made much more money wrestling than playing for Green Bay.

— **Faces Major Wrestling Stars**

During the fall 1955, Afflis appeared in main events against three individuals who would later become significant wrestling associates both in and out of the ring. Those three individuals were Verne Gagne, The Sheik of Araby, and Reggie Lisowski.

Bruiser would lose his first main event against Gagne in Toledo on Thursday, September 8, 1955, with Gagne winning the first and third falls. Gagne and Afflis remained closely associated for the next 30 years when Gagne bought ownership of the Minnesota territory.

On Friday, September 23, 1955, at the Armory in Gary, Indiana, Afflis was booked against Reggie Lisowski, a Milwaukee native, who would later wrestle simply as "The Crusher" and become Bruiser's most important tag team partner. Lisowski probably was Bruiser's best friend in the wrestling business, as well.

On Wednesday, November 23, 1955, at Memorial Hall in Racine, Wisconsin, Bruiser defeated The Sheik of Araby, who would later become both an in-the-ring opponent and out-of-the-ring business competitor. (see page 53 for ad)

In all cases, Afflis was featured in main events within his first year as a full-time wrestler and rubbing shoulders with older and more experienced mat veterans.

In the fall 1955, Bruiser crossed paths with newcomer Dick Beyer, who played college football for Syracuse University. Afflis and Beyer became roommates for a short while at the Hotel Chateau at 3838 N. Broadway in Chicago, located just a block from the Marigold. The two made a few trips together to Milwaukee and Indianapolis and wrestled each other there. Years later, Beyer told the author that he and Afflis would go out drinking, downing beers mixed with V-8 juice. It is assumed the concoction must have more vitamins and minerals than pure beer. Beyer later gained international mat fame as The Intelligent, Sensational Destroyer, as well as Doctor X in the Midwest.

WRESTLING

GARY ARMORY
Sept. 23 — 8:30
PEE WEE JAMES
vs.
LORD BEAVERBROOK

Tag Match
Gardini vs Len Rossi
Gypsy Joe vs DeSounza

Return Grudge Match
REGGIE LISOWSKI
vs.
DICK THE BRUISER

For Reserve Tickets
Call 284-W Hobart

Gary, Indiana • Sept. 23, 1955
First ad found using the term "Dick the Bruiser"

— **Returns to Indianapolis**

During this time, Afflis wrestled professionally for the first time in Indianapolis. Indianapolis had a respectable professional wrestling history in the '40s, and was the site of an NWA world heavyweight title change when Lou Thesz won the belt from Wild Bill Longson on July 20, 1948, at the Fairgrounds Coliseum. Newspaper ads show the legendary Buddy Rogers appeared at the Indianapolis Sport Arena in 1949, then located in the 5000 block of North Meridian Avenue. The key wrestling entrepreneur in Indianapolis in those days was a man named Billy Thom. Thom (1900-1973) was a legendary amateur wrestling coach for both Indiana University and the 1936 U.S. Olympic team. Thom had a hand in training the patriarch of the famous wrestling Funk family, namely Dory Funk, Sr. Since 1979, there is a Billy Thom Award given out annually by the Indiana High School Wrestling

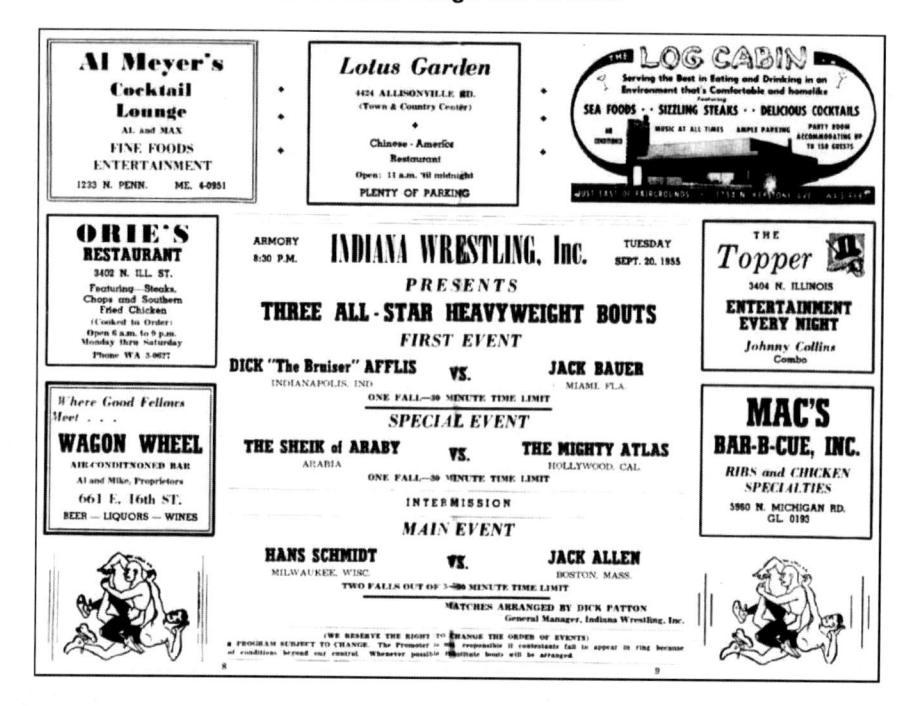

Coaches Association to honor a wrestler, coach, or contributor to amateur wrestling in Indiana. In the mid '50s, Thom sold his interests in the promotion to James Barnett and Fred Kohler. Under the management of local promoter Dick Patton, Dick Afflis made his debut at Tyndall Armory in Indianapolis on September 20, 1955, against Jack Bauer, in the preliminary bout.

— National Publicity

In October 1955, Bruiser was the subject of a four-page publicity article in the self-proclaimed "America's Wrestling Magazine," known more commonly as *Wrestling Life*. This magazine was published monthly by WAYLI, Inc. WAYLI stood for *Wrestling As You Like It*, the same name as a predecessor publication that had been discontinued in 1955. *Wrestling Life* was published out of the same office as Fred Kohler's wrestling operations at 817 W. Grace Street in Chicago. The magazine's purpose was to promote news of wrestling events and wrestlers appearing in the Midwest, but it also covered the wrestling scene across the entire United States. In the October 1955 edition, the magazine's advertising manager, photographer, and writer, Robert Alden Luce, engaged in masterful promotional writing. The headline on page nine read, "The Romans had their great gladiators ... Medieval history had its mighty torturers ... and we have The Bruiser." Luce recounted a somewhat embellished sequence of Afflis' athletic career, including football achievements in high school, college, and Green Bay. For publicity purposes, Luce claimed Afflis was All Pacific Coast for Nevada (even though he never suited up for Nevada). Professional wrestling is staged athletic drama with wrestlers portraying fictional characters, so a little hype for show purposes was standard fare in those days. The article included a photo of Afflis using only one arm to suspend a young lady (lady wrestler Rose Roman) high above his head, and another of him getting into his new

Chapter 5 • 53

Fred Kohler Enterprises, Inc. mailing envelope

Source: Chris Parsons

automobile, a Packard 400, a sponsor of *Wrestling Life* magazine. Bob Luce would later follow-up with another promotional feature on Bruiser in the May 1956 issue of *Wrestling Life* entitled "*Matdom's Terrifying Goliath.*" Dick the Bruiser became such a dominating personality that his photo appeared on the envelopes sent out by Fred Kohler's wrestling office.

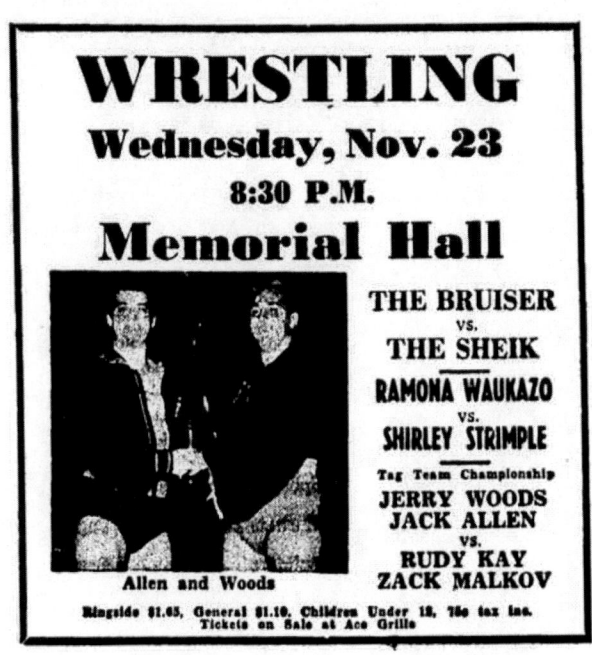

WRESTLING
Wednesday, Nov. 23
8:30 P.M.
Memorial Hall

THE BRUISER
vs.
THE SHEIK

RAMONA WAUKAZO
vs.
SHIRLEY STRIMPLE

Tag Team Championship
JERRY WOODS
JACK ALLEN
vs.
RUDY KAY
ZACK MALKOV

Allen and Woods

Ringside $1.65, General $1.10, Children Under 12, 75c tax inc.
Tickets on Sale at Ace Grille

Racine, Wisconsin • November 23, 1955

Chapter 6
A Voice Like A Ruptured Foghorn — 1956

As 1956 rolled in, less than one year after his full-time debut, Afflis was being regularly featured in the main events, an accomplishment few in professional wrestling ever achieved. On Saturday, January 14, 1956, at the Auditorium in Milwaukee, Bruiser lost (via disqualification) his first NWA world championship challenge match against Lou Thesz before a sellout of 6,187 fans.

— Amphitheatre Main Event

About two weeks later, on Friday, January 27, 1956, Bruiser challenged NWA U.S. TV champion Verne Gagne in Chicago. Bruiser and Gagne shared top billing that night with NWA heavyweight champion Lou Thesz and the challenger Hans Schmidt.

The Bruiser vs. Gagne match was a two-of-three-falls affair with a 60-minute time limit, and was refereed by Jim McMillen, a former professional wrestler and executive with the Chicago Bears. While both wrestlers shook hands just before the opening bell, it was an intense match and got rough at times. Bruiser was lean and mean in those years and was no thicker than Gagne. Bruiser won the first fall with a body press, while Gagne won the second with an early version of his sleeper hold. Well into the third fall, Bruiser took big bumps after two consecutive flying drop kicks from Gagne. After the third dropkick, Bruiser's momentum sent him reeling backwards into referee McMillen, who was subsequently "knocked out" for almost 15 seconds. During that time, Gagne had Bruiser pinned flat on his back for almost 10 seconds, but there was nobody there to make the three-count. Bruiser escaped and turned the tables, putting

Milwaukee • January 14, 1956
Source: Robert Luce family

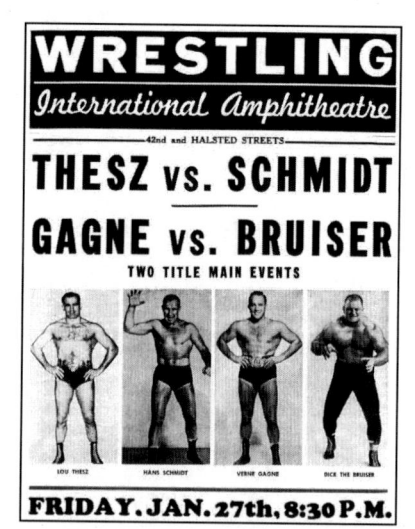

Chicago • January 27, 1956
Source: Robert Luce family

Gagne on his back, just as McMillen regained his composure. McMillen made a quick count, resulting in Bruiser winning the third and deciding fall. The crowd was outraged by the decision. An official from the Illinois Athletic Commission climbed into the ring, had a discussion with the referee McMillen, and called ring announcer Eddie Glick into the discussion. Eddie Glick raised his arm and hand to the crowd:

> "Ladies and Gentlemen, the time was seven minutes and ten seconds when Dick the Bruiser pinned Verne Gagne. Jim McMillen ... HOLD IT! HOLD IT! Jim McMillen was knocked semi-conscious and couldn't count. Gagne had Bruiser down for ten seconds. The winner ... VERNE GAGNE."

Dick the Bruiser vs. Verne Gagne • Chicago, Illinois • January 27, 1956
Source: Chicago Film Archives

In response, Bruiser shoved and screamed at the official. The finish to that match in Chicago, that of a semi-conscious or kayoed referee, would be used over and over again for decades in the professional wrestling industry. In the 1980s, WWE Hall of Famer wrestler/booker Dusty Rhodes would use a variation of this gimmick finish so frequently that it became known as "The Dusty Finish."

— Wilbur Snyder, Opponent

The next distinctive main event for the Bruiser was on Tuesday, March 20, 1956, at the Northside Armory in Indianapolis. This time, his opponent was Wilbur Snyder. In the ring, Snyder became one of Bruiser's frequent opponents and, to the fans, they were bitter enemies. Behind the scenes, though, Snyder became one of Bruiser's closest associates in the wrestling business. Snyder, billed as "The World's Most Scientific Wrestler," hailed from Woodland Hills,

56 • BRUISER: The World's Most Dangerous Wrestler

California, and played college football at the University of Utah and Canadian football for the Edmonton Eskimos.

With all three of these early main event scientific masters of the mat (Thesz, Gagne, and Snyder), Bruiser was honing his skills as a first-rate villain in the business.

A rare black-and-white film of a match between Bruiser and veteran Bill Melby, filmed at the International Amphitheatre on April 6, 1956, is still in existence today. Ringside that night looked vastly different from the WWE ringside of the new millennium as most of the spectators were grown men who wore suits and ties. There was no throng of children at ringside, or audience members holding up signs and posters. On that night in 1956, Bruiser generated loud boos from

Wilbur Snyder vs. Bruiser • 1957
Source: Robert Luce family

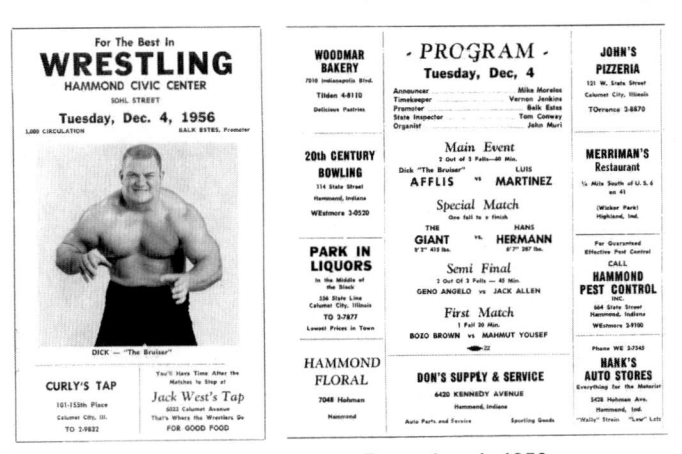

Hammond, Indiana • December 4, 1956
Source: William Estes

the crowd even before he was introduced. He shook his clenched fist at the crowd in defiance. Wearing long tights and a ring jacket, Afflis initially shook hands with opponent Melby, but gradually drifted into his classic bad guy repertoire. He used standard bad-guy tactics, like pulling hair, choking Melby, or not breaking cleanly when the ref so instructed. Those methods were played masterfully by Bruiser. He also showed impressive agility as he flew around the ring, the recipient of repeated arm drag take-downs and four consecutive flying dropkicks. The Bruiser also took arching backdrops from Melby when called to do so. The match ended with Melby injuring himself when he missed an attempted flying tackle against the Bruiser. Melby was unable to continue and the match was awarded to the Bruiser.

Eight nights later at the Marigold, Bruiser was booked to wrestle Billy Wicks, a legitimate shooter who had been in the wrestling business less than a year, but had several years taking on all-comers in carnivals. Wicks told about the experience in a 1998 interview with Scott Teal.

> "*I didn't get to talk with (Bruiser) before the match, or after for that matter. They just told me to go in there and lay down* [lose the match] *when I was ready. Bruiser charged across the ring and tore into me. I just moved around and took him down. I got up and he starts stomping and kicking me. I wasn't used to being abused like that. He started stomping the shit out of me and I'm going,* 'Wait a minute now. This is supposed to be a work.' *Of course, he didn't want to let me have anything, so I just started screwing up every time he tried anything. He picked me up and slammed me. He picked me up to slam me again, but I got a little heavier for him that time. The third time, I small packaged him up, then let him go. Well, he didn't like that too much. I thought,* 'Hell, what's going on here?'
>
> *The referee says,* 'Slow down, kid.'
>
> *Anyway, I did the job and made $800.*

— **Publicity in *Life* Magazine**

In 1956, Bruiser received some of the first national publicity for pro wrestling in *LIFE* magazine, one of the most popular publications in this country. A full pictorial on page 102 in the May 7, 1956, edition showed an "awesomely muscled"

Bruiser in a test-of-strength demonstration by a 67-year-old, 109 lb., former bantamweight champion boxer named Johnny Coulon. Other athletes pictured with smaller images in the article with Coulon were Jack Dempsey, Gene Tunney, Primo Carnera, Joe Louis, and Rocky Marciano — all boxing legends. Bruiser's image with Coulon was the biggest, illustrating Bruiser's thick thighs that looked like tree trunks.

— Milwaukee County Stadium

By the summer 1956, Bruiser's drawing power was evident as he was booked into one of the two main events in one of the biggest-drawing professional wrestling cards of the decade, held on Saturday, August 4, 1956, at County Stadium in Milwaukee. Co-promoters Fred Kohler and Johnny Heim booked a U.S. TV title match featuring title-holder Wilbur Snyder against Verne Gagne. The special referee for that match was former heavyweight boxing champion Jack Dempsey, then known as "The Manassa Mauler." Dempsey was brought in to maintain order if combatants Gagne and Snyder got out of hand. Based on past encounters, while Gagne and Snyder were mainly scientific wrestlers, emotions would get the best of them and the rulebook would go out the window. Dempsey arrived in town in advance of the card to promote the show, telling an audience, "*Wrestlers give you a show, and boxers seldom do.*"

Wilbur Snyder • 1950
Source: Estate of
Shirlie Montgomery

In the second main event, Dick the Bruiser teamed with Hans Schmidt against Reggie and Stan Lisowski. A special stipulation of the match stated the referee would officiate from the outside of the ring. The Sunday, July 29, 1956, edition of the *Milwaukee Journal* featured a six-man photo spread headlining page three of the sports section — Melby, Bruiser, Snyder, Gagne, (Angelo) Poffo, and Schmidt. The newspaper used many of the wrestlers' standard publicity stills, illustrating the clout of wrestling promoters in those days within the mainstream print media. By Friday, August 3, 1956, advance sales for the card exceeded $20,000, and the following day, promoter Johnny Heim predicted the crowd would exceed 20,000 fans.

On the night of Saturday, August 4, 1956, a very respectable crowd of 16,069 turned out, paying $33,689, one of the largest gates for an outdoor wrestling card in the U.S., although it was far short of the $103,278 plus gate for Lou Thesz vs. Baron Michele Leone in Los Angeles on May 21, 1952. While Jack Dempsey was brought in to ensure a controlled bout, nothing like that happened. Dempsey disqualified champion Wilbur Snyder, handed the title belt to Gagne, and left the ring. There's no record of how signals got mixed, but that couldn't have been the planned finish to the match. Under NWA rules, a title belt cannot change hands by disqualification, so the belt should have remained with Snyder. Why Dempsey presented the belt to Gagne is a mystery. As a result, Fred Kohler had to get into the ring and explain to the fans that Snyder was still the champion.

For the main-event tag bout, *Milwaukee Sentinel* columnist Bryl described the mayhem that ensued:

> "Saturday night was the rowdiest night of the week — at the stadium, anyway. ... Hans Schmidt and Dick the Bruiser visited the first and third base line in pursuit of Reggie and Stan Lisowski in their tag match tele-a-tete. Reggie and Stan, the world champs in this category of matdom, returned the honors shortly thereafter. To make matters even more unpredictable, the ring was barren of arbiters. However, two were stationed just outside the ring. When the battlers were too tired to continue (no 'official' wrestling had yet taken place), things were called to a halt, and lo and behold, the Lisowskis had retained their laurels."

On this big card, a relatively young Bruiser, Snyder, Gagne, and Reggie Lisowski set the stage for decades of headline wrestling performances in the Midwest.

— Feud with Antonino Rocca

Also in mid-1956, the Bruiser began a program with one of the biggest names in the history of professional wrestling — the legendary Antonino Rocca. In June 1956, Bruiser found himself in Hammond, Indiana, in a tag bout against Rocca, followed by a singles match three days later in Janesville, Wisconsin. Black and white film survives of a September 14, 1956, match from Chicago's International Amphitheatre. The bout featured Verne Gagne, Wilbur Snyder and Antonino Rocca against Dick the Bruiser, Reggie Lisowski and Stan Lisowski. Two referees were required to maintain order during this wild two-out-of-three-falls contest.

Announcer Russ Davis warned viewers, "*Bar the door. This is going to be a donnybrook.*" The Bruiser took great bumps that night — leg sweeps, back flips, and arm drags. In a trademark maneuver, Rocca leaped into the air onto Bruiser's shoulders as announcer Davis cried out, "*Let's play horsey.*" Rocca then somersaulted down, rolled the Bruiser over, and proceeded to pound his fists into Bruiser's stomach. Later in the match, when the Bruiser growled at one of the referees, announcer Davis posed the question, "*Doesn't he have a nice voice?*" Davis said Bruiser's voice sounded "*like a ruptured foghorn.*"

Fellow wrestler Stan Lisowski wrestled on many cards with the Bruiser during these early years and remembers the money paid to professional wrestlers in those days. When asked if wrestlers in those days were paid more than a ditch digger, Stan answered, "*Not too much more. I could tell you some stories about how much a guy earned, sometimes in the ring three times in one day. It didn't pay. Today, people think the guy was on TV and made a fortune — a fortune my eye! I don't know how many times I went and drove quite a ways to do a show for TV and got twenty-five bucks.*"

WRESTLING
HAMMOND
CIVIC CENTER
WORLD'S CHAMPIONSHIP
MATCHES
Tues., Nov. 13th, 8:30 P.M.
SPECIAL EVENT
VERNE GAGNE
vs.
"THE BRUISER"
GIRLS
JOAN BALLARD vs. Ilse SCHMIDT
ANGELO vs. MALKOV
LUIS Martinez vs. JACK WILSON
Ringside $1.50—General Adm. $1.20
Student 50c
Tickets on Sale . . .
Dave's Camera Mart, 214 Russell St.

Hammond, Indiana
December 4, 1956

Chapter 7
A Night To Remember — 1957-1958

— Madison Square Garden Debut

In November 1956, Dick the Bruiser made his first appearances on the eastern seaboard, namely in Washington DC, during which time he appeared on five consecutive weekly TV appearances under the promotion of Capitol Wrestling Corporation, a forerunner of the WWF. Eventually, the Bruiser was booked in the main event at one of professional wrestling's meccas, Madison Square Garden in New York City, on Monday, November 26, 1956. His opponent was the undisputed most-popular wrestler on the east coast at the time — Antonino Rocca. It had been more than eleven months since wrestling had been held in the Garden and fans were anxious to see some hot action. East Coast fans had not seen Bruiser on the DuMont Network because he had never appeared on the nationally broadcast show. Even though Rocca won the match, it was quite an accomplishment for Dick the Bruiser to be headlining in New York City in what was only his second year as a full-time professional wrestler. Bruiser would return to the Garden many times during the next 12 months.

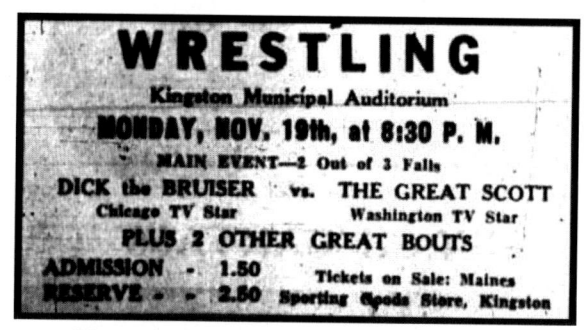

Kingston, New York • November 19, 1956

— Fundraiser in Boston

In 1957, Bruiser once again found himself booked on the east side of the USA and Canada. On Tuesday, October 22, he made a special appearance outside of the ring at the Parker House Hotel in downtown Boston. The event was a benefit dinner for the local Abou Ben Adhem Temple — Knights of Pythias, a predecessor of the Shriners Organization, dedicated to helping crippled children. Bruiser was in the midst of a wrestling program with French-Canadian Edouard Carpentier. They had an upcoming match scheduled for Monday, October 28, 1957, at the Boston Arena. The New England promoter, Paul Bowser, also was at that dinner and was shown in photos of the event. Several days later, the now defunct *Boston Evening American* featured a photo of Bruiser holding up a 4-year-old boy named Paul Yanetti from suburban Chelsea. Fifty-seven years later, Paul Yanetti, now a government contract officer, reminisced about that night with the help of his still-living mother:

Chapter 7 • 61

"I talked to my mother about the charity dinner. She was not a sports or wrestling fan, so she didn't know about Dick the Bruiser beforehand. She never saw him on TV. She said he was very charming and courteous, down to earth, and very much a gentleman at the dinner. Yes, I wore leg braces until I was about ten years old or so. When I grew up, I started running and have run probably a hundred road races and two marathons. So things worked out well for me, thanks to charitable celebrities like Dick who helped raise money and awareness."

Shriner's benefit • Boston, Massachusetts • 1957
Source: Boston Herald

Decades of professional wrestling cards at Madison Square Garden have been painstakingly documented in the book, *Wrestling in the Garden — The Battle for New York — Shoots, Works, and Double-Crosses*, written by Scott Teal and J Michael Kenyon. The compilation notes that Bruiser appeared on ten wrestling cards at Madison Square Garden. He had a mixed win-loss record during his run in both singles and tag team actions, and usually was booked on one of the top three bouts of the card. While out east, Bruiser also picked up payoffs for appearances in places like White Plains, New York, and Bridgeport, Connecticut.

MAT FANS RIOT IN GARDEN

— Riot in New York City

Bruiser's highest-profile match in New York City took place on Tuesday, November 19, 1957, at Madison Square Garden. In the seventh and final bout of the card, Bruiser was originally scheduled to team with Killer Kowalski against Antonino Rocca and Edouard Carpentier, opponents he was very familiar with. On the morning of that show, newspaper ads noted that Dr. Jerry Graham would substitute for Kowalski. The match was scheduled for two-out-of-three falls to a finish with Bruiser billed as being from the state of Montana.

Professional wrestling historian Fred Hornby, who was present at that card when he was a teenager, wrote in 2011 that *"it was a night to remember."* Hornby added that rain most of the day kept the crowd to 12,987, in a building that could hold up to 20,000 fans. Journalist Gordon S. White Jr. covered the wrestling card for the *New York Times* on that memorable night, a rare assignment for him as he was usually assigned to college sports and golf. White's headlines in the *New York Times* the next morning read, "Wrestling Ends In Riot At Garden" and "Two Policeman Hurt as Fans Storm Ring and Throw Chairs and Bottles."

What happened? The mayhem began during the second fall of the match, after Bruiser and Graham had already lost the first fall after 18 minutes and 27 seconds. Gordon White Jr. reminisced in 2012:

> "I remember the riot very well and what really precipitated it. That was when Rocca, angered by being truly injured and bleeding, grabbed Graham around the neck in a bear hug and ran him all the way across the ring into the brass ring post, splitting open the top of Graham's head. Blood poured into his bright blond (dyed) curls and the crowd went crazy."

Fred Hornby remembers *"watching chairs, cans and bottles tossed from the balcony regions."* Hornby added, *"Bruiser and Graham stood back-to-back, tossing their attackers* [the fans] *out of the ring onto the floor."* Hornby escaped personal injury by retreating from ringside shortly after the conflict began. The riot attracted the attention of *Life* magazine, which ran a pictorial story in the December 2, 1957, issue, along with the headline, "Wrestling Script Goes Awry." The pictorial featured a full-length photo of Dr. Jerry Graham with blood streaming down his face. In March 2011, back-up referee Ed Gersh retold his experiences of that 1957 riot night.

> "A good friend of mine was Antonino Rocca. I was a dean of a school in Harlem and used to bring in the wrestlers to speak to students on moral values. I was a seasoned referee and had been hit many times accidentally.

I was a former fighter and knew how to take care of myself. I wasn't concerned about myself, but I was concerned about the spectators who would be getting out of hand. That's why I tried to settle things up in the ring and calm things down."

When he realized the crowd was getting out of control and referee Danny Bartfield was unable to keep order, Gersh decided to run into the ring and help. Gersh also was concerned that the ensuing chaos wouldn't sit well with the New York State Athletic Commission. The bedlam received widespread coverage in all the New York City newspapers. In addition, the December 2nd issue of *Time* magazine noted that *"only when real blood fell on the canvas did the crowd realize that it was watching a real fight for a change; few in the Garden wanted to waste the rare opportunity as beer bottles sailed ringward."*

MADISON SQUARE GARDEN
OFFICIAL PROGRAM
TUNE IN CHANNEL 5 EVERY THURSDAY NIGHT
FOR THE BEST WRESTLING SHOWS

TUESDAY, NOVEMBER 19, 1957
TAG TEAM MATCH TWO OUT OF THREE FALLS TO A FINISH

Antonino ROCCA So. America AND Eduardo CARPENTIER France	**vs.**	Killer KOWALSKI Canada AND The BRUISER Montana

TIME LIMIT

| Miguel PEREZ
Porto Rica
Won | VS | Danny McSHANE
Ireland
Time |

TAG TEAM MATCH

| Eduardo CASTILLO
Spain
AND
Luis MARTINEZ
Mexico
Won | **vs.** | Karl VON HESS
Prussia
AND
Ludwig VON KRUPP
Germany
Time |

TIME LIMIT

| Pat O'CONNOR
Australia | | Don EAGLE
Indian Chief |

TIME LIMIT

| Skull MURPHY
Ireland
Won | VS | The GREAT SCOTT
Camden, N. J.
Time |

TIME LIMIT

| Dr. Jerry GRAHAM
California
Won | VS | Bob LONGEVIN
Canada
Time |

TIME LIMIT

| Paul BERGER
Germany
Won | VS | Chief BIG HEART
Oklahoma
Time |

Four Wrestlers in Riot Fined $2,600
— State Athletic Commission

Gersh was certainly correct that the riot would not sit well with the New York State Athletic Commission. On Friday morning, November 22, 1957, the commission held a hearing on the riot at its offices then located at 226 W. 47th Street in Manhattan, a few short blocks from Madison Square Garden, the site of all the trouble. Commissioner Julius Helfand canceled the next wrestling event at the Garden scheduled for November 30, 1957, during which time Rocca was booked to face Chief Big Heart. Helfand warned that if commission rules were not followed, the commission might take action that would "endanger the future of wrestling" in the state of New York. Rocca and Graham were fined $1,000 each, while Afflis was fined $500 and Carpentier was fined $100. Fortunately, the wrestlers were not banned from the ring in New York State. In order to get some mileage out of the publicity, though, Bruiser later claimed the commission "banned him for life." However, he made three more appearances on subsequent Madison Square Garden cards.

Afflis reflected on the "riot" experience later in 1981 in his interview with Dick Mittman:

"They said I started the riot, which I had no more to do with than anybody else in the ring. There were twenty thousand fans there, I was beating up their idol, and they charged the ring. Everybody fled the ring and I got caught in there. I couldn't get out of it. The policemen and myself were in the ring, and it looked like the Alamo. Most of them [fans] had those umbrellas, and they had the ends of them sharpened. They were trying to stab you with those things. I didn't get a scratch out of it, but many people got hurt."

Chapter 8
No Lilacs, Bobby Pins, or Peroxide — 1958

— Faces Gorgeous George

During his early career as a wrestler, Dick the Bruiser had brushes with greatness when he faced 1950s wrestling icons like Thesz, Gagne, Rocca, and Carpentier. However, he didn't cross paths with one of the biggest and brightest stars in the business until Friday, July 11, 1958, at Chicago's International Amphitheatre. That superstar was Gorgeous George. Born George Raymond Wagner in 1915, George had been wrestling professionally since 1934, and his previous Chicago appearance had been almost four years earlier on September 10, 1954. Fueled by television exposure of his bleached blond hair, elaborate orchid ring robes, golden bobby pins, accompanying valets, and outrageous personality, Gorgeous George was a national celebrity. The valet role — that of taking care of George's robe and spraying the ring with perfume — was now filled by his girlfriend and future wife, Cherie Dupre, who weighed in at around 94 lbs.. The *Chicago Daily News* jokingly wrote, "*The Amphitheatre's air-conditioning may dispel the mist.*"

Gorgeous George & Cheri Dupre
Photo by Tony Lanza

Promoter Fred Kohler and his associate, Bob Luce, went all out in promoting that first meeting between George and the Bruiser. The pre-match, multi-dimensional publicity campaign probably was more noteworthy than the match itself.

— One-Man Parade

During the week of the wrestling card, Lions Club International was in town, complete with their own parade scheduled for downtown. Gorgeous George was denied his request to participate in the parade, so publicity ace Bob Luce staged a "one-man parade," starting at the Marigold Arena on the north side of Chicago, passing through downtown, and returning back to the Marigold ... not once, but twice. The

Gorgeous George & Cheri Dupre
Courtesy Scott Teal Collection

newspaper coverage was heavy as the *Chicago American* featured the headline, "Gorgeous Still At It; Antics Tie Up Traffic." Columnist Gene Kessler of the *Chicago Sun Times* said, "*Bruiser is a one-man crusader bent upon ridding the mat world of effeminate characters.*" Kessler quoted Bruiser as saying, "*No sissy who marcels bleach blond hair, has a lady valet, and tosses orchids to the female fans, belongs in the same ring with me.*"

George and Cherie had their photograph taken and published at the chic Chez Paree nightclub with one of Hollywood's leading beauties, Kim Novak. George's schedule included appearances on radio talk programs, at neighborhood community festivals, and at Honolulu Harry's Waikiki supper club, which also was a loyal advertiser for *Wrestling Life*. Ironically, Dick the Bruiser appeared in many of the supper club's advertisements for years on the back cover of the magazine.

— Bruiser Defeats George

The match that Friday night led off with a three-man bagpipe ensemble marching down the aisles. All the tried-and-true routines — throwing out bobby pins and orchids, and spraying the ring with perfume — were performed by George and Cherie. The newspaper headlines the next day in the *Chicago Tribune* read, "Bruiser Wins Over Gorgeous George, 2 to 1." The crowd attendance was reported as being 6,002 and gross gate receipts were $14,705.68. The *Chicago Daily News* proclaimed, "Same Old Act Still Good" as Cherie tended to the defeated George and "combed his messed-up locks and gave him a sniff of smelling salts." The event, however, even with all the hoopla, failed to garner a fraction of the anticipated fan reaction and interest. Dick the Bruiser was pictured snarling at Cherie Dupre on the cover of the August 1958 edition of *Wrestling Life*, but it would be just a one-night stand in Chicago. The *Chicago Daily News* reported: "He [George] lost the first fall, came roaring back to win the second fall in 58 seconds flat, but went down hard to defeat in the third and final fall."

— Fort Wayne Sequel

Their next meeting was scheduled for the following Friday, July 18, 1958, at Zollner Stadium in Fort Wayne, Indiana. (ad at left) Gorgeous George previously drew 3,684 fans to Zollner four years earlier and the local newspaper proclaimed him as "wrestling's all-time box-office attraction." The *Fort Wayne Journal-Gazette* reported on the July 18 fiasco, saying, *"The more than two thousand fans at Zollner Stadium last night enjoyed the unique showmanship of Gorgeous George, nationally-known*

TONITE 8:30

Gorgeous

GEORGE

Vs.

The

BRUISER

ZOLLNER STADIUM
8:30

-- ALSO --

Hans Herman
Vs.
Bobbie Managoff

and

Carl Engstrum
Vs.
Swede Karlsson

Tickets on Sale
Tri-State Ticket
Office, Hotel
Keenan E-7371

Stadium Open
7 p.m. Call A-8408

FORT WAYNE NEWS-SENTINEL FRIDAY JANUARY 9, 1959

RECORD WRESTLING CROWD AT THE COLISEUM – Here's how the Memorial Coliseum looked on Thursday night as a record crowd for wrestling in Indiana was on hand for the three match program which featured a "death" struggle between Hans Schmidt and Dick (The Bruiser) Afflis.

ESTIMATE 3,000 TURNED AWAY
It Happened: Sellout for Wrestling
By Bud Gallmeier

They said it couldn't be done – sell out the Coliseum for a wrestling match. But it happened Thursday night as 9,039 fans jammed into the big building to see Hans Schmidt and Dick (The Bruiser) Afflis wrestle to the "death". An estimated 3,000 were turned away. Schmidt won the battle. But Schmidt, who is the "meanest man in the world" except when he is sent in against the Bruiser, and Afflis (who is the meanest man in the world all the time), had to play second fiddle to the crowd. They provided the most entertainment and the real story in this craziest of all developments in the world of sports for Fort Wayne.

Five months ago, Tri-State Promotions was seriously considering dropping wrestling from its list of promotional ventures. People didn't apparently want wrestling. But suddenly, the sport caught on again. Last night's show was the seventh of the indoor season. The total attendance for the seven shows was been 39,839. This averages out to 5,691 per program. Probably the happiest guy about the whole thing is Coliseum Manager Don Myers. Since the transfer of the Pistons to Detroit, it has been no secret that Myers has been a little concerned about the future of the big building. The Coliseum's cut from last night's show should approximate $2,500. The rent alone was $1,476. There were about 2,500 cars on the parking lot which brought in about $600. The Coliseum's cut of the concessions should just about match that figure.

And the State of Indiana should be happy too. The state's cut was $1,000. The crowd set a record for attendance at a wrestling match in Indiana. The previous high was 5,500 established in Indianapolis in December. The fact that Fort Wayne and area fans are seeing wrestling's greatest stars at bargain prices is emphasized by the difference in the gross gate for this record crowd and that for the one in Indianapolis. The gross gate last night was $10,370. The gross at Indianapolis, where a $3.60 top is paid, was $30,000. Maybe that's the secret of Phil Olofson's success.

REPRINTED COURTESY OF THE FORT WAYNE NEWS-SENTINEL.

platinum-haired grappler, but they left very unhappy over the outcome." The article continued with, *"George called at seven o'clock p.m. from Dyer, Indiana, saying his car had broken down, but he chartered a plane out of Chicago."* In the meantime, Dick the Bruiser was running late, so promoters matched up Gorgeous George with Gypsy Joe, who had wrestled earlier that night. Rain was threatening, so promoters decided they couldn't wait for Bruiser to show up. When he did, promoters announced that Gorgeous George would face Dick the Bruiser in a one-fall match. After Bruiser won the fall and *"charged after Gorgeous George who retreated to the dressing room,"* the crowd was left grumbling over somewhat of a screwball finish.

They met again on Saturday, August 2, 1958, at Buck Lake Ranch in Angola, Indiana, which was followed by a rematch at Zollner Stadium for Thursday, August 21, 1958. Print publicity in local newspapers was classic, claiming George "canceled two television interviews for July 17 in favor of a three-hour session in the beauty shop." On Friday, the *Fort Wayne Journal-Gazette* post-match headlines read, "George-Afflis Scrap Declared No Contest." Referee Dick Patton, former Indianapolis wrestling promoter, declared the match no contest *"because the two were doing more wrestling and fighting outside the ring than within."* The following week, the newspaper reported, *"The police wanted to avoid any difficulty with the ringside fans, who were in a threatening turmoil."*

With no conclusive finish that night, George and Bruiser were booked the following week for Zollner's summer season finale, this time for a tag team match. George and Bobby Managoff were scheduled to wrestle Bruiser and Karl Karlson in the main event. However, the match never took place. George told promoters he had "an abscessed tooth which required surgery" and didn't show up that night. The two local newspapers reported an estimated 18 out of 750 customers asked for refunds due to Gypsy Joe substituting for George.

Gorgeous George's short program with Dick the Bruiser did nothing to turnaround George's sagging professional wrestling career. Wrestling historian Don Luce pointed out that *"in his heyday, he* [George] *was really something as far as a drawing card as he could set his own price all the time."* Unfortunately, Luce added, *"Gorgeous George had a drinking problem and 'no showed' a lot of matches, and a lot of promoters did not put up with that."* By this stage in the game, George was trying to live off his previous national reputation as one of the pioneers of the revival of professional wrestling on a television stage. As Luce pointed out, *"You can only stay on top so long and they* [promoters] *start pushing somebody else."* That "somebody else" was Dick the Bruiser, and the Bruiser's career would continue to grow and expand.

Chapter 9
I Created a Monster — 1959-1963

On January 2, 1959, someone broke into the trunk of Bruiser's parked car in Indianapolis. They stole a suitcase full of clothes, a .25 caliber Colt automatic, and some wrestling trunks.

Wrestling fans from as far east as New York and Washington, and as far north as Montreal and Boston, were witness to wrestling's new phenomenon. In March 1959, a major Midwest city — Detroit, Michigan — experienced the beginnings of its own wrestling renaissance. Detroit wrestling historian Rob Bauer remembers the big names who appeared on wrestling cards in Detroit in early 1956 under the promotion of Harry Light; Antonino Rocca, Lord James Blears, Verne Gagne, and Hans Schmidt headlined mat shows during that time. A card on May 24, 1956, featured former world heavyweight boxing champion Joe Louis against Brute Bernard, and a semi-final match between Buddy Rogers and Lou Klein. That card, however, would be one of the last wrestling events held in Detroit until April 1959.

Detroit, always a powerhouse of the automobile industry and a city with a population of 1.5 million, was the home of a major indoor sports venue called Olympia Stadium. Built in the late '20s, the Olympia was most famous for being the home of the Detroit Red Wings of the National Hockey League. It was located on Grand River Road at McGraw, several miles northwest of downtown Detroit.

Olympia Stadium, Grand River Road • Detroit • 1956
Source: Artist of Detroit

— Doyle and Barnett Launch Promotion

Unfortunately, major professional wrestling in Detroit disappeared until early 1959. At that time, two established veterans of professional wrestling, Johnny Doyle and James Barnett, formed a new wrestling promotion that promised a "new era in wrestling in Detroit" in its promotional material. James Barnett had previous dealings with Dick the Bruiser during the mid-'50s when Barnett worked for Chicago wrestling czar Fred Kohler. Subsequently, a television program was arranged through outlet CKLW-TV in Windsor, Ontario, Canada, under the name *Big Time Wrestling* on Channel 9. Modern day Detroit wrestling columnist and coach, Kurt Schneider, remembers:

"*Growing up in Detroit, I watched* [the Bruiser] *on Channel 9, just like everybody else. I remember this, but was just a kid. That TV program* [on CKLW-TV] *was the preeminent wrestling program of its time.*"

Ticket stub for CKLW TV • 1960

CKLW-TV hosting duties were assigned to Sam Menacker, a long-time professional wrestler, promoter, and personality. Menacker wrote in the event programs that Doyle and Barnett "*have at their fingertips, access to the world's best wrestlers.*" He added, "*cost is no object as far as they are concerned*" as "*they only bring the finest to Detroit.*" Menacker's inimitable hype promised "*Olympia fans will see the world's most exciting wrestling on regular cards presented every three to four weeks ... There will be no let-down in the excitement or the quality of the wrestlers.*"

Before a live card was presented at the Olympia, several weekly wrestling telecasts originated from CKLW-TV and were broadcast in the metropolitan area. Detroit major newspapers, such as now defunct *Detroit Times*, covered professional wrestling extensively on its sports pages. Reporter Charles P. Ward described one of the early telecasts in the *Detroit Times* by writing, "*Virtue, good sportsmanship, and that sort of thing were triumphant again today after last night's wrestling jamboree at CKLW-TV in Windsor.*"

Doyle and Barnett used television to build up the two initial feuds that would showcase their first card at the Olympia: Wilbur Snyder versus Angelo Poffo and, of course, Dick the Bruiser versus Yukon Eric. Reporter Ward commented that the Bruiser "*looks a good deal like James Cagney might look after somebody bounced a brick off his noggin*" and may be "*a guy who might scowl in his sleep.*" Ward added, "*Bruiser didn't sign the contract* [to wrestle Yukon Eric] *until customers taunted him with charge he couldn't sign because he couldn't write.*"

The first big card at the Olympia was scheduled for Saturday, April 11, 1959, with steady build-up featured in the print media. Much of the hype surrounded the match-up between Wilbur Snyder and Angelo Poffo, who had underhandedly defeated Snyder during a match telecasted on CKLW-TV, whereby Poffo's manager, Bronco Lubich, clubbed Snyder with his cane. Announcer Sam Menacker claimed, "*Thousands of fans wrote indignant letters, acidly protesting*

WILD ACTION!

Motor City Wrestling, 3:30 pm

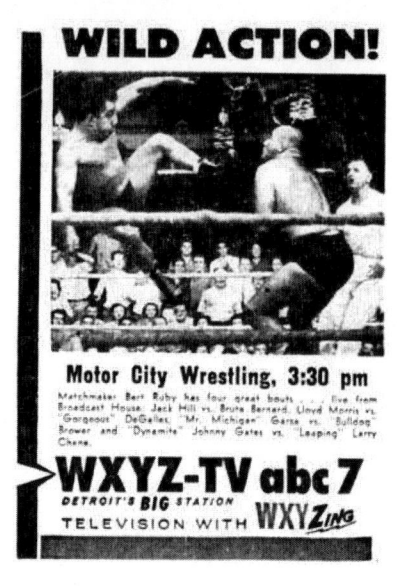

WXYZ-TV abc 7
DETROIT'S BIG STATION
TELEVISION WITH WXYZing

Poffo's foul tactics." Bruiser got his share of publicity by badmouthing Yukon Eric, saying, *"He can't be too smart. Although there is no snow on the ground, he wears lumberjack boots into the ring and then wrestles in his bare feet."*

Even officials from the Olympia got involved, such as Louis Marudas claimed in the *Detroit Times*:

"I walk down the street and friends stop me to give me money for tickets. We have received mail from Flint, Saginaw, Port Huron, Ann Arbor, Milan, Lapeer, Owosso, Lansing, Jackson, and dozen other places in Michigan. We have received orders from Chatham, Sarnia, Windsor, and Blenheim in Ontario, and as well as from Toledo."

Author's note: Louis Marudas was the person in charge of arranging and scheduling boxing and wrestling at the Olympia. In newspaper reports, he was listed as "matchmaker," although Jim Barnett and Johnny Doyle were calling the shots. Years later, when Bruiser ran opposition to the Sheik in Detroit, Marudas acted as his front man.

The broadcast signal from CKLW-TV did, indeed, go as far as Toledo, about 60 miles to the south, and there, a young boy named Jerry Jaffee would be exposed to Dick the Bruiser and to professional wrestling in general. Jaffee remembers seeing Bruiser during that time. By the time he was in his mid-20s, Jaffee would be working for Dick the Bruiser in Indianapolis, eventually using the ring name Dr. Jerry Graham, Jr.

— Opening Night at the Olympia

Saturday, April 11, 1959, marked the beginning of the new era in wrestling in Detroit, and what a success it was. The *Detroit Times* reported "16,266 Fans Jam Olympia" — the largest wrestling crowd in over 20 years and the biggest box office gross of any wrestling event ever at the Olympia — $40,394.

While the main event featured U.S. heavyweight champ Angelo Poffo defending his title against Wilbur Snyder, it was Dick the Bruiser who stole the show. When Bruiser tied up Yukon Eric's neck between the ropes, the *Detroit Times* noted, *"Irate fans threw tomatoes, peanuts, paper cups, and whatever objects they had into the ring."* About a dozen spectators tried to get into the ring "to give Yukon Eric a hand," as well. One report noted, "*A cordon of policemen stationed*

WRESTLING TONITE

and every
**THURSDAY
9 - 10 p.m.**

Featuring Tonite
**DICK "THE BRUISER"
and
WILBUR SNYDER**

CKLW-TV channel **9**

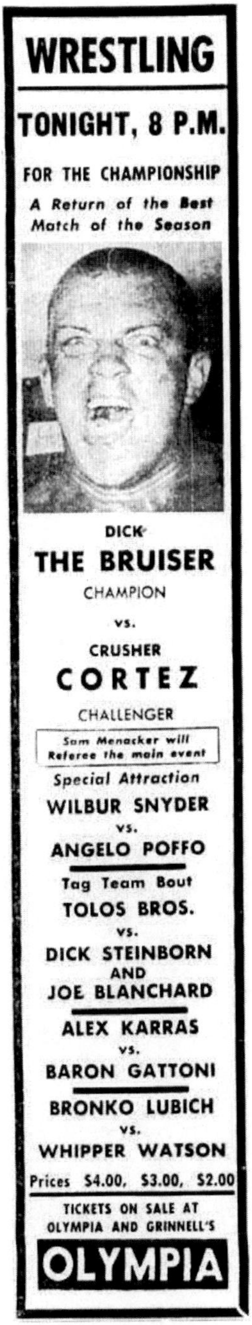

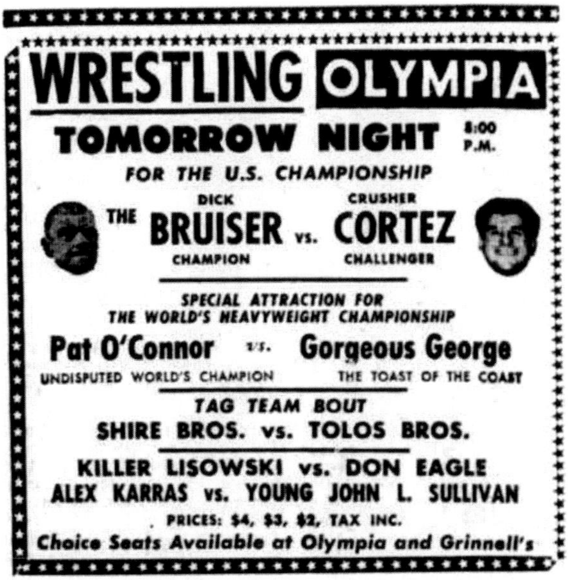

Chapter 9 • 71

WRESTLING
TONIGHT, 8 P.M.
FOR THE CHAMPIONSHIP
A Return of the Best Match of the Season

DICK THE BRUISER
CHAMPION
vs.
CRUSHER CORTEZ
CHALLENGER

Sam Menacker will Referee the main event

Special Attraction
WILBUR SNYDER
vs.
ANGELO POFFO

Tag Team Bout
TOLOS BROS.
vs.
DICK STEINBORN AND JOE BLANCHARD

ALEX KARRAS
vs.
BARON GATTONI

BRONKO LUBICH
vs.
WHIPPER WATSON

Prices $4.00, $3.00, $2.00

TICKETS ON SALE AT OLYMPIA AND GRINNELL'S

OLYMPIA

WRESTLING OLYMPIA
TOMORROW NIGHT 8:00 P.M.
FOR THE U.S. CHAMPIONSHIP

DICK THE BRUISER vs. **CRUSHER CORTEZ**
CHAMPION — CHALLENGER

SPECIAL ATTRACTION FOR THE WORLD'S HEAVYWEIGHT CHAMPIONSHIP
Pat O'Connor vs. Gorgeous George
UNDISPUTED WORLD'S CHAMPION — THE TOAST OF THE COAST

TAG TEAM BOUT
SHIRE BROS. vs. TOLOS BROS.

KILLER LISOWSKI vs. DON EAGLE
ALEX KARRAS vs. YOUNG JOHN L. SULLIVAN

PRICES: $4, $3, $2, TAX INC.
Choice Seats Available at Olympia and Grinnell's

Wrestling at the Olympia

WRESTLING
TONITE (SAT.) 8:00 P.M.
FOR THE CHAMPIONSHIP

Dick the BRUISER
U.S. CHAMPION
Vs.
Dr. Big Bill MILLER
No. 1 CHALLENGER

World's Championship Tag Team Match
THE SHIRE BROS.
vs.
RAOL ROMERO and YUKON ERIC

SPECIAL ATTRACTION
Jiu Jitsu Match with Jackets
BRONKO LUBITCH
vs.
KINJI SHIBUYA

Angelo Poffo vs. Killer Kowalski
Pepper Gomez vs. Mitsu Arakawa

PRICES: $4, $3, $2 Tax Incl.
Choice Seats Available at Olympia and Grinnell's

OLYMPIA

WRESTLING
FRI., DEC. 30 8:00 P.M.
FOR THE WORLD'S TAG TEAM CHAMPIONS

DICK THE BRUISER
AND
KILLER KOWALSKI
vs.
ANTONINO ROCCA
and
VERNE GAGNE

SPECIAL ATTRACTION
WILBUR SNYDER
vs.
ERNIE DUSEK

Larry Hamilton vs. Emil Dupre
John Pisek vs. George McArthur
Luis Martinez vs. Dick Garza

PRICES: $4, $3, $2 TAX INC.
Choice Seats Available at Olympia & Grinnell's

OLYMPIA

(above, clockwise)
January 15, 1960
January 2
November 26
December 30

themselves around the ring and got some exercise repelling spectators who tried to get into the act." Dick the Bruiser won his match against Yukon Eric that night.

Wrestling historian Rob Bauer attended this debut and reminisced about the atmosphere at the Olympia:

> "There was no entrance music, no female valets, and no fireworks — just good old school wrestling. The old Olympia pipe organ would be played during the intermission, giving a real sport feel. There were programs for sale, but no marketing gimmicks [posters, photos, etc.]. There probably [could have] been a lot of Bruiser t-shirts and action figures sold because he was that popular, even though he was a heel."

The Bruiser faced Yukon Eric the following week on Wednesday, April 22, 1959, at the Arena in Windsor, Ontario, Canada. Now billed as being from Chicago, this was Bruiser's first appearance at this venue in more than three years. The *Windsor Daily Star* reported the combatants "*produced thirteen minutes of wild action, but all they gained for their effort was a 'no disqualification' decision from* [the referee]."

From the Detroit "premiere" night on April 11, 1959, through July 14, 1961, Dick the Bruiser appeared on 39 out of 41 wrestling cards held at the Olympia. In addition, there would be two other cards at alternate locations, Tiger Stadium and suburban Hazel Park Raceway. During that time, Bruiser held the U.S. heavyweight title during the overwhelming majority of that period, dropping the title a few times, but usually winning the belt back during a rematch.

Rob Bauer commented on the Bruiser era in Detroit:

> "A lot of wrestling fans were born because of him. He had that gravel voice and wild tactics, something the people here had never seen before. They would boo him but try to see him all the time. People would come [to] the Olympia to see Bruiser lose the belt. He was definitely the showpiece of the promotion."

— A Who's Who of Wrestling

The list of wrestling opponents Bruiser wrestled reads like a "Who's Who of Wrestling" during the '50s and '60s — Wilbur Snyder, Cowboy Bob Ellis, Haystacks Calhoun, Verne Gagne, Dr. Bill Miller, Killer Lisowski (aka Reggie), Joe Brunetti, Don Eagle, Ricky Cortez, Raoul Romero, Pat O'Connor, Bobo Brazil, Angelo Poffo, Pepper Gomez, Larry Chene, Antonino Rocca, Killer Kowalski, Leo Nomellini, and Fritz Von Erich.

With all these matches, there are many standouts over this 28-month period, illustrating the creative planning of promoters Doyle and Barnett and the flawless performance of Dick the Bruiser. On the second wrestling card of the new Olympia era, Saturday, May 2, 1959, Wilbur Snyder defeated Angelo Poffo in the main event to capture the U.S. heavyweight title, with Dick the Bruiser winning over Cowboy Bob Ellis in the semi-final, setting up a perfect rematch for the next show. Then, on May 23, Bruiser won two out of three falls from Wilbur Snyder to win the U.S. title. Wilbur's young son, Mike Snyder, made several trips with his dad to the Olympia in those days. Mike recalled, "*Wilbur would assign a policeman to me and* [then] *would hand me his billfold.*" Mike remembered that Wilbur later also told him, "*If I ever go home and your mother ever reiterates what happens in these dressing rooms, you'll never go with me again.*" In other words, "What happens in Detroit, stays in Detroit." Wilbur got his rematch on June 13, but was unsuccessful in regaining the belt.

Throughout 1959, Bruiser fought through his formidable string of opponents. On November 6, 1959, promoters staged an elimination tournament with the ultimate winner getting a title shot against Bruiser on November 28. One of the participants was Dick Steinborn, son of long-time wrestler Milo Steinborn and frequent wrestler in Detroit during the Bruiser era. Steinborn never faced Bruiser in the ring in Detroit, though. Steinborn shared a story with the author involving promoter Jim Barnett. Barnett was sitting in the TV control room watching Bruiser in the ring when he suddenly cried out loud, "*I created a monster.*" Besides Steinborn, other participants in the tourney were Gorgeous George, Roy Shire, Ray Shire (aka Ray Stevens), Joe Blanchard, Bronco Lubich, Hans Schmidt, and Joe Brunetti. The referee had the power to declare a winner if neither wrestler won the match within the prescribed time limit. The final two

WRESTLING OLYMPIA
TONIGHT AT 8:00 P.M.
International
ONE NIGHT **TOURNAMENT**
16 BOUTS
17 GREAT STARS ★ INCLUDING:
ANGELO POFFO ★ MAX PALMER 6'8"
GORGEOUS GEORGE ★ NICK BOCK
HANS SCHMIDT ★ BRUNETTI BROS.
SHIRE BROS. ★ BRONKO LUBICH, etc.
PRICES $4, $3, $2, TAX INC.
Choice Seats Available at Olympia and Grinnell's

survivors were Brunetti and Roy Shire, with Brunetti ultimately winning to earn the shot at Bruiser. Bruiser, however, would successfully defend the belt against Brunetti.

On March 6, 1997, Scott Teal conducted a round-robin interview session with several wrestlers, including Dick Steinborn and Dick Beyer. The following is an excerpt from the transcript:

— Steinborn:

Hey, I went to Indianapolis for [Jim] *Barnett. He had big stars like* [Dick] *the Bruiser. He used to go to Detroit on Saturday night. There used to be a late flight that went back to Indianapolis. We're all on the plane and the girl is looking for her last passenger. There's like eight of us there. Here he comes. He walks up the steps like this. She says,* 'Are you going to Indianapolis?'

(gruff voice) 'No, I'm going to Chicago.'

'Well, this plane doesn't go into Chicago.'

He says, 'It goes to Chicago tonight,' *and walks into the plane. She walks to the front and I'm witnessing this from the back. It's like a theatre.* (laughs) *She says,* 'We got this guy that blah-blah-blah.'

The pilot says, 'Oh, that's Dick the Bruiser.' (all laugh)

He made the trip every two weeks to Detroit. Here's what I remember.

The plane only seats about forty-five or so and several of them are businessmen returning home. I'm standing in the back and, when I look up, everything's dark, except for one little light way up on the left side. It's Jim Barnett. He's got this little light on and Dick sits next to him. Dick's looking down at what Barnett's reading. Evidently, Barnett was showing Bruiser his little record book.

(imitates Barnett) 'Well, you drew this here and you drew that there.'

Evidently, in those days, Bruiser was so powerful that he'd say, (imitates Bruiser) 'Look, you want me at the matches? I'll be there, but I want to know what the house is and I want my money when I walk out of the building.'

I think that's what they were doing. Barnett must have said, 'I'll catch you on the plane coming back from Detroit.'

He got on the plane and showed him what he did in Louisville, what he did in Detroit. This is about two o'clock in the morning. All of a sudden, the quiet of the plane is shattered when Bruiser screams, 'WHAT!!!??' (laughs) *If you can imagine Woody Allen ... that's what Barnett looked like. What a cartoon Bruiser was!*

— Beyer:

He did that all the time, although it wasn't only in Detroit. He did that with every airplane he ever got on."

— Steinborn:

He always had an attaché case. He had a jockstrap, which he never washed. He had a pair of trunks, which he never washed. He had a towel, which he never washed. He used to bring it in the dressing room, put it next to you, and open it up. Jeez!"

— University of Detroit

On Wednesday, November 11, 1959, Bruiser was invited to the Union Ballroom at the University of Detroit by fraternity Alpha Kappa Psi. Bruiser spoke to the students "in character" and maintained his incorrigible demeanor. The University's student newspaper, The *Varsity News,* quoted Bruiser as saying, "*Just because I'm wearing a tie and a coat, I'm still a dirty rat.*" The *Detroit Times* added a follow-up quote of "*all professional wrestlers are a bunch of dirty rats, but I'm the leader of the pack.*" Bruiser bragged about hitting the Purdue coach with his football helmet and roughing up rowdy gamblers at Harold's Club in Reno. Bruiser was accompanied to the presentation by CKLW-TV commentator Sam Menacker, who dutifully asked why Bruiser continues to tear away on TV opponents after they are clearly beat up and worn down. Bruiser replied, "*I can't stand the idea of having people sit at home watching television while I'm here wrestling. It makes me mad. TV wrestling is only practice for me.*" Bruiser closed the program by claiming, "*I wondered how the smell of a university would strike me again. Well, it's just as rotten as I remembered it.*"

Source: The Detroit News

Wrestling

Linton-Stockton High School Gymnasium
THURSDAY, DEC. 17th
FIRST EVENT · 8:00 P. M. CST

Wrestling

MAIN EVENT
DICK THE BRUISER vs JOE BLANCHARD

SEMI-FINAL MATCH
GORGEOUS GEORGE vs DICK STEINBORN

OPENER
GINO ANGELO vs BILL DROMO

RINGSIDE $2.00 — SPONSORED BY L.H.S. BOOSTER CLUB — GENERAL ADMISSION $1.25

Lipton, Indiana • December 17, 1959

Bruiser eventually dropped the U.S. title to his frequent foe, Wilbur Snyder, on February 5, 1960, but won the belt back during the rematch on February 21. The next logical step for promoters Doyle and Barnett was to bring in the NWA world heavyweight champion to the Olympia. At the time, the champion was New Zealander Pat O'Connor, who won the NWA belt on Friday, January 9, 1959, from Dick Hutton at the Kiel Auditorium in St. Louis, Missouri. The scientific O'Connor was booked to put his title on the line against roughneck Bruiser on April 30, 1960. On that night, 10,635 fans paid $23,306 to see the match end in a one-hour draw. That visit by the NWA champion coincided with the month of the first anniversary of "Bruiser" wrestling at the Olympia.

The March 21, 1960, edition of the showbiz bible, *The Billboard* magazine, chimed in by saying, *"This year's wrestling bouts alone brought in $471,000, which is attributed to this season's star of the ring — Dick the Bruiser."*

— Cowboy Bob Ellis

For Bruiser's next challenger, Doyle and Barnett rekindled the feud between Bruiser and Cowboy Bob Ellis. This latest chapter began when Ellis defeated Bruiser in a nontitle bout on television from CKLW-TV in Windsor. After the match, wrestling fans presented Cowboy Bob Ellis with a brand new cowboy hat, which Bruiser immediately destroyed, setting up the big arena bouts. Ads for the June 11 card reminded fans, *"Ellis beat the Bruiser last week."* Bruiser, however, withstood the challenge and told the *Detroit Times* a few weeks later:

> *"These promoters are not too bright. I'm the biggest box office in wrestling, yet they keep trying to get me beaten. Don't they like the money?"*

Bruiser would go on to defeat Ellis in the rematch on June 25th in a bout that would take place "in the fence" with chicken coup fencing surrounding the ring. Ads for the match read, "The Bruiser can't run; the ring will be fenced in." Decades later, wrestling author Greg Oliver would interview Bob Ellis for this biography about his long history with the Bruiser.

> *"He was one of the best as far as getting the heat. You could depend on him, and we had sensational matches. He knew how to get the job done. He helped me more than any other wrestler I can think of. A lot of the boys said he got stiff-er-oo with them. He punched a little hard, but he and I got along. He was the mainstay of Jim Barnett's whole outfit. They would just have to mention our two names together, and boom, it would be a sellout."*

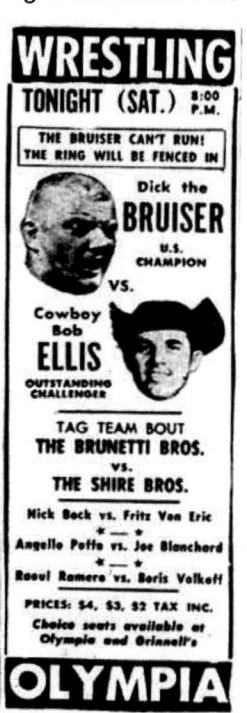

WRESTLING
TONIGHT (SAT.) 8:00 P.M.

THE BRUISER CAN'T RUN!
THE RING WILL BE FENCED IN

Dick the
BRUISER
U.S. CHAMPION

VS.

Cowboy Bob
ELLIS
OUTSTANDING CHALLENGER

TAG TEAM BOUT
THE BRUNETTI BROS.
vs.
THE SHIRE BROS.

Nick Bock vs. Fritz Von Eric
* — *
Angelo Poffo vs. Joe Blanchard
* — *
Raoul Romero vs. Boris Volkoff

PRICES: $4, $3, $2 TAX INC.
Choice seats available at Olympia and Grinnell's

OLYMPIA

— **Leaping Larry Chene**

One of the most violent bouts during Bruiser's run in Detroit happened when he was wrestling Leaping Larry Chene, a native of Detroit's East Side and a long-time Detroit high-flying headliner. On September 10, the *Detroit Free Press* noted Chene's appearance when they wrote, "Leaping Larry Chene is replacing chili suppers as a fundraiser for the volunteer fire department." The support of Detroit wrestling fans was overwhelming as 15,468 fans paid $38,046 to see the bout stopped by the referee due to heavy bleeding by both men.

Historian Rob Bauer remembered:

> "This was my all-time favorite match, almost one hour long. Larry Chene was normally hooked up with the Motor City promotion that would sometimes merge their talent [with Barnett and Doyle]. The Bruiser faced Larry Chene, who wrestled barefoot that night. They [the fans] were on their feet the whole night. It was a very packed card and a very long card that lasted almost to one in the morning. Doyle and Barnett never let the fans go home disappointed."

A photo of Bruiser, battered from his bout with Chene, graced the cover of the October 1960 issue of *Wrestling Life*. Bruiser and Chene each won one fall. The gory bout was photographed at ringside by Chicago-based ace photographer Bob Luce and several of the photos were used for publicity purposes into the next decade. Larry Chene would never face Dick the Bruiser again and would tragically pass away on October 1, 1964, in a late night automobile accident near Ottawa, Illinois. Chene had just wrestled Larry Hennig at Wharton Fieldhouse in Moline, Illinois, and was trying to drive all night back home to Detroit.

> **Author's note:** I went to St. Joseph's College in Indiana at the same time as Donna Beauchene, Larry Chene's daughter. She saw me on campus with a wrestling magazine that had the Sheik on the cover and yelled to me, "*That's my uncle Ed!*"

— **Antonino Rocca Returns**

The spectacles from Doyle and Barnett continued the following Friday, September 30, 1960, as the legendary Antonino Rocca was brought back to Detroit to face the seemingly unbeatable Bruiser. The headline in the *Detroit Times* the day before the match proclaimed "The Bruiser vs. Rocca and Moore" — Moore being light heavyweight boxing champion Archie Moore, who got the referee assignment that night. *The Detroit Times* continued: "*Dick the Bruiser considers all referees his natural enemies and he is always prepared to do battle with them.*" Bruiser then made comments about Moore. His printed rants were classic:

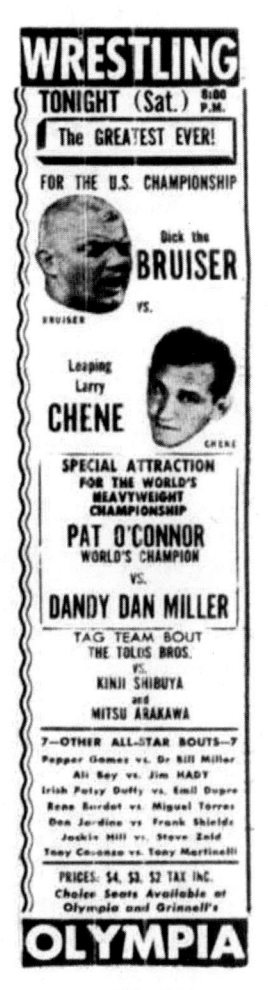

"He's the referee and supposed to be neutral, yet he's already telling everybody what he's going to do with me. He doesn't scare me. If he tries to slug me, I'll show him a few things about wrestling. I don't like to pick on old folks, but I'm going to protect myself. A good wrestler can flatten a boxer anytime, and I'm the best wrestler there."

The *Detroit Times* described the outcome the next day:

"After each wrestler had taken a fall, both mat men fell out of the ring. Archie Moore, the light heavyweight boxing champion, who was the referee, ordered both back into the square, but Bruiser wouldn't cooperate. Bruiser sat on Rocca and wouldn't budge, so Moore disqualified him at 6:21 minutes of the deciding fall."

— **Ongoing Feud with Bobo Brazil**

In early 1961, a new challenger was brought to face Dick the Bruiser ... his first black opponent, Bobo Brazil, a native of Benton Harbor, Michigan. The match was scheduled for Saturday, January 28, 1961. The report in the *Detroit Times* the following morning said:

"16,852 Fans See Bruiser Banned." Brazil was cast as the winner, but by disqualification, not a fall. The Bruiser stayed outside the ropes too long in the third act. A rematch is indicated. The big crowd paid a gross gate of $41,013.

Brazil's victory gained some nationwide notoriety as the next month, an article in the *Pittsburgh Courier* trumpeted "Tan Wrestlers Gain Detroit Mat Spotlight." They continued with, "The negro wrestler is finally coming into the limelight and is on his way up the ladder." Brazil and other black wrestlers, like Bearcat Wright, were mentioned, as well. The article also played up Brazil's key maneuver, the "Koko Bump, a modern weapon of the game" — also known as the head butt.

The February 25 rematch promised to be a "fight to a finish." Newspaper ads duly noted Bobo Brazil as the U.S. champion and regular ticket prices of $4, $3, and $2 prevailed. Historian Rob Bauer recalled what happened that night:

"Detroit got hit by one of the worst ice storms ever that afternoon and it went right into evening. I remember how slow it was driving and I left an hour early to get to this match. The Bruiser and some of the wrestlers were stranded and didn't get into Detroit. Bobo did show up, but Bruiser didn't, so the promoters put together a makeshift card for the fans. They [the fans] were told to save their ticket stubs from Saturday, February 25 ,because on Monday, February 27, they would get in free for the main event — Bruiser vs. Bobo — with a complete undercard. Can you imagine the cost there? [The promoters] showed a lot of class in order to do that. On February 27, there was no ice problem and Bruiser took the belt back."

The *Detroit Times* described the key elements of the rematch:

Chapter 9 • 79

| A NEW FEATURE | "RINGSIDE CAMERA" |

". . . Matdom's Famous "Butcher" Finally Runs Headlong Into A Famous Negro GOLIATH! And All Hell Breaks Loose In The Midwest!"

Dick the Bruiser vs Bobo Brazil

Bruiser stars unloading his heavy fists on Bobo and the gigantic negro star wades in with his own two-fisted barrage. Above, Brute heads for neutral ground outside the ropes in double-time! Said newsmen: "Brazil was the aggressor all the way."

Source: Robert Luce family

"A crowd of 16,363, not at all disappointed in the two-day postponement of the match from Saturday night, saw the Bruiser get his lumps early. In the fight to a finish in which falls didn't mean a thing, Bobo owned a three-to-one advantage over the Bruiser before missing a dropkick and landing on the back of his neck, 33 minutes into the bout. Olympia officials said more than 10,000 fans were turned away, but they weren't fretting. The card drew a gross gate of $42,256."

Other professional wrestling promotions would not have been as considerate or treated the fans to a free show. Most promoters would have invoked the standard policy, whereby they were not responsible if wrestlers did not appear due to events beyond the promoter's control. However, Barnett and Doyle were different than others, even though there was still some box-office appetite for more of Bruiser vs. Bobo.

80 • BRUISER: The World's Most Dangerous Wrestler

Bruiser next withstood formidable challenges from Killer Kowalski on March 25, Leo Nomellini on April 15, and (again) the reliable Cowboy Bob Ellis on May 6.

An interview Scott Teal conducted with Southern wrestler/promoter Buddy Wayne in March 2000 revealed a different side of Bruiser; one not normally seen by the general public:

> I was in Atlanta at the Ponce de Leon ballpark on May 27, 1961. Argentina Rocca was there, Yukon Eric, Dick the Bruiser. Me and Bruiser were in the dugout. That's when he was hot as a firecracker. This little girl, maybe four or five years old, eased over and said in a shy voice, 'Mr. Bruiser, can I have your autograph?' He looks all around, reaches over for the paper, writes on it, hands it back to her. 'Thank you,' and she walks off. Dick looks all around again and goes, 'I don't guess nobody saw that, did they? I couldn't tell a pretty little girl like that no.'

A RECORD GATE?
Great Outdoors Calling Bruiser

While Bruiser continued to travel and wrestle around the nation, promoters were planning a wrestling spectacle for Bruiser that had the potential of being the biggest blockbuster for the Bruiser at that point in his seven-year career.

— Tiger Stadium

In May 1961, *Detroit News* columnist George E. Van pointed out that wrestling exhibitions had drawn 435,000 spectators and grossed more than a million dollars at the Olympia since April 1959, and credited that successful revival to Dick the Bruiser and Bobo Brazil. Co-promoter Johnny Doyle told Van, "*We need a larger place for this pair now and we're going to Tiger Stadium* [on] *June 23 with them.*"

Doyle expanded on his plans for the extravaganza:

> "We plan to use all the gimmicks that have proved successful here, like the Texas death match, jiu-jitsu, the Indian styles — all of them. Women and children are number one fans. That's why we scheduled this show on Friday. If the weather's bad, we can go the next day."

Doyle estimated the third confrontation between Bruiser and Brazil would draw more than 30,000 fans to Tiger Stadium,

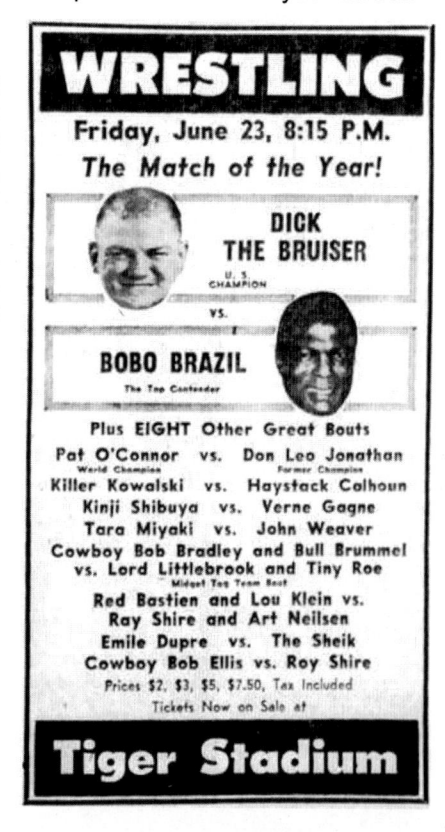

WRESTLING
Friday, June 23, 8:15 P.M.
The Match of the Year!

DICK THE BRUISER
U.S. CHAMPION
vs.
BOBO BRAZIL
The Top Contender

Plus EIGHT Other Great Bouts
Pat O'Connor vs. Don Leo Jonathan
   World Champion   Former Champion
Killer Kowalski vs. Haystack Calhoun
Kinji Shibuya vs. Verne Gagne
Tara Miyaki vs. John Weaver
Cowboy Bob Bradley and Bull Brummel vs. Lord Littlebrook and Tiny Roe
   Midget Tag Team Bout
Red Bastien and Lou Klein vs. Ray Shire and Art Neilsen
Emile Dupre vs. The Sheik
Cowboy Bob Ellis vs. Roy Shire
Prices $2, $3, $5, $7.50, Tax Included
Tickets Now on Sale at

Tiger Stadium

including 2,000 seats at $10 each around the infield of the stadium. Doyle expressed his philosophy when he said, "*To sustain good crowds, you must entertain the fans.*" Doyle and Barnett were hoping for the biggest gate in the history of professional wrestling, noting the previous record gate of $103,278 at Gilmore Stadium in 1952 in Los Angeles with Lou Thesz and Baron Leone, which Doyle also promoted. The *Detroit Free Press* commented, "*As anybody can plainly see, promoter Doyle thinks quite highly of the way Detroiters have responded to their indoctrination into the baffling and pseudo-sporting world of rassling.*" *Detroit News* columnist Doc Greene interviewed Bruiser close to the match date and wrote, "*Dick Afflis starred on television last evening wearing a scabbed right eye, a flamboyant cigar, and a pinner collar around a redwood neck and shoulders ... Dick is wrestling's greatest actor and, perhaps, its greatest athlete, and certainly, its most intelligent business performer.*"

Friday, June 23, 1961, started out as a rainy day in Detroit, and a decision was made to go ahead and run the show that night at Tiger Stadium, even though an alternate rain date was available the following night. Promoters were hoping for 30,000 people and a gate around $100,000. However, threats of inclement weather suppressed the crowd to only 11,097 and a gate of $36,886. Bruiser successfully defended his championship against Bobo, while Pat O'Connor retained his NWA world title against the challenge of Don Leo Jonathan.

The depressed attendance for Detroit wrestling continued when they returned to the Olympia three weeks later (July 14) as only 5,371 fans turned out to see Bruiser defeat Yukon Eric in a lumberjack match. Promoters began to question whether or not Bruiser's star was fading after more than two years of good business.

The following week, on July 21, Verne Gagne took the U.S. belt from Bruiser at the Hazel Park Raceway. At that time, Gagne was in the early stages of building his own territorial promotion, the American Wrestling Association (AWA), headquartered out of Minneapolis, Minnesota. It is believed the wrestling scene in Detroit needed a little shaking up with a title change; although the long-term availability of Gagne in Detroit would not be likely as he had just launched the AWA.

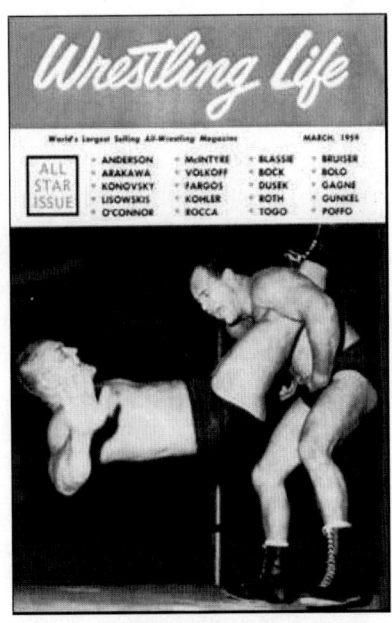

Bruiser vs Verne Gagne
Source: Robert Luce family

Barnett and Doyle switched venues in Detroit and began promoting their shows at the newly constructed Cobo Hall convention center and arena, in downtown Detroit overlooking the Detroit River. Beginning on August 11, Bruiser and Gagne would subsequently have several rematches, with Bruiser winning back the belt on September 23. Nine weeks later, on December 1, Bruiser would drop the strap to Fritz Von Erich. Von Erich, who normally was hated by the fans, was reported to have played "the unusual role of hero in their wrestling exhibition at the Convention Arena."

Chapter 10
I Got In A Fight — 1963

Throughout 1962, the Bruiser would make steady appearances in Detroit, facing a new crop of top-name talent, such as Bearcat Wright, Ray Stern, The Sheik, and the newly appointed play-by-play TV announcer Lord Athol Layton (one of the most interesting rivalries). Layton was born in England and had previously wrestled at Maple Leaf Gardens in Toronto. The combination of Layton's British accent and Bruiser's gravel voice must have been hilarious to hear.

— Feud with Lord Athol Layton

The first of the three main events took place on Saturday, August 4, 1962, at Cobo Arena, where Bruiser entered the ring as the U.S. heavyweight champion. An impressive 11,575 fans paid $32,090 to see Layton declared the winner as the ringside physician stopped the bout due to Bruiser's bleeding head wound. Hundreds of fans had been turned away from the card, so promoters Doyle and Barnett booked the rematch at the larger Olympia Stadium for Saturday, September 15, 1962. Layton won the rematch via disqualification before 15,521 fans as Bruiser twisted Layton's head between the ring ropes and refused to break the hold. The final confrontation was presented on Saturday, December 29, 1962, again at the Olympia. Layton once again won via disqualification before 15,267 fans. Newspaper reports indicated Bruiser knocked out the referee to cause a disqualification. The Bruiser-Layton feud was one of the hottest series; however, the biggest event in Detroit was yet to come.

Detroit program June 29, 1963
Source: Author's collection

— Detroit Sports, 1963

The Detroit professional sports scene was pretty hot during Bruiser's run in Detroit. The Detroit Tigers major league baseball team was led by future Hall of Famer Al Kaline, who played his entire professional career with the Tigers from 1953 to 1974. The Detroit Red Wings of the NHL had no less than six players (Gordie Howe, Alex Delvecchio, Norm Ullman, Bill Gadsby, Marcel Pronovost, and

Terry Sawchuk) and its coach (Sid Abel) who wound up in the Hockey Hall of Fame. The Detroit Lions of the NFL had two future Hall of Famers on their 1962 team, linebacker Joe Schmidt and defensive back Dick (Nightrain) Lane, as well as another standout player who was one of the best, but who never got into the Hall of Fame, defensive tackle Alex Karras.

Karras was an All-American at the University of Iowa and moved on to the Lions, with whom he played in several Pro Bowl games, and co-owned a local sports bar — The Lindell Athletic Club, then located at the corner of Cass and Bagley in downtown Detroit. Karras even dabbled in pro wrestling from time to time. Karras was, in all respects, a local celebrity.

In April 1963, Doyle and Barnett signed Karras to face Dick the Bruiser in the main event of the April 27 show. What would happen after that signing in an unrelated event would shock the sports world.

— Karras Suspended by NFL

On Wednesday April 17, Pete Rozelle, NFL commissioner fined and levied a one-year suspension against both Alex Karras of the Lions and Paul Hornung of the Green Bay Packers for betting on NFL games, including the 1962 championship game between the Packers and the New York Giants. The Lions team itself was fined for negligence, as were five other Lions players. Legendary head coach of the Packers, Vince Lombardi conceded, "*There was no evidence of criminal intent, that is, the shaving of points and so forth.*" It also was reported that the other professional football leagues, the CFL in Canada and the AFL in the United States, would not permit Karras and Hornung to play in their games while under NFL suspension. Karras' initial reaction was unrepentant as he proclaimed, "*This is guilt by association and innuendo ... I've done nothing to be ashamed of.*" In Karras' 1977 autobiography, *Even Big Guys Cry*, Alex and his co-writer, Herb Gluck, brought up another controversy. Karras had been observed by law enforcement personnel associating with "gamblers, bookmakers, hustlers" while he ate and drank in various establishments in downtown Detroit. Karras' association with people like that, which United Press International referred to as "known hoodlums," drew the ire of the NFL.

Karras eventually responded to the suspension with the comment, "*Maybe I'll go into wrestling for the rest of my life.*" Almost immediately, promoter Johnny Doyle offered Karras a $40,000 per year contract. On April 22, 1963, UPI reported that "*the huge tackle, who's still numb over his indefinite suspension by the NFL, is mulling over the forty thousand dollar one-year pro wrestling contract.*" Doyle noted that Karras wasn't all that enthusiastic about the offer and was quoted by UPI:

"He [Karras] *sure didn't jump at the offer, but it must help his spirits. He doesn't have to worry about money. He's only twenty-seven now. If he stays in shape and has some luck, he could wrestle until he's forty-five, and no football player ever lasted that long.*"

— Lindell Athletic Club

Late on the night of Tuesday, April 23, Dick the Bruiser paid a visit to the Lindell Athletic Club, where Alex Karras and one of his partners, James Butsicaris, were hanging out with patrons. The *Detroit News* later that day printed a police account of the events which unfolded, whereby Afflis entered the bar around one a.m., verbally attacked Butsicaris and Karras, was refused service, grabbed Butsicaris by the shirt, and swung his fist. A brawl erupted that involved patrons and, eventually, the police. During the fracas, two policemen were injured, Andrew H. Meholic (broken wrist) and James Carolan (torn elbow ligament).

Interview transcripts from the Bruiser's 1981 interview with Dick Mittman offered the Bruiser's recollections of what led up to the fight:

> "He [Karras] *saw the crowds I had and all the money I was making in the Detroit area. I don't know whether you've ever followed Karras. If you read his book, he always mentions this Butsicaris. This guy was the owner of the place where this happened. He and Karras were partners. That little Greek kind of guided him. They had easy access to the press because the* Detroit Free Press *was just a block away. Everybody on their breaks, that's where they came to eat and drink. So they got the word in, he was a better wrestler than I was. These sportswriters ate that up, that I was just a so-so football player and that's why I became a wrestler. He was building himself up because it was so easy because he had access to all these writers. So, anyway, I told him to stop doing that and a big story, that he was going to clean up wrestling around there, and that Dick the Bruiser was just a bum and so forth.*
>
> "I got arguing with Butsicaras, and then Karras happened to come by, and the first thing, we got in a fight — not much of a fight. Karras and I threw a couple of punches, maybe. Karras got between us and we all fell on the floor. Pretty soon, everybody was against me because they were hitting me on the head with pool cues, all the goofs that were shooting pool. During this time, the police arrived. Everybody took off from the fight but me. They had so many police trying to knock me down or cuff me. They couldn't do it. It was just like a comedy. They couldn't push me over because there were too many on this side and that side, and I was stuck in the middle. They finally put shackles on my feet and tripped me. Then when they got me down, it was all over."

LANDS IN JAIL AFTER BAR BRAWL
Bruiser Loses 'Tag Match' with 8 Police

— **The Morning After**

On Wednesday morning, April 24, Bruiser pled *"not guilty"* to assault-and-battery charges before judge Joseph A. Gillis, who scheduled a trial date for Monday April 29.

Michigan boxing commissioner David Gudelsky promised fines and suspensions, as well. However, Gudelsky didn't cancel the upcoming Saturday night wrestling card at the Olympia *"only out of fairness to innocent people who are staging it and the people who bought tickets."* What wasn't said was canceling the show would deprive the commission of a good deal of revenue they received from the event. Gudelsky also said Karras' NFL suspension wouldn't result in the suspension of Karras' wrestling license since he thought he could *"help straighten Karras out."*

On April 26, the night before the Bruiser-Karras showdown at the Detroit Olympia, Bruiser faced NWA world champion Lou Thesz in St. Louis. Long-

After the Alex Karras brawl
Source: The Detroit News

time St. Louis wrestling authority Larry Matysik was then a teenager watching at ringside at Kiel:

> "Thesz won two out of three falls from Dick the Bruiser when the third fall was stopped because Bruiser was bleeding so badly. Bruiser went berserk at the decision, requiring Bobby Bruns, Bill Longson, Rock Hunter, Bill Dromo, Lorenzo Parente, and Ray Gordon to restrain him."

— Grudge Match at the Olympia

Pre-bout publicity for the April 27 showdown between Bruiser and Karras kicked into high gear with two newspaper ads; one featuring a photo of Bruiser and the other of Karras.

WRESTLING AT OLYMPIA
APRIL 27, SAT. 10 BIG BOUTS

Alex KARRAS
vs. Dick the Bruiser

INCLUDING WORLD CHAMP
LOU THESZ
VS. DR. BIG BILL MILLER

Mark Lewin vs. Ray Stevens
Von Erich vs. Skyscraper Evans
Bob Stanley vs. Argentina ROCCA
Emil Dupre vs. Hans Schmidt
Jim Hady vs. Steve Stanly
Joe Blanchard vs. Bob Nander
Chief Kit Fox vs. The Sheik
Angelo Savoldi vs. Manny King

ALEX KARRAS

CHOICE SEATS IN ANY PRICE RANGE.
BOX OFFICE OPEN DAILY 12-8 P.M. $2 $3 $4

The undercard lineup on Saturday April 27 was impressive. Lou Thesz was on hand to defend his NWA title against Big Bill Miller, a match that, on any other card, would have been the main event. On this night, however, it took second place against the Bruiser-Karras face-off. The card was stacked with top names from around the country — Ray Stevens, Mark Lewin, Fritz Von Erich, Hans Schmidt, Antonino Rocca, and The Sheik. Tickets were priced at $2, $3, and $4, with the first match (which the *Detroit News* called "the first skit") scheduled for 8:30 p.m.

Karras was accompanied to the ring by his business partner, James Butsicaris, along with a midget named Major Little. According to the caption underneath the UPI photo, the match lasted 11 minutes and 21 seconds. To nobody's surprise, Bruiser's hand was raised at the conclusion of the match.

The turnout and the match itself were disappointing. In the *Detroit News* two days later, columnist Doc Greene quoted a fellow spectator at the event, who (supposedly) said to him, "*Embarrassing, isn't it?*" Green noted all the build-up, including the NFL suspension and the saloon brawl, didn't culminate in anything special.

Russell Leonard, former editor and publisher of *Big Time Wrestling* magazine, attended the match. He reflected on the failure of the event 50 years after the fact:

> "*Perhaps people up there did not regard Karras as too much of a wrestler as the Bruiser had a big reputation. Karras was just this football player who had been banned for gambling by the NFL. Maybe fans figured it wouldn't be much of a match, and maybe that's why they didn't go.*"

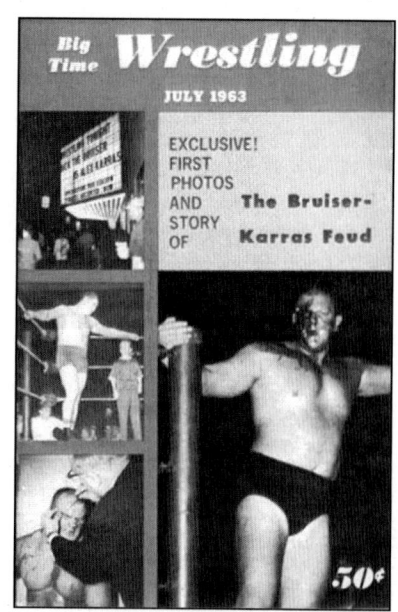

Big Time Wrestling
JULY 1963

EXCLUSIVE! FIRST PHOTOS AND STORY OF **The Bruiser-Karras Feud**

Big Time Wrestling • July 1963
Source: Russ Leonard

Bruiser Pins Karras in Bloody Duel

Promoter Johnny Doyle visited with reporters in the dressing room after the match and expressed his disappointment since "*everybody thought it would be a sellout.*" Karras was paid $4,500 that night, a huge payoff for the time, but still hadn't decided whether or not to accept Doyle's one-year contract offer. The UPI story quoted Karras on his future plans:

> "*I've got to make up my mind what I'm going to do now, whether I should take the one wrestling offer I have and go on the road, and maybe wrestle Bruiser again. Or, I have a public relations offer here in town that pays pretty good money and will keep me at home and I can still work at my bar.*"

— Legal Headaches

The following week, on May 8, the Associated Press reported that Alex Karras had turned down the wrestling offer and opted to apply for reinstatement to the NFL for the 1964 season. As for Dick the Bruiser, the assault-and-battery charges were dismissed the following week after he agreed to contribute $400 to the police pension fund. Those monies were returned to Bruiser the following month after a police official called the payment "blood money."

The most lasting aftermath and impact on Bruiser would be the lawsuits filed against him by the two policemen injured in the bar fight. It is believed a $10,359 judgment was awarded to James Carolan in September 1965 and, in May 1966, U.S. district judge Fred Kaess ordered Bruiser to pay $15,000 damages to Andrew H. Meholic.

Three years later, in July 1966, Bruiser appeared before U.S. judge William Steckler to explain why he should not comply with the Carolan judgment and make the payments ordered by the judge. The hearing was covered by Carolyn Pickering, a journalist for the *Indianapolis Star*, who noted Bruiser's response was evasive when he was asked about his financial status. He claimed he was "*so broke that all I have is forty dollars cash and a wardrobe worth less than a hundred bucks.*" Bruiser claimed the $40,000 home he lived in was owned by his wife, who also owned the Cadillac. Bruiser also refused to answer a question about his purported gambling activities on grounds of self-incrimination.

The Bruiser won a continuance until the following month, but those lawsuits would continue to haunt him for years to come. Years later, the son of officer Meholic, Andrew H. Meholic, Jr., would reveal to the author that his father had to retire early from the police department, but was given money by the law firm that handled his case. Patrolmen Meholic also told his son the police weren't told the so-called "brawl" at the Lindell Athletic Club in April 1963 was a publicity stunt.

Bruiser eventually paid out the judgment, with Meholic's law firm retaining most of those funds. It is believed wrestling promoter James Barnett, who, by that time, had left Detroit and was promoting in Atlanta, reimbursed Bruiser for some of the money he lost during the drawn-out scenario.

H.E. (Duke) West wrestled on small independent shows in Indiana during the '70s. In his book *Long Days and Short Pays*, he remembers several incidents involving Bruiser and the police, but one stood out:

"Then there was the night when Dick the Bruiser was led away by the police. I can't remember for sure who he was wrestling, but it was a much-hated heel like Fritz Von Erich or the Sheik. It was the most heat I had ever witnessed in a match. They wound up outside the ring and continued to go after each other. Some of the ringside fans decided to put in their two cents and chairs began flying toward the wrestlers. Fists began flying among the spectators at ringside and the police rushed up to the ring.

"One of the cops, Jack Mann, had the reputation of being the "biggest and baddest" cop in the Muncie Police Department. Jack stood about six-foot-six and easily weighed in the 270-pound range. He had as big a reputation for breaking up bar fights as the Bruiser had for being in them. Jack ran up behind the Bruiser and grabbed him. I think Bruiser thought it was one of the fans as he suddenly turned and punched Jack. I remember seeing Jack's hat fly off of his head. The next thing I knew, Jack's size fourteens could be seen sticking straight up in the air. Seeing one of their own in trouble, all the cops piled on, and the next thing you know, Dick was on his way to a ride in a police car.

"The next morning, I was shocked to see Dick the Bruiser's mug shot on the front page of the Muncie Star, with headlines declaring that he had been charged with battery to a police officer. Subsequent reports said the charges were dropped, but he paid a hefty fine for disorderly conduct. Years later, I got to know Officer Mann pretty well, but he never would discuss the incident. From what I've heard, the same thing happened in other places, as well, leading me to believe his arrest had been a publicity gimmick. More than likely, Dick the Bruiser was driven around the block and dropped off at the back of the tents that served as dressing rooms. I never could substantiate that, but I strongly believe that's what happened."

In mid-1963, Bruiser made somewhat of a babyface turn in Detroit, and even teamed up with Lord Layton, one of his most hated enemies, on June 29 and August 31. On September 28, though, the two wound up against each other in a grudge match at Cobo, no doubt stemming from problems they may have had when they teamed up on August 31.

Detroit, Michigan • August 31, 1963

— JFK

Dick the Bruiser would make five more wrestling appearances in Detroit in 1963. On November 22, he found himself scheduled in a six-man tag team match in St. Louis with Rip Hawk and Bill Miller as his tag team partners against Wilbur Snyder, Cowboy Bob Ellis, and John Paul Henning. Almost every American knows about the tragic event that occurred in Dallas that afternoon as President John F. Kennedy was assassinated. That night, wrestling cards booked in Buffalo, Atlanta, Los Angeles, and other cities, all went on as scheduled. St. Louis wrestling promoter, announcer, and author Larry Matysik was a teenager helping out the St. Louis Wrestling Club at that time and remembered a lot of what happened that night in St. Louis.

"There was a question as to whether there would even be a show. Everything in the country came to a standstill. Sam [Muchnick] later told me that he talked to the mayor and to Congressman Mel Price of Illinois. Both told him to run the show. The city probably needed it right now. [Muchnick was told that] if he could get the guys there, run the show. I remember it was a very distracting evening. The country, for the rest of the year, was in shock."

Wrestler Reggie Parks remembers phoning in from Kansas City and being told the card would be going on as scheduled. Anne Kakacek, wife of wrestler Johnny Kace, remembered:

"I recall that we were on Hunt Club Road when the announcer came on the car radio. I was driving John to the airport [O'Hare in Chicago] to fly to St. Louis. There were not many people at the wrestling match in St. Louis that night."

The low attendance in St. Louis was a good indicator of the shock Americans were in over the assassination, especially in view of the fact that NWA heavyweight champ Lou Thesz was there to defend his title against Fritz Von Erich.

The assassination was particularly devastating for the Bruiser's mother, who had been a loyal Democratic supporter and high level department head for years. That afternoon, her pastor, William Hudnutt, from the 2nd Presbyterian Church of Indianapolis, would visit. He remembers, *"I found her prostrate and grieving on the floor of her living room."*

Dick the Bruiser didn't realize it as 1963 came to an end, but he would be facing new directions in his career and financial risk-taking in the year that lay ahead.

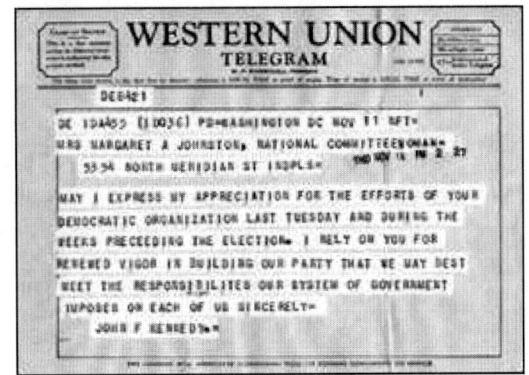

Source: Indiana State Museum

Chapter 11
Spreading the Mayhem — 1959-1963

While Dick the Bruiser made wrestling history in Detroit during these years, his wrestling activities were by no means confined to the Motor City.

— Bruiser as a Heel

Dick the Bruiser's nasty ring persona in those days was legendary, and it had an infuriating effect on wrestling fans. That situation was skillfully described by Tim Replogle, who would later wrestle with the Bruiser in the late '80s as the Golden Lion. In the early '60s, Replogle's father, Karl Replogle, was a licensed wrestling referee for the State of Indiana. In that capacity, he found himself the appointed ring official for Bruiser's main event at Naponee, Indiana. The finish called for referee Replogle to turn a blind eye to the unpopular Bruiser's misdeeds and erroneously award him the victory, thereby agitating local wrestling fans. Bruiser's opponent on that night was one of the top babyfaces (good guys) of the day, Cowboy Bob Ellis. After the match, Tim and his father ignored verbal abuse from the fans as they fought their way to their car through a dark parking lot. A gang of rowdy teenagers followed them home to Fort Wayne and pulled their car alongside them. Mr. Replogle got out of the car and landed a hard right jab to the chin of the guy in the passenger seat. The driver immediately sped off.

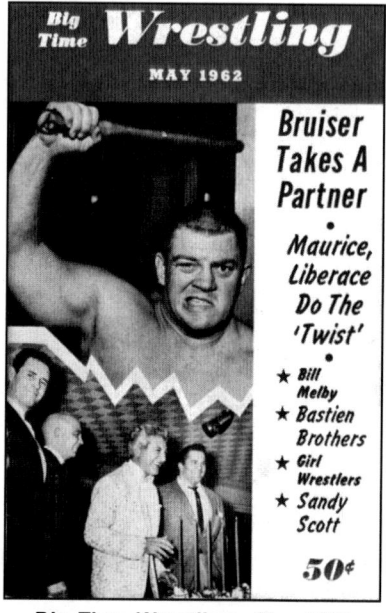

Big Time Wrestling • May 1962
Source: Russ Leonard

— Indianapolis

The Bruiser made appearances in other wrestling cities during his Detroit heyday. On August 6, 1959, he was booked in Indianapolis at Victory Field, the home of the Indianapolis Indians, a minor-league baseball team. That night, Bruiser and his partner, Angelo Poffo, won a tag-team tournament and the local tag belts against the Shire "brothers," Roy and Ray. Ray would later achieve nationwide notoriety as Ray (The Crippler) Stevens. Promoters raked in a $23,330 gate from 10,200 fans that night. Photos of the card showed a film crew present, footage that would be considered priceless if it could be located.

The following month, on September 22, Bruiser returned to his small hometown of Delphi to wrestle a big-city opponent, Cowboy Bob Ellis. Four days later in Detroit, he teamed with Reggie Lisowski (wrestling as Killer Lisowski) against

Verne Gagne and Wilbur Snyder. It is believed this was the first time Bruiser and Lisowski ever teamed up. They lost the match, though, when they began to fight with each other. Three weeks later, they met in a main event grudge match with the ring surrounded by a fence and commentator Sam Menacker acting as special referee.

— **Atlanta**

In 1961, Bruiser headlined wrestling cards at Ponce De Leon Ballpark in Atlanta, including three against fellow Purdue alumnus Ray Gunkel and a match with Antonino Rocca on July 4, 1961. Reverend Danny Goddard, now of New Castle, Indiana, was then the president of the "Sputnik Monroe Fan Club." More than 50 years later, Goddard looked back on the Bruiser's appearances in Atlanta, especially a match-up against Lou Thesz on August 23, 1964:

> "I was around eight years old when I saw the Bruiser for the first time. He was in the main event in Atlanta for the NWA world championship. I remember it was two out of three falls [and] each had one apiece. I remember that during the rest [between falls], the Bruiser went out to the fans and sat between two women who were frightened out of their wits. The Bruiser often attacked his opponent before the bell, many times with the announcer's microphone, wrapping the cord around their neck and hitting them with it. He would go down a row of ringside seats, sending people jumping over in front or behind them."

Long-time Atlanta referee Charlie Smith remembered more of the Bruiser's antics at the ballpark.

> "He came into the ring carrying a can of beer in his hand, poured it all over himself, and then smashed the can on his forehead. The crowd went wild. All the time in Georgia, he was a heel."

— **Los Angeles**

The Bruiser had one notable wrestling gig in Los Angeles on October 7, 1961, as promoter Johnny Doyle tried unsuccessfully to "invade" an existing territory with a card at the LA Sports Arena. Bruiser was booked against Cowboy Bob Ellis in a card loaded with stars like Ray Stevens, Bobo Brazil, Wilbur Snyder, and Killer Kowalski. The short-lived effort unsuccessfully utilized local television outlet KTLA-TV as a promotional tool.

— **Cincinnati**

At times, television could be a tremendous promotional tool and pay big dividends. Judge H. Kenneth Johnson of Indianapolis remembered one such publicity stunt:

"Dick the Bruiser was the man we loved to hate when I was growing up in Cincinnati. The memory of one night stands out, even now. There was another wrestler named Cowboy Bob Ellis. He played the part of a 'good guy' against the Bruiser's 'bad guy.' Cowboy Bob wore bright trunks with a horseshoe on his rump. One night, my mom and I were settled in to watch the Bruiser do his thing when the TV screen went to a studio just off the arena. Two crippled children were there with a birthday cake to wish Cowboy Bob a happy birthday when, who should burst into the studio ... but the Bruiser himself. He reached over and took a big handful of cake and mashed it into Cowboy Bob's face, and then, amidst the screams and howls of the announcer and the poor children, starting throwing hunks of cake at the announcer and all around the studio. It was so over the top, but terrifically entertaining. I nearly choked to death laughing so hard. Sweet mom was overwhelmed with such boorish behavior and began screaming at the TV screen. Our family laughed at this for many years to come."

Cincinnati was also the site of a 1959 lawsuit filed against Bruiser, promoter Jim Barnett, and the local arena — Cincinnati Gardens. During a wrestling card on April 25, 1959, a post-polio paralytic woman in a wheelchair named Catherine Brown was sitting at ringside in the fifth row. That night, in the main event before 8,127 fans, Dick the Bruiser teamed with Angelo Poffo against Yukon Eric and Wilbur Snyder. A Cincinnati newspaper reported, *"Afflis left the ring, seized the wheelchair, and pushed it, causing her to thrown forward so that her feet where caught in the wheels."* The lady claimed the actions resulted in *"a bruised leg, fear, and shock."* The newspaper noted Brown's complaint *"alleges that Afflis was a person of uncontrolled temper and violence."* Brown claimed to be *"made sick, sore, and lame."* The lawsuit also sought reimbursement for related medical expenses. The eventual result of the lawsuit is unknown, but it is believed to have been settled privately. The Cincinnati Boxing and Wrestling Commission also revoked the Bruiser's wrestling license and suspended him indefinitely. In spite of this, promoter Jim Barnett was quoted as saying, *"Afflis is a great villain-type worth $4,000 a show."*

— Louisville

The Bruiser's exploits in Louisville, Kentucky, were witnessed firsthand by a youngster who would grow up to become a wrestling legend named Cowboy Bob Kelly in the Gulf Coast territory. Cowboy Bob grew up in Louisville and was a self-proclaimed "mark" — a true believer fan. At the time in Louisville, the wrestling scene was populated with teams like Karl and Kurt Von Brauner and Art and Stan Neilson, and Cowboy Bob Kelly sometimes would be the referee. Kelly looked back about 50 years ago at his memories of Dick the Bruiser:

Louisville, Kentucky • April 18, 1959

"Dick the Bruiser was one of the best as people were terrified of him. He was believable, and everything he did was believable. He was one of the toughest in the business as far as I'm concerned. He was also an all-around nice guy on a personal level."

— San Francisco

In 1962, the Bruiser traveled to San Francisco to wrestle at the Cow Palace for Roy Shire. While there, he was reunited with Don Manoukian, his old YMCA weightlifting buddy from Reno. Manoukian remembered that Dick the Bruiser was angry at him and, 50 years later, looked back at the incident:

> "A promoter from Hawaii named Al Karasak named me "The Bruiser." We absolutely plagiarized the name from Dick. Years later, Ray Stevens and I were on top at the Cow Palace. Dick was traveling and Roy Shire booked him as a courtesy one night. Afflis refused to talk to me. Stealing his ring name really hurt his feelings. It was a bittersweet moment for me. I felt we missed a great opportunity to reminisce. I had known Afflis for many more years than anybody else in the locker room. Never saw him again."

— St. Louis, The One-Town Territory

It would be neglectful to chronicle the wrestling career of Dick the Bruiser without discussing his legacy in St. Louis, Missouri. To many, the most important NWA-affiliated city was St. Louis, where long-time NWA president Sam Muchnick promoted wrestling for almost 40 years. St. Louis drew historically impressive gates for wrestling, in spite of not being a major city in terms of population, like New York, Chicago, Philadelphia, or Los Angeles. St. Louis was not a wrestling territory with multiple towns on a regular circuit, but rather a stand-alone town. The primary venue, the Kiel Auditorium, was located at 15th and Market Street. St. Louis also was the site of the renowned *Wrestling at the Chase* television show on KPLR-TV Channel 11, which debuted in May 1959 and ran until 1983. The legal entity for Muchnick's wrestling enterprises was the St. Louis Wrestling Club, in which Muchnick held a controlling majority of shares until his retirement in 1982. KPLR-TV covered production costs for the program and had a handshake deal with Muchnick over money matters that lasted for decades. From 1959 to 1967, the program originated from the Khorassan Room, the formal ballroom facility at the Chase Park Plaza Hotel. Men wore dinner jackets and women wore formal gowns to the tapings. The original TV announcer for the program was famed broadcaster and St. Louis native Joe Garagiola, who called the play-by-play before going to NBC's *Today Show* in 1963. Former NWA heavyweight champion Dory Funk Jr. said, "*St. Louis was the cream of the crop* (and where) *you wanted to get over and make it big in wrestling.*"

— Debut in St. Louis

Dick the Bruiser made his first appearance on *Wrestling at the Chase* on January 19, 1963, wrestling Emile Dupre. Long-time St. Louis wrestling broadcaster and author Larry Matysik, then an enthusiastic teenage wrestling fan, shared his early impressions of the newly-arrived Dick the Bruiser:

> "Bruiser was the original wild man and looked like Triple HHH at his most muscular, with slabs of muscle across his chest and arms. Bruiser wasn't as tall at Triple HHH, maybe six-feet-tall at his best, but was just a monster and unpredictable."

Bruiser debuted at the Kiel Auditorium on February 1, 1963, against Ray Gordon, and returned on February 15 to battle to a double disqualification ruling against

John Paul Henning. Bruiser's fellow wrestlers and referees were required to pull apart the two brawlers. Bruiser and Henning were rematched on March 1, with Bronko Nagurski as the special referee, to draw a sellout of 12,695 fans.

Dick the Bruiser certainly made a big splash during his initial appearances in St. Louis. Matysik described some of Dick's early antics in the St. Louis ring: *"Bruiser grabs the timekeeper's chair and pitches it into the ring, and then grabs the ring announcer's chair and pitches it into the ring."* Both Matysik and veteran wrestler Reggie Parks remember instances where the Bruiser poured a fan's beer all over himself, to the delight of the audience.

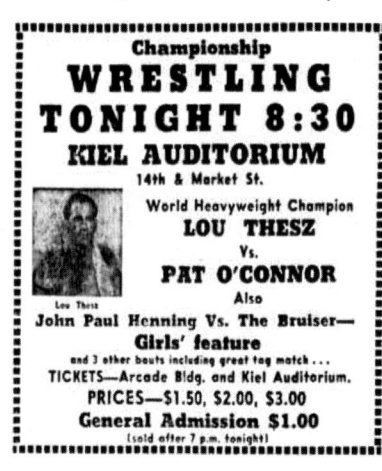

— Feud with Fritz Von Erich

Bruiser's first major feud in St. Louis was with a standout tough-guy wrestler of the era, Fritz Von Erich, whose family name attained legendary status in the professional wrestling business in Texas from the '60s to the '80s. Von Erich had been a football star at Southern Methodist University and used a facial claw hold as his signature finishing maneuver. After an initial double disqualification on June 15, 1963, they wrestled four more times in St. Louis over the next two years. According to Larry Matysik, they had "one of the hottest feuds ever."

— Warning from Sam Muchnick

Bruiser's style of wrestling wasn't typical for St. Louis. Shortly before leaving to wrestle on *Wrestling at the Chase* in fall 1963, he received a cautionary, but polite, letter from Sam Muchnick dated September 9, 1963. Muchnick welcomed the Bruiser and envisioned him to be *"an important part of our programs."* Muchnick spoke frankly and said, *"I know you are a rough wrestler and no one is attempting to curb your style — except there are certain rules that MUST be obeyed."* Muchnick warned, *"If they are not, then I must tell you reluctantly that we must come to a parting of the way."* The letter ended with, *"Kindest personal regards, Sam Muchnick."* It is believed that letter set the tone for a fruitful and respectful relationship between Muchnick and Bruiser that lasted nearly 20 years.

On Friday November 8, 1963, a handicap match featured Dick the Bruiser against both Cowboy Bob Ellis and Von Erich. Matysik noted that Bruiser agreed to win one fall from each of his two opponents *"within the time limit or forfeit the decision."* Ellis won a coin toss, faced the Bruiser alone during the first fall, and lost in 10:52. Von Erich immediately came into the ring, administered three consecutive flying dropkicks, and pinned Bruiser only 32 seconds into the fall. As a result, Von Erich earned a shot at NWA heavyweight champion Lou Thesz on the following card.

On February 15, 1964, Bruiser and Fritz attempted to set aside their differences when they teamed up to face The Bavarian Boys, Rudi Jacobs and Harry Wenzel, in a televised match. After Fritz won the first fall, he and Bruiser began fighting each other, effectively ending the match. When Muchnick ordered them to wrestle each other, things got out of control and their fellow wrestlers were called in to pull them apart. The lineup for the February 21 Kiel Auditorium card was already set by that time, so Muchnick booked Fritz and Bruiser on the March 6 main event. In that set-to, Fritz applied his claw hold on Bruiser, only to be pinned while he was doing so.

Matysik wrote this detailed report of that match:

"Neither combatant was portrayed as the classic babyface or the terrible heel in the situation, nor had it been in previous confrontations between the two. They were just two of the roughest, meanest, and nastiest competitors in the ring, and they did not get along. The Kiel was rocking and absolutely roaring. When these two clashed, the audience seemed to be split basically 50/50 for whom they were cheering."

By this time, the wrestling matches at Kiel Auditorium were being broadcast on radio via KMOX-AM at 1120 with legendary baseball announcer Jack Buck calling the action.

The feud was finally settled on April 17 in a "Texas death match" that lasted six falls before a sellout crowd of 12,204. Matysik's records noted that the Bruiser's leap off the top rope was a legal maneuver in this type of match and helped Bruiser win a fall. Bruiser "supposedly" injured his knee when he attempted the move again. Fritz used the claw on Bruiser to win the sixth fall. Bruiser was unable to continue due to the injury and was carried out of the ring by the referee and ring attendants.

— Minneapolis

In late 1963, Bruiser started a new and important chapter in the history of tag team wrestling when he teamed up in the AWA with his old acquaintance Reggie Lisowski, who now was wrestling as "The Crusher." Minnesota wrestling historian George Schire remembers this being the first time Bruiser referred to Crusher as "my cousin." Bruiser and Crusher began their first major tag-team rivalry against the dastardly Russians, Ivan and Karol Kalmikoff. Schire noted that both teams were bad guys at the time and their match was billed as *"The Battle of the Butchers."*

On August 20, 1963, Bruiser and Crusher won the AWA tag team titles from the Kalmikoffs at the Auditorium in Minneapolis. The feud was short-lived as they had only two rematches (Sept. 7 and Oct. 5) following the title change as Bruiser and Crusher spent little time in the AWA until February 9, 1964, when Bruiser and Crusher dropped the tag belts to Verne Gagne and Moose Evans. Nonetheless, their feud with the Kalmikoff Brothers was the beginning of what would become a legendary mid-career boost for both Bruiser and Crusher as they became tag team icons in the Midwest.

Dick the Bruiser at home

Source: Russ Leonard

— At Home in Indianapolis

In 1963, publisher Russell Leonard and photographer Tim Halcomb of *Big Time Wrestling* magazine visited the Bruiser at his home and later published a seven-page pictorial feature entitled "Dick the Bruiser At Home." The Bruiser proudly showed off his gun collection, boat, sports trophies, and an extra-large king-size bed. The story was the bed was so large that it had to be loaded into the house before the outside wall was finished. Russell Leonard remembers it was Bruiser who invited them to his house on North Kessler Boulevard in Indianapolis. One photo that accompanied the feature article showed Bruiser diving upside down into his swimming pool while drinking a can of beer. The spread also included a photograph taken in 1963 at the Marott Hotel showing Bruiser posed with motion-picture sex symbol Jayne Mansfield and her husband, strongman Mickey Hargitay, who knew the Bruiser years earlier in Indianapolis. The long-rumored, often-told joke went this way — Bruiser was jealous of Jayne because she had bigger chest measurements.

PART III
CO-EXECUTIVE PRODUCER & CO-STAR

Chapter 12
Build A Better Mousetrap — 1964

In 1964, several new developments came about in the life of Dick the Bruiser. Bruiser had spent the previous nine years perfecting his brawler wrestling style and hardcore personality, while selling his services to some of the most prominent wrestling promoters in the nation. One of Bruiser's long-time in-ring rivals, Ox Baker, shared his memory of something Bruiser once told him: *"Bruiser said it was better to be a boss than get paid [by a promoter] because then he could get the kind of money he wanted."* Longtime wrestling publicist Jeff Walton added, *"Dick the Bruiser was a smart businessman who knew he had a fabulous persona, but his time was limited, and [he] knew he could make money promoting."*

— Indianapolis Wrestling

For many years, the Indianapolis territory was controlled by James Barnett and promoted by Balk Estes, who frequently utilized the services of Dick the Bruiser and Wilbur Snyder in their own main events. As far back as 1957, wrestling aired on WTTV-TV Channel 4 with Chuck Marlowe handling the play-by-play and conducting the promotional interviews. Marlowe would later recall, *"Barnett would come to Indianapolis from Louisville (Kentucky) and give me the schedule of matches."*

Chris Parsons, the foremost expert on old-school wrestling in Indianapolis, provided these insights on the formation of this new promotion:

Balk Estes
Source: Willliam Estes

"The announcement about Wilbur Snyder and Dick the Bruiser starting their own promotion came in the form of a print ad in an Indianapolis newspaper. It said that since Dick and Wilbur had taken out a license to promote wrestling, they were being stripped of the local tag team title they held for Barnett and Estes. It was stated that, according to Indiana state law, wrestlers couldn't hold a promoter's license and wrestle at the same time."

In early 1964, there were only two small venues for staging professional wrestling, both of which were National Guard armories. Tyndall Armory, also called Northside Armory, was located just north of downtown at 711 N. Pennsylvania. The other was Southside Armory, located at 2015 S. Pennsylvania. The largest indoor sports venue in Indianapolis was the Fairgrounds Coliseum located at 1202 E. 38th Street. Unfortunately, a horrific propane gas explosion killed 74 people and caused major damage to the building during an ice show on October 31, 1963, so the building was closed for many long months.

Chuck Marlowe remembers:

> "The Coliseum disaster in 1963 was a real setback for spectator events in Indianapolis. I had four tickets to the [show] that night and called my wife to see if she would like to take our older son to see the show. She reminded me that it was a school night, so we didn't go. The section that blew up was the same section which held our seats, and there's a good chance we could have been seriously injured had we been there."

Partners in the wrestling business Dick the Bruiser & Wilbur Snyder
Source: *Detroit News*

— Bruiser and Snyder Become Partners

Wilbur's son, Mike Snyder, looked back at the change that took place between his dad and Dick the Bruiser in 1964, which coincided with the Snyder family moving permanently to Indianapolis.

> "They [Dick and Wilbur] later formed a bond and decided they could take over this territory [Indianapolis]. I remember a guy named Balk Estes ... We must have been good friends with that family because I became friends with the twin sons [of Balk Estes]. I remember playing at their house as they were older than I was. That's where their partnership started and they tried to take over that territory. Back in Indianapolis, Dick and Wilbur were able to get better talent and they put it together."

While they were business partners in Indianapolis, that fact was not known to fans in other wrestling territories since they were often booked against each other. In the eyes of those fans, Bruiser and Snyder were bitter enemies, intent on destroying each other.

Sometime in early 1964, promoter Balk Estes saw wrestling posters hanging in windows around town and realized Bruiser and Snyder were going to promote their own shows. William Estes, the son of Balk and now an attorney in Texas, was a teenager at the time and remembers Bruiser and Snyder failing to show up for a Barnett-Estes card on which they had been advertised. Young Estes remembers, "*That really pissed us off — very seriously.*" William and his twin brother were given the job of ripping down the Bruiser/Snyder posters. "*We would go out after school, but Wee Willie Davis* [the promoter in Louisville] *caught us tearing them down.*"

Winnipeg, Manitoba, Canada
March 31, 1964

— Bruiser Goes to Los Angeles

Before going full speed ahead with his ambition as a wrestling promoter, Bruiser had business to take care of in the Los Angeles territory. The wrestling business in LA in 1964 was under the control of Cal and Aileen Eaton. Aileen, one of few women in the pro wrestling business, had two sons, Mike and Gene LeBell, who also were involved in the business. Their prime wrestling venue was the Olympic Auditorium, located at 18th and Grand Avenue in downtown Los Angeles, where the Eatons also promoted professional boxing. Author Bill Libby described the atmosphere of the Olympic during those years in his book, *Best of Sport: 1946-71*:

> "*The Olympic Auditorium in downtown Los Angeles is a monument to days sadly gone by. It sags and creaks. Its ten thousand upholstered seats leak out their insides from a thousand knife slashes. Its stairs are slippery from blood and spit and spilled beer and millions of shuffling feet. Its air is stale with smoke and sweat, and heavy with the echoes of cheers and boos and profanities.*"

Wrestling shows ran twice weekly at the Olympic in Los Angeles with a "live" TV broadcast on Wednesday nights and a non-televised card on Friday night. Other California towns on their circuit included San Bernardino, Long Beach, Bakersfield, and San Diego. The Los Angeles wrestling scene was highly influenced by matchmaker Jules Strongbow, who had been involved in the 1950s nationwide television wrestling program originating from Hollywood Legion Stadium, a venue in which Wilbur Snyder had many of his early matches. The owners relied on the expertise of Strongbow and, later, his associate Charlie Moto (who wrestled for many years as Mr. Moto), to handle the details of running the promotion. Two other local celebrities were involved with the Los Angeles wrestling scene. The television play-by-play announcer was long-time Hollywood character actor Dick Lane, while the "live" ring announcer at the Olympic was Jimmy Lennon, uncle of the famous Lennon Sisters singing act. The Olympic Auditorium's telephone number — RIchmond 9-5171 — was legendary and as well-known to the general public as the wrestlers themselves.

Bruiser's clash in Detroit with Alex Karras made the national newspapers, and it had been well-covered by both the *Los Angeles Times* and *Los Angeles Herald Examiner*, so his reputation in Los Angeles was definitely established by early 1964.

At the time, the leading heel in Southern California was Classy Freddie Blassie, known throughout his career as the "Hollywood Fashion Plate" and for a "blood and guts" style in the ring. On June 12, 1961, Blassie headlined against Edouard Carpentier and drew a record indoor wrestling gate of 13,000 fans paying $40,169. Veteran LA wrestling photographer Dr. Mike Lano remembers Blassie having to leave the Southern California wrestling scene when the bloodletting and overexposure began to "get stale."

Jeff Walton offered another perspective on the status of Blassie and the territory bosses. *"Strongbow and Moto wanted to send a message to Blassie that he wasn't the only act in town and could be replaced. Blassie eventually moved on to the Northeast to work for Vince McMahon Sr. and feud with their champion, Bruno Sammartino."*

Both Walton and Lano agree that Bruiser had another motive for traveling to the Southern California territory. Bruiser wanted to get work as an actor in Hollywood, like fellow wrestlers Hard Boiled Haggerty, Woody Strode and Mike Mazurki. One has to admit that Bruiser had been acting in quite a captivating role since he began wrestling professionally. Walton remembers Bruiser auditioning for the *Dennis the Menace* TV series, but not getting the part. Bruiser's photograph with the star of the series, youngster Jay North, was published in *Big Time Wrestling* magazine in 1964 and was showcased in Bruiser's trophy room in his Indianapolis home. Bruiser's visits also were designed to help him secure future wrestling trips to Japan via connections matchmaker Charlie Moto had with wrestling promoters in Tokyo. It is said that wrestler Dick Beyer, who roomed with Bruiser in Chicago in 1955 and was wrestling in LA as The Sensational, Intelligent Destroyer, recommended Bruiser to the LA promoters.

Bruiser vs. Freddie Blassie
1964
Source: John Greensmith family

Bruiser made his return to LA on February 28, 1964. Wrestling historian Steve Yohe described that night when fans were warned in advance to not touch Bruiser or get near him.

"Bruiser was the first wrestler in LA to be led to the ring by a police escort. Once in the ring, he really put on a show — running around, shaking the ropes, and stomping the boards to make sure the ring would hold up during his assault. Bruiser was in his prime, and I thought he was the meanest looking wrestler I had ever seen. He wrestled Edouard Carpentier and just destroyed him. The finish had Dick doing his stomp off the top rope onto Ed and he [Bruiser] got the pin standing, just holding Carpentier down with his foot. It put Bruiser over like crazy."

— Bruiser Wins WWA Title

Bruiser returned to Los Angeles for a high-profile match on April 22, at which time he defeated Fred Blassie to win the WWA world title. Bruiser made a big splash in the territory and attracted the attention of the mainstream media. He even became the subject of a long article by columnist Jim Murray of the *Los Angeles Times*. Some of the highlights of Murray's column included these comments:

> "*Combine the worst aspects of the Japanese fruit fly, the rose aphids, rabies, or the giant spider, together with the best of Benito Mussolini, you can get an idea what kind of man Dick Afflis is.*
>
> "*Dick the Bruiser is his ring name. He wrestles for a living and hates for fun. He's the kind of guy who would put Albert Schweitzer adrift in a lifeboat, then poke a hole in his canteen.*
>
> "*... He is such a mass of muscle, he looks as if he should have tramways running down the sides. If he had to have an operation, you'd have to have a plow.*
>
> "*His favorite 'hold' is a kick in the teeth. He has so many stitches on top of his head, he looks as if he cut his hair with a lawn mower.*"

New Champ
Dick The Bruiser displays the Worldwide Wrestling Alliance championship belt he won Wednesday night in Los Angeles from Fred Blassie. Tonight Bruiser teams with Wilbur Snyder in the feature event against the Miller Brothers in the debut of wrestling at the Southside Armory, 2015 S. Pennsylvania. Other matches on the 8:30 p. m. card are: Joe Brunetti vs. Nicoli Volkoff; Roger Kirby vs. The Mongol; Tony Parente vs. Angelo Poffo and Roy Gordon vs. Billy Goelz.

Los Angeles program
April 29, 1964

— Debut of WWA in Indianapolis

A few days after this victory over Blassie, a photo of a cigar-chomping Dick the Bruiser appeared in the April 25, 1964, edition of the *Indianapolis Times* with Bruiser displaying his newly-won WWA championship belt. The timing of this LA victory was masterfully orchestrated to coincide with a big event booked in Indianapolis that night — the first Indianapolis wrestling card staged under the auspices of Dick the Bruiser and Wilbur Snyder. Dick and Wilbur were finally "their own boss" in Indianapolis.

Chapter 13
Championship Wrestling, Inc. — 1964-1965

In his book *Long Days and Short Pays*, former wrestler H.E. (Duke) West explains how the "new" Bruiser was not much different from the "old" Bruiser:

> "I always found it amazing how a wrestler would "turn" and go from babyface to heel, or vice versa. I can remember when I first watched wrestling on TV and saw Dick the Bruiser. I still remember him wearing the long black tights on those shows out of the Chicago Amphitheatre. At least, I think they were black. There was no color TV back then, so they looked black to me. The "heel" Bruiser was really scary. He would trounce the babyfaces and he seemed to be unstoppable. He struck fear into the hearts of many a fan just walking to and from the ring. I think he was responsible for more than one riot at the venues he worked. I sure wouldn't have wanted to cross his path in a dark alley ... or for that matter, a light one.
>
> "One day, out of the blue, Bruiser did a run-in and trounced one of his fellow heels. From that day on, he was one of the good guys. His style of wrestling didn't change one iota. He was still scary. He still went after the opponent with reckless ferocity, both before and after the bell rang. And yet, the fans all loved him."

— Bruiser and Snyder Go Into Business

Dick the Bruiser and Wilbur Snyder were 50/50 partners in the Indianapolis promotion. Duties that fell upon the shoulders of the owners and day-to-day managers of the business included hiring and firing of wrestling talent, scheduling matches, creating storylines, renting buildings in which to stage the events, producing and paying for television programs and airtime, and the proverbial "counting the beans" — keeping financial records of income and expenses.

All sources indicate that Dick the Bruiser was the more dominant of the two owners. Mike Snyder told the author, "*Dick the Bruiser was Dick the Bruiser.*" The author believes Wilbur could be described more accurately as mild-mannered Clark Kent. Johnny Valiant shared his thoughts on Wilbur:

> "My take was Wilbur was more of a clerical and bookkeeper type. Dick was the colorful guy who was in the trenches with the talent. Wilbur was a legitimate wrestler and played for the Edmonton Eskimos football. He was a collegiate type. I always equate him with a Burt Lancaster type. He was a Marine Corp type person. You know he had a red jacket with "SNYDER" on the back, not "THE GREAT WILBUR SNYDER."

Mike Snyder remembered his father had a home office and kept the books for the company. The corporate address of Championship Wrestling, Inc. — 5928 Northland Road, Indianapolis — was, in fact, the Snyder family home for several years, until Wilbur built his dream home in suburban Carmel. The function of hiring and firing was a shared responsibility as both owners had a say in what wrestlers would work for the company. However, all the wrestlers interviewed for this biography said Dick the Bruiser was the main guy in charge of talent relations.

In his autobiography, *The Hard Way*, Don Fargo gave his take on Bruiser and Snyder:

> "There was as much difference between Bruiser and Snyder as there was space between Jupiter and Mars. They were nothing alike. They were like night and day. It was comical to watch them together.
>
> "Bruiser was a brute. He was wild. He lived on the edge. He ate chicken with his fingers and wiped his fingers on his shirt. He drank beer and whiskey from the bottle. Snyder, on the other hand, was from high society. He was prim and proper. He picked the meat off the bones with his fork and wiped his fingers on the napkin he had tucked into his shirt collar. He sipped on cocktails and margaritas with his little finger sticking up into the air."

— **Booking Calendar**

To keep a handle on what needed to be done, Bruiser maintained a detailed booking calendar for each year of operation. Each monthly spread showed the venue and wrestling line-ups for each card scheduled on any particular day. The main events would be listed on top, followed by the semi-main event, and then the mid-card and preliminaries. It appears that the winner of the match was frequently listed first within each match-up, but no details regarding finishes appear. Each day with an event would have a circle surrounding a dollar sign and a number, indicating Bruiser's payoff for that event. The Bruiser's airline carrier, flight number, and departure time also were recorded. At times, the calendar would show Bruiser's dividend compensation as a promotional co-owner, whether from Indianapolis, Chicago, or Milwaukee, even when Bruiser didn't actually wrestle on a card. It is believed Bruiser bought or was given points or shares in Fred Kohler's promotion in Milwaukee around 1964 or 1965.

Veteran WWA worker, Tom Lynch, remembers how wrestlers would find out where and when they were scheduled to wrestle:

> "The call at noon was on Monday to get your bookings. Sometimes, I would wait on that phone. You couldn't call before noon. You would keep dialing and finally you would get through. I would ask Bruiser, 'Do you have any bookings?' We would not know who our opponent was, just where the show was and what time it started."

One wrestler said newly arrived talent were often set up as victims of a prank when they were instructed to call the Bruiser at home around seven a.m. because "*Bruiser is an early riser.*"

On their debut show at the Southside Armory, Bruiser and Snyder booked themselves into the main event as tag team champions against Big Bill Miller and Dan Miller, real life brothers and legitimate amateur wrestlers. Local

Championship
WRESTLING
Southside Armory
2015 S. Pennsylvania
FREE PARKING

TONITE
First Event 8:30

★ **MAIN EVENT** ★
World's Tag Team
Championship Match
DICK THE BRUISER
and
WILBUR SNYDER
vs
BIG BILL MILLER
and
DAN MILLER

★ **SEMI-WINDUP** ★
Joe Brunetti vs
Nicoli Volkoff
Roger Kirby vs
The Mongol
Tony Parente vs
Angelo Poffo
Roy Gordon vs
Billy Goelz

Advance Tickets: Claypool
Ticket Agency, ME 5-7533
and Harem Lounge, 2208 N.
Meridian, or call WA 6-9569

Ad for Bruiser & Snyder's first card April 25, 1964

newspapers carried advance articles promoting this inaugural event, even noting that Bruiser and Snyder were instrumental in setting up a new legal corporate entity — Championship Wrestling, Inc. Chris Parsons explained, "*Dick and Wilbur christened their promotion the WWA, or Worldwide Wrestling Alliance* [later shortened to World Wrestling Association] *taken from the Los Angeles promotion, Worldwide Wrestling Associates.*" Parsons added, "*To get around the promotional license issue, the wrestlers put the license in their wives' names.*" Wrestling historian and author Tim Hornbaker managed to uncover corporate regulatory filings from 1965 showing the company directors as Louise Afflis (president, Dick's wife), Shirlee Snyder (vice president, Wilbur's wife), and Margaret Afflis Johnston (secretary-treasurer, Dick's mother).

Corporate Form No. 1 (Mar. 1950)—Page Three

ARTICLE VII

Voting Rights of Capital Stock

Every owner of the capital stock of the Corporation shall have the right, at every shareholders' meeting, to one vote for each share of stock standing in his name on the books of the Corporation.

ARTICLE VIII

Paid-in Capital

The amount of paid-in capital, with which the Corporation is beginning business, is $ 1000.00

ARTICLE IX

Data Respecting Directors

Section 1. Number. The number of Directors of the Corporation shall not be less than three (3) nor more than five (5), the exact number to be specified by the code of By-Laws but in no event shall the number be less than three (3), and in the absence of any By-Law provision, the number **Section 2. Qualifications.** Directors need not be shareholders of the shall be Corporation. A majority of the Directors at any time shall be citizens of the three. United States.

ARTICLE X

Further Data Respecting Directors

Section 1. Names and Post-Office Addresses. The names and post-office addresses of the first Board of Directors of the Corporation are as follows:

Name	Number and Street or Building	City	Zone	State
S. Snyder	5928 Northland Road	Indianapolis,		Indiana
L. Afflis	4930 N. Kessler Blvd.	Indianapolis,		Indiana
M. A. Johnston	5354 N. Meridian St.	Indianapolis,		Indiana

Section 2. Citizenship. All of such Directors are citizens of the United States.

Articles of Incorporation, Championship Wrestling, Inc.
Source: Tim Hornbaker

The new entrepreneurs booked a follow-up card with a return tag-team match against the Miller brothers on Saturday, May 9, 1964, at the same Southside Armory.

— **Harem Lounge**

The address of the wrestling office was 2208 N. Meridian Street in Indianapolis, the same address as the Harem Lounge, a saloon and nightspot owned by Dick and/or his wife. Several wrestlers called the establishment a "Go Go" bar with dancing, but there was no nudity or stripping, and local musical acts were occasionally booked to provide entertainment. Wrestler Les Thatcher remembers that *"Bruiser was a great host and welcomed the boys"* at the Harem. Most of the wrestlers who worked for Bruiser would hang out and drink at the Harem, and some met new girlfriends there. Wrestling fans who wanted tickets to the wrestling events could get them at the Harem or a ticket office at the Claypool Hotel in downtown Indianapolis. For many years, the phone number of the Claypool wrestling office was Melrose 6-1375.

When Bruiser and Snyder first began to tape local TV wrestling in 1964, the tapings were done at one of the two National Guard armories in Indianapolis — Northside (Tyndall) and Southside. Those armories were dark, dingy, and not designed for television production. In the early days, audience attendance was minimal, and the TV shows almost always consisted of "squash matches," whereby a highly talented and main-event wrestler or tag team would face a not-so-talented preliminary wrestler or "jobber." In Bobby Heenan's first autobiography, he claimed the audio track of the taping was beefed up with tape recordings of crowd noise from Chicago Bears football games. More than likely, that's accurate because a viewing of older tapes shows the audio level to be much higher than what the sparse crowd could generate.

Bruiser was able to utilize his wrestling tapes over and over throughout the years because the commentators made no references to specific dates or places within the narrative of the play-by-play. The matches were generic and, while some fans knew they came from Indianapolis, knowing that wasn't necessary to follow the action. The WWA heavyweight and tag team championship belts were never displayed while video tape was rolling. There were several reasons for that, but the primary reason was that the televised matches were regularly broadcast in Chicago, where only the AWA title belts were recognized. Another reason for avoiding use of the WWA belts was because, at times, there were different WWA champions in different towns for short time spans.

> **Editor's note:** As an example, Sailor Art Thomas was recognized in Detroit as the WWA champion on February 4, 1972, reportedly having defeated Baron Von Raschke in Minneapolis. However, Raschke continued to be recognized as the champion in Indianapolis until Billy Red Cloud won the title on March 21, 1972. Raschke regained the Indianapolis version of the title back from Red Cloud on June 2, 1972, then appeared in Detroit on the next night, June 3, 1972, to regain the title from Art Thomas. Art's best recollection of the dual title situation is that, due to his job responsibilities, he didn't have the time to travel to Indianapolis, so they split the title for a short time.

Over time, the TV tapings increasingly utilized head-to-head competition with top good guys against top bad guys, giving fans a chance to get a glimpse of what a match between Bruiser and Ernie Ladd looked like at the house (i.e. arena) shows. A big match on television, though, would never show the conclusion or resolution of a storyline.

— **Television Interviews**

Bruiser's calendar also kept detailed records of various aspects of running the company, such as tracking the daily advance ticket sales for upcoming wrestling cards. In addition, every Tuesday or Wednesday, the television promotional interviews (i.e. promos) were videotaped in Indianapolis for the various cities on the regular circuit, such as Chicago, Indianapolis, Fort Wayne, Elkhart, Terre Haute, and Hammond. On the videotaping day, detailed records were kept as to the broadcast dates and towns for the various interview segments, all geared to generating fan interest in each market. Most of the top wrestlers on the payroll would gather at WTTV-TV Channel 4, and later at WRTV-TV Channel 6, for the videotaping marathon, all produced by Dick the Bruiser. Bruiser's TV announcer would introduce each wrestler, or group of wrestlers, and ask them about their upcoming match in whatever town was on the schedule. The wrestlers had to think on their feet and spontaneously come up with interesting threats or promises that would stimulate fans to buy tickets to the "live" matches.

Chuck Marlowe, The voice of Indianapolis wrestling from 1957 to 1971

For several years, the TV studio set had an old, stand-up locker in the background, making the TV audience think they were looking into the dressing room of a wrestling arena. At other times, the background consisted of blown-up posters of Bruiser and other wrestlers in the territory. The videotaped interview segments were inserted into the video tapes of the televised matches and sent on to the local television stations for broadcast. The town of Hammond was promoted on television out of the Chicago broadcast outlets. At times, Bruiser would appear in a promotional interview on television, frequently during the final minute of the program. He would go berserk as the TV announcer would interrupt and say, "*I'm sorry Dick, but we have run out of time.*"

From a 1970 Indianapolis 500 raceday program magazine
Source: Indianapolis Motor Speedway

Miss Bunny Love, lady wrestler and valet of Paul Christy in the late '70s, remembered an incident during the interview tapings:

"*We did interviews, promos, and stuff in Indianapolis. The Bruiser wanted to see how good I could be under pressure ... to see if I could blow a promo. I was standing there, and the Bruiser picked up a cricket off the ground and threw it at me. It landed on my chest, and it's crawling down my dress and into my hair. After the interview, I flung the cricket off, and the Bruiser laughed his butt off. He thought it was hysterical because I didn't crack. He was pretty impressed.*"

For a while, the two wrestling promotions ran simultaneously in Indianapolis. Les Thatcher remembers "*When Dick and Wilbur started as partners, we* [Les and Roger Kirby] *worked for both offices."* On the shoot interview Scott Teal conducted with Dennis Hall for his *Shooting with the Legends* DVD series, Dennis Hall recalls being warned by a representative of the existing promoters about working for Bruiser and Snyder and threatened with unemployment if he did so. Others, like Bill Frazier said, *"I was never threatened by either side of the dispute."*

In an interview conducted by Scott Teal on May 25, 1995, Dennis Hall remembers a trip he and Roger Kirby made with Bruiser:

"Roger and I used to drive to Indianapolis and meet the Bruiser, then ride with him to do St. Louis TV. The first time we went down with him, of course, he was tan, because all he did was wrestle. Well, we had these jobs, and were just part-time. Bruiser drove a Cadillac convertible with the top down. Me and Kirby took our shirts off on the way because it got hot. We got red as lobsters. From the waist up, we were blood red, and our legs were bone white."

— **Ballpark Spectacular**

In a brilliant business move, Bruiser and Snyder booked a big extravaganza show at Victory Field for Friday, May 29, 1964, the night before the world-famous Indianapolis 500 auto race, and enlisted the sponsorship of the Kroger Company, a national grocery-store chain based in Cincinnati. The retailer distributed a half million free gift certificates to customers at their central Indiana outlets. The official program for that night listed the promoter as "L. Afflis" — Dick's wife, Louise. There were two main events that evening, the first being co-owner Wilbur Snyder and Cowboy Bob Ellis against Angelo Poffo and Nicoli Volkoff. The headline event, though, was newly-crowned WWA champion Dick the Bruiser defending his title against Freddie Blassie, the man Bruiser took the title from the previous month. Bruiser and Blassie had what might be called a dress rehearsal for the Indianapolis card on May 27 in Los Angeles.

Kroger Presents:
Championship Wrestling
Dick the Bruiser vs. Freddie Blassie
Fri., May 29th—8:30 p.m., Indpls., Victory Field
FREE! 50¢ Off Gift certificate available at any Kroger Store.

When a wrestling show was booked at Victory Field, Bruiser and Snyder dealt directly with Max Schumacher, president of the Indianapolis Indians ball club at that time, a position he still held while this biography was being written.

In May 2010, president Schumacher talked about transforming the ballpark for wrestling events:

"When the Indians were playing at home, we would not have wrestling, but when they were on road trips, we would set up the ballpark for wrestling. We would put up the ring at home plate. Then we would put up chairs all around between home plate and the pitcher's mound, and down towards first [base]*, and down towards third* [base]*, and behind home plate and the*

108 • BRUISER: The World's Most Dangerous Wrestler

backstop. Those were ringside seats, then people could sit up in the grandstand."

Schumacher had positive things to say about business owners Bruiser and Snyder:

"One thing I'll say about Dick and his partner, Wilbur ... they were reputable, good businessmen from my experience with them. We would meet with them a week or ten days before the event. They would tell us what they

Kroger Presents:

Championship Wrestling
TONIGHT:

Copyright 1964 — The Kroger Co.

L. Afflis—Promoter
Johnny King—Matchmaker and Announcer
Timekeeper—Edward Smith
Attending Physician—Michael Kosanovich
Referee—Johnny Schoen

INDIANA STATE ATHLETIC COMMISSION
Dr. J. B. Daugerty—Chairman
Merle Ahe—Secretary
Dr. L. J. Holliday, M.D.—Commissioner
Don L. Parker—Commissioner

MAIN EVENT

Dick the Bruiser Indianapolis, Ind.—240 lbs.	vs.	**Freddie Blassie** St. Louis, Missouri—240 lbs.
Wilbur Snyder Indianapolis, Ind.—240 lbs.	and vs.	**Cowboy Bob Ellis** Amarillo, Texas—245 lbs.
Angelo Poffo Chicago, Illinois—235 lbs.	and	**Nicoli Volkoff** Russia—237 lbs.
Joe Blanchard Dallas, Texas—245 lbs.	vs.	**Bobby Managoff** Chicago, Illinois—242 lbs. (former World's Champion)
Joe Brunetti Salt Lake City, Utah 230 lbs.	vs.	**Mike Paidousis**
Bill Miller Columbus, Ohio—280 lbs.	vs.	**Bob Whitlow** Indianapolis, Ind—246 lbs.
Bobby Graham Detroit, Michigan—226 lbs.	vs.	**Billie Geolz** Chicago, Illinois—222 lbs.
The Mongol Tibet—237 lbs.	vs.	**Dennis Hall** New Castle, Ind—226 lbs.

MIDGET TAG TEAMS

Pewee Lopez Puerto Rico—105 lbs.	and vs.	**Chico Santana** Puerto Rico—95 lbs.
Marcel Semard Montreal, Canada—102 lbs.	and	**Little Boy Blue** Richmond, Virginia—97 lbs.

"The management reserves the right to make last-minute substitutions, through any unforeseen circumstances, in any of the regular-scheduled bouts. In such events, it regrets any inconvenience caused to fans.

Kroger Tenderay Brand Beef!

Tendered Naturally ... The only beef you don't trim again at home! ... Every cut of Kroger's exclusive Tenderay Beef goes from package to pan the way you unwrap it—juicy, lean and trimmed close to the rosy red. That's because Tenderay Beef is trimmed with conscience as well as care. Triple-trimmed, in fact, of excess fat, bone and waste according to precise standards laid down in the 250-page Kroger Meat Cutting Manual. Triple-trimmed before weighing and pricing!

Kroger Tail-less T-Bone

Note the Kroger Tail-less trim on this Tenderay T-Bone Steak. Long, wasteful "tail" is removed ... all but enough fat for flavor is cut off ... excess bone and waste are trimmed away. You pay only for tender, juicy, full-flavored meat you can eat.

KROGER TENDERAY BEEF

Source: The Kroger Company

wanted in terms of ticket sellers based on anticipated crowds — how many ushers, how many gate men, and how many security people. Then we would arrange for all that, and then when it was all over, we would send them a bill and, by return mail, we would always get the check. There was never a problem with a single dollar with dealing with Dick Afflis and Wilbur Snyder."

The wrestlers (both good and bad guys) would all use the visiting team dressing room behind first base since the Indian's dressing room was filled with uniforms and equipment. The ballpark would charge a minimum guarantee against a percentage of the box office receipts. Schumacher also was amazed on how the professional wrestlers would affect the live audience:

"The crowds would be worked into a real lather as there would be apparent mayhem in the ring. I remember one of our electricians would work the wrestling shows to make sure all the microphones and the lights were turned on. He was sitting at ringside. A fan apparently had carried in a large rock, or piece of concrete. I only theorize that was on the top of the grandstand and he spotted something he did not like in the match and was going to test out his throwing arm. He threw this rock or concrete at the wrestler he didn't like, but it fell short and hit our electrician and cut him badly. We had to call an ambulance and take him to the hospital to get stitched up."

This first card at Victory Field for Bruiser and Snyder was dutifully reported the next day in great detail in the *Indianapolis Times*:

"Dick the Bruiser retained his world heavyweight wrestling championship before some 5,000 chilly fans at Victory Field on Friday night by throwing Freddie Blassie out of the ring in the third and deciding fall. Blassie won the first fall with a hangman, but the Bruiser came back with one of his patented knee drops from the top rope to set the stage for the furious last-fall action. During the third fall, Blassie was warned repeatedly against hitting the Bruiser low, and was finally tossed out of the ring by the champion. Blassie could not get back in time to continue the match."

A crowd of 5,000 can surely be considered a success when you note that each of the armories in town barely held a few thousand. Wilbur Snyder's son, Mike Snyder, remembered "*the Victory Field promotion as very successful and I remember selling programs throughout the stands that night."*

It isn't known where this story took place, but H.E. (Duke) West shared an amusing anecdote told to him by Moose Cholak:

"*Bobby* [Golden], *Chief* [Lone Eagle], *and I had a tradition of lighting up a cigar when we arrived at [a] venue. When we strolled into the locker room one night, Moose Cholak began chuckling. He told us to either finish or get rid of our stogies before our match. He recalled a time when Freddie Blassie lit up a big cigar in the dressing room. He was still enjoying it when the time came for him to hit the ring. He carefully tamped it out and put the remainder on top of a locker so he could retrieve it when he returned.*

"One of the wrestlers sharing the dressing room that night was none other than Dick the Bruiser. Bruiser had quietly watched Freddie's ritual. As soon as Freddie was out of the room, Bruiser strolled over and grabbed the cigar. He then dropped his trunks, methodically twirled the end of it in his butt crack, and placed it back on top of the locker where Blassie had left it. Bruiser calmly sat back down, not having said one word the entire time.

"When Blassie returned, he retrieved the cigar and sat down on the bench. After going on and on about the match, he lit the cigar and took several puffs. Suddenly, with a puzzled look on his face, he held the cigar out in front of him and said, "This tastes like shit!" Of course, the entire dressing room broke out in laughter."

— **Wrestling Business in Indianapolis**

Bruiser and Snyder encountered the same issues all start-up businesses have, such as drawing enough customers to generate sufficient revenue, and controlling labor expenses while trying to retain key employees. They likely realized that having their own business also meant having to subsidize operating losses when revenues didn't cover operating expenses (including the cost of television production).

Wrestler Bill Frazier remembers seeing Bruiser deal directly with one of the most common problems for wrestling promoters — the never-ending debate over payoffs to the wrestlers. Frazier remembers an incident when a veteran wrestler was complaining to Bruiser in the dressing room about his payoff. The wrestler, Boris Volkoff, was teamed with his ring "brother," Nicoli Volkoff. The instant the protest came out of Volkoff's mouth, Bruiser turned around and hollered, "*Hey, Frazier. How long would it take for you to grow a beard and become a Russian?*" Soon afterwards, Frazier grew out his beard and began to wrestle as Ivan Volkoff, a character named after a real-life minister of sports in Russia. From that day on, the original Volkoff brothers found themselves booked less and less frequently.

Long-time mat veteran Dennis Hall remembers witnessing another issue the new promoter/owners had to deal with:

"The chief of police and the mayor came to the arena. I overheard a conversation with Snyder. They wanted a part of the gate because they said anything that went on in [the town], they got a part of. They [Bruiser and Snyder] *decided not to run there anymore because they weren't going to pay kickback money there.* Snyder told the mayor and the chief of police, 'We got a license to run anywhere we want in Indiana as long as we rent out a building.' The chief of police said, 'Yes, but we control the parking around here, and we can put no parking signs up around this area, and we can tow the cars if anybody tries to park going to the matches'"

— **Reliable Employees**

Bruiser and Snyder began surrounding themselves with reliable and talented performers who would regularly come in and out of their territory for the forseeable future. "Nature Boy" Roger Kirby was born and grew up in nearby Dunkirk,

Indiana, and found himself working for Bruiser many times. Roger reflected on working for Bruiser. *"I had the ability to do whatever he wanted me to do and I never questioned him."* Each time he returned to the territory, Kirby would ask Bruiser, *"What can I do to get you where you want to go."* Kirby also remembered his treatment from the older veterans like Snyder, Gene Kiniski, and especially Bruiser in those early days:

"There were a number of times when Bruiser would come by and pick me up and ask me, 'Do you have enough money to pay your rent, or, do you have enough food?' When I was hurt, he would come by and give me money. He was such a giving person."

In *The Hard Way*, Don Fargo also had good things to say about Bruiser as a person:

"I have to say something about Dick the Bruiser. He was a really good guy. He always had beer in the dressing room for the boys, and since Snyder was too uppity to drink beer, Bruiser made sure he always had a couple of bottles of champagne in the cooler. Bruiser never acted like he was better than any of the boys who worked for him. In fact, he treated us as equals. He made sure we knew who ruled the roost, but he didn't lord his position over us."

One young rookie to whom Bruiser gave a start was Tom Jones, a black wrestler who had once been a fan in Indianapolis. He had been trained in Boston and had only a handful of matches under his belt when he decided to return to his job at Sanford Industrial in Indianapolis. In an August 1996 interview with Scott Teal, Tom said:

"They had matches one night in Indianapolis ... well, what happened was when I worked with Bull Curry, there was some pictures taken. I took them with me. The only guy I could talk to there was Bruiser. Snyder was a hell of a guy after he got to know me. Snyder was kind of funny, but after he got to know you, and you got to know him, he was a good guy. Bruiser would talk to anybody. I talked to Snyder that night. As a matter of fact, I finally got into the dressing room at the Fairgrounds Coliseum. Snyder just kind of looked at them [photos], rolled his eyes, and said, 'Uh, I'll talk to you later.' Prince Pullins was there and said, 'Go over and talk to Dick. You'll get more out of him.' Dick stood up and shook my hand, then I showed him the pictures.

"He said, 'Yeah, I know Bull. Give me about a week and I'll give you a call.' Sure enough, he called me. My first match in Indianapolis was at Northside Armory and I worked against Dick. I only weighed about one-hundred-ninety pounds. I mean, I was pumping iron and trying to gain weight. I finally did, and now I can't get rid of it. (laughs)

"The first trip I ever made was to Louisville, Kentucky with Bruiser. It was 1965. He said, 'Hey, kid. What name do you want to use?'

"I said, 'Well, I don't know.'

"'What name have you been using?'

"'Bearcat Jones.'

"He said, [low, gravelly voice] *'Bearcat Jones? Aw, that won't work. We've got Bearcat Wright coming in here. I'll think of a name.' By the time we got there, he said, 'I know what I'll call you. I'll call you Tom Jones, okay?'*

"I said, 'Yeah, whatever you want, Dick.' *(laughs)*

"I was so green. I thought, 'If I don't say yes, this guy's liable to pull over and beat my ass.' I found out different because Dick was a sweetheart."

Another long-time mat veteran Bruiser would hire back repeatedly for decades was John Steele Hill, who had numerous ring names under Bruiser — Assassin #2, Guy Heenan, Guy Mitchell, The Masked Strangler, Mad Man Mitchell, and Gentleman Jerry Valiant. In the 1980s, John Steele Hill would even supervise occasional out-of-town spot shows, including supervising the wrestlers, handing out match finishes, and handling all the cash receipts. Steele's widow, Carolyn Hill, remembers the special relationship between Hill and the promoters in Indianapolis:

"They [Wilbur and Dick] *knew John from seventeen years old and up when they brought him from Canada to Indianapolis on the green card. They knew his ethics and values. They knew he was a straight arrow. They knew what they were getting and who was worth it.*"

— Expanding the Territory

According to former wrestler Tom Hankins, who was still just a fan in June 1964, Bruiser and Snyder ran two shows in Cedar Rapids, Iowa, at Veterans Memorial Coliseum against established Kansas City promoter Gust Karras and local promoter Art Mitchell. Bruiser was featured in the main event against Bobo Brazil on the first show and against Ellis on the second, with Bruiser winning both matches. In his yet-to-be-released autobiography, Tom writes:

"*Bruiser stacked his cards with main-event talent like Bill Miller, Wilbur Snyder, Joe Blanchard, Bobby Managoff, Art Thomas, Moose Cholak, and more. I even told Art* [Mitchell] *how much better it was than the local show, and he didn't disagree with me. He didn't disagree with me because, no doubt, he knew it was true. For all I knew, and I had my suspicions, Art may have been in cahoots with Bruiser in his efforts to take the cities. Bruiser drew double what Karras did and Art may have sensed larger profits for himself down the line. That's all speculation, though. I did wonder, though, why Art didn't seem upset when I told him Bruiser's show was better. He never said anything bad about them, either.* Surprisingly, Bruiser's presence didn't affect the size of Art's crowd by any measurable amount. Bruiser drew a thousand or more fans — about double the business the Kansas City promotion was doing.

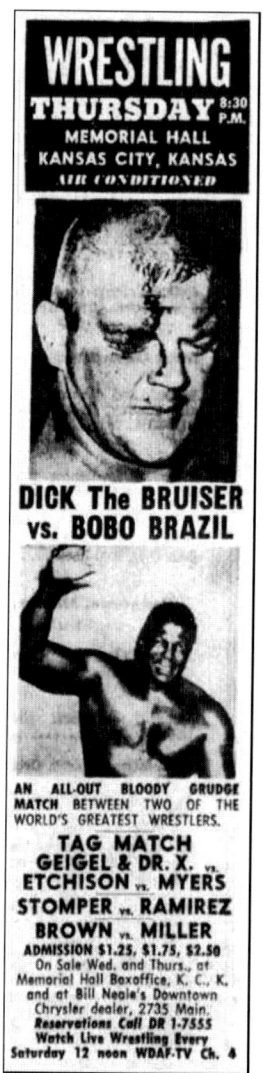

"The Kansas City promoters [Karras, Bob Geigel and Pat O'Connor] *eventually reached some kind of agreement with Bruiser and Snyder because*

they pulled out after those two cards. Eleven years later, Gust Karras told me how furious he had been at Bruiser for coming into his city and he still had a deep resentment for him. Sam Muchnick gets the credit for convincing Gust to use Bruiser in Kansas City after that. That seems strange to me because I never understood why Muchnick didn't stop Bruiser from invading Iowa in the first place. Bruiser was a good drawing card, so Gust did bring him into Kansas City and Des Moines, but he used him sparingly."

— **Supporting Cast**

Many people fail to realize the supporting players behind the scenes who help promoters run their companies. In many cases, a local promoter did the legwork and took care of the logistics of running a show. People in that capacity in Bruiser's territory included Phil Olaufson (Fort Wayne), Mike Mercurio (Richmond), Ralph Hamilton (Terre Haute), and Bob Luce (Hammond). At other times, promoters would schedule a wrestling card known as a purchased or paid show, in which an organization or sponsor would pay Bruiser and Snyder a flat fee to put together a wrestling card and provide the wrestlers and a ring.

The WWA also had a steady group of guys who would truck the wrestling ring from town to town. Their job was to set up the ring and dismantle it afterwards. Many people got into the business in just such a fashion, including Mike Snyder, Tom Lynch, Steve Regal, Spike Huber, and Dick's own son, Karl Afflis. Bruiser and Snyder also employed a crew of part-time referees who became distinctive personalities in their own right. Little Connie (The Golden Greek) Marker owned a Greek restaurant in Richmond, plump John Shoren from Plainfield was a beverage driver for 7-Up, and lanky Bob Wingo from Bedford worked for a railroad company. Bruiser also had a long-time buddy named Dennis Reidlinger, who provided cold beer to the dressing rooms in Indianapolis and sat quietly at ringside during Bruiser's matches.

— **Finishing Up in Los Angeles**

While Bruiser and Snyder had their hands full getting their promotion off the ground, there were still loose ends for Bruiser in Los Angeles. With so much to be done in Indianapolis, there was little time for Bruiser to be a full-time champion in Los Angeles, but he popped in and out of the LA territory. In all, Bruiser made eight trips back to the territory to defend the title in Los Angeles, Bakersfield, and San Diego, some of which were rematches against Blassie. On Wednesday, July 22, 1964, at the Olympic Auditorium, a televised main event pitted him against The Destroyer, Bruiser's short-term ex-roommate Dick Beyer. Wrestling historian Steve Yohe recalled the event of that evening:

"There was a good build up for this match on the TV news with the two Dicks being interviewed beside a hotel swimming pool. The match was okay, but it wasn't anything special.

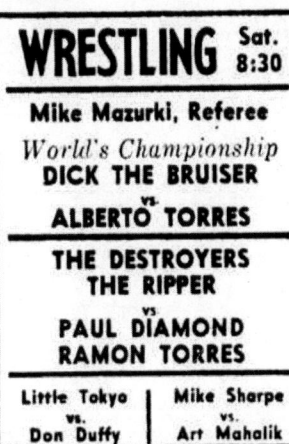

WRESTLING Sat. 8:30

Mike Mazurki, Referee

World's Championship
DICK THE BRUISER
vs.
ALBERTO TORRES

THE DESTROYERS
THE RIPPER
vs.
PAUL DIAMOND
RAMON TORRES

Little Tokyo	Mike Sharpe
vs.	vs.
Don Duffy	Art Maholik

SAN BERNARDINO **ARENA**
137 S. G St.

Sat. Only After 10 A.M. **TU 5-9169**

San Bernardino, California
June 27, 1964

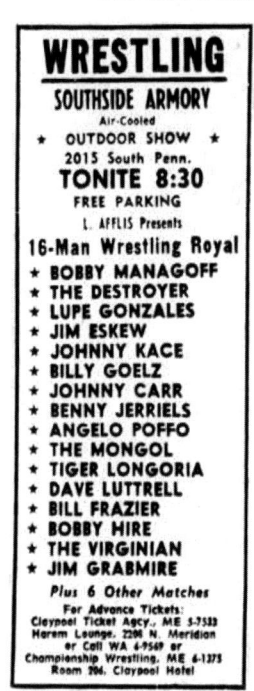

114 • BRUISER: The World's Most Dangerous Wrestler

WRESTLING
SOUTHSIDE ARMORY
Air-Cooled
★ OUTDOOR SHOW ★
2015 South Penn.
TONITE 8:30
FREE PARKING
L. AFFLIS Presents
16-Man Wrestling Royal
★ BOBBY MANAGOFF
★ THE DESTROYER
★ LUPE GONZALES
★ JIM ESKEW
★ JOHNNY KACE
★ BILLY GOELZ
★ JOHNNY CARR
★ BENNY JERRIELS
★ ANGELO POFFO
★ THE MONGOL
★ TIGER LONGORIA
★ DAVE LUTTRELL
★ BILL FRAZIER
★ BOBBY HIRE
★ THE VIRGINIAN
★ JIM GRABMIRE
Plus 6 Other Matches
For Advance Tickets:
Claypool Ticket Agcy., ME 5-7533
Harem Lounge, 2206 N. Meridian
or Call WA 4-9569 or
Championship Wrestling, ME 6-1373
Room 206, Claypool Hotel

Back-to-back cards
in Indianapolis
September 11, 1964
Jim Barnett, above
Bruiser-Snyder, below

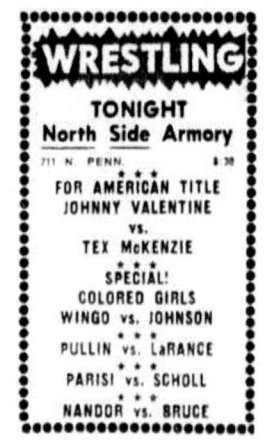

WRESTLING
TONIGHT
North Side Armory
711 N. PENN.   8:30
* * *
FOR AMERICAN TITLE
JOHNNY VALENTINE
vs.
TEX McKENZIE
* * *
SPECIAL!
COLORED GIRLS
WINGO vs. JOHNSON
* *
PULLIN vs. LaRANCE
* *
PARISI vs. SCHOLL
* * *
NANDOR vs. BRUCE

[Cowboy] *Bob Ellis was standing at ringside. As the Bruiser and the Destroyer were fighting outside the ring, Beyer fell down and Bruiser's punch hit Ellis, and they began to brawl. The Destroyer rolled into the ring and the Bruiser was counted out. The Destroyer claimed the belt and took his argument to the WWA commission."*

Weeks later, TV viewers in Los Angeles were told the WWA commission ruled The Destroyer won the match in July via count-out and was the new WWA champion. It had been a nice run for Bruiser as it gave him an additional boost to his status in the wrestling business. Bruiser would continue to claim the WWA world title when he returned to Indianapolis, at which time two separate lineages of the title began. Bruiser's version of the WWA title became the most-important title in the Indianapolis territory and had no ties to the California version.

Bruiser's name would surface in the *San Diego Union* newspaper article nine months later. In an article about wrestling promoter Hardy Kruskamp, he mentioned Bruiser. *"Dick the Bruiser?"* said Hardy. *"He represents the back-alley brawler. But don't think Dick the Bruiser is dumb. After all, he went to six or seven universities — uh, briefly."*

— The Fate of Barnett and Estes

The partnership of Bruiser and Snyder was formidable competition for incumbents Barnett and Estes. There was an initial rivalry for the wrestling fans' dollars in mid-1964 with Bruiser and Snyder using the Southside Armory and Barnett and Estes using the Northside Armory. It appears the drawing power of big stars Bruiser and Snyder was too much to handle.

Chris Parsons, the foremost expert on the WWA, points out that one Barnett/Estes card at the Northside Armory on July 4, 1964, had to be cancelled when the promoters were "not able to secure enough talent for the undercard." Bruiser and Snyder continued plugging along with weekly or bi-weekly events, even though Barnett and Estes occasionally brought in respectable main-event talent.

Both promotions ran head-to-head events on September 11, 1964, and newspapers reported "sparse" crowds at both shows. The Barnett/Estes card featured Johnny Valentine defending his American title belt against the challenge of Tex McKenzie. Bruiser and Snyder's feature was a 16-man, over-the-top-rope, battle royal with the winner to get a shot at Dick the Bruiser's "world heavyweight title."

Chapter 13 • 115

The final card for Barnett and Estes was held on September 18, 1964, at the Northside Armory. Barnett next traveled to Australia to launch a new wrestling promotion while Estes moved to Amarillo, Texas, to book wrestling cards under the auspices of Dory Funk Sr. The war seemed to end as fast as it began.

— Back to Detroit

In January 1965, Bruiser and Snyder decided to expand their territory into a nearby Midwest city — Detroit, Michigan — a city in which both of them had spent a lot of time since 1959. The previous year, the territory had been purchased from the previous owners by Ed Farhat, better known as The Sheik.

The invasion began by filming wrestling matches at the Leland Hotel in downtown Detroit and airing them on WKBD-TV, Channel 50. It was hoped the exposure on television would garner enough interest in the new promotional group to entice fans to attend the live cards at Olympia Stadium. The first 90-minute TV program was taped on Friday, January 22, 1965. The show was peppered with performers from the Indianapolis roster — Angelo Poffo, Bill Miller, Pat O'Connor, Guy Mitchell, Bill Frazier, and others, with either Bruiser or Snyder appearing on the telecasts. Indianapolis TV wrestling commentator Chuck Marlowe remembered working on some of those programs.

WRESTLING TONIGHT
North Side Armory
711 N. PENN. 8:30
FOR AMERICAN TITLE
JOHNNY VALENTINE
vs.
TEX McKENZIE
* * *
MILLER vs. NANDOR
* * *
PARIS vs. BRUCE
* * *
SPECIAL TAG BOUT!
PULLIN & THATCHER
vs.
GALLION & BAD BOY JOE

Final Barnett card in Indianapolis
September 18, 1964

Detroit wrestling historian Allan Cooper kept meticulously detailed notes of all thirteen weekly cards. Occasionally, a videotape of a non-Detroit match was shown, such as February 4 when Larry Hennig and Harley Race were featured in a TV studio match from Minneapolis, Minnesota. On Thursday, March 4, a substitute wrestling program aired, the top-rated *Wrestling at the Chase* show from St. Louis. Gene Kiniski, who would win the WWA world title from Bruiser in August, appeared on three of the telecasts in February and another on March 11.

The debut house show was scheduled for Friday, March 26, at the Olympia. On television the night before the card, Hennig, Race, and Verne Gagne all made appearances to promote the show. That night, Bruiser successfully defended his WWA world title against Pat O'Connor, while Hennig and Race held off a challenge from Joe Blanchard and Gagne. Kiniski was commonly matched up against Wilbur Snyder, his old Canadian Football League teammate, during this series. Three more Olympia cards followed — April 24, May 8 and May 22. After the fourth show, Bruiser and Snyder pulled out of Detroit and concentrated on their home turf.

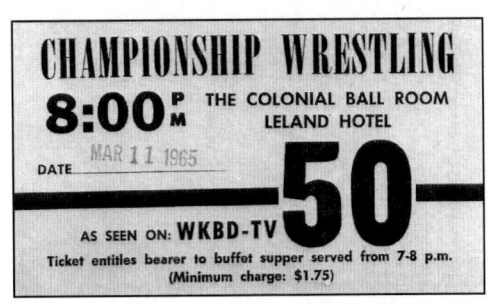

CHAMPIONSHIP WRESTLING
8:00 P.M. THE COLONIAL BALL ROOM
LELAND HOTEL
DATE MAR 11 1965
50
AS SEEN ON: WKBD-TV
Ticket entitles bearer to buffet supper served from 7-8 p.m.
(Minimum charge: $1.75)

Wrestling admission ticket • 1965
Source: Chris Parsons

— First Card at Fairgrounds Coliseum

Bruiser and Snyder continued to build up their promotion in Indiana, occasionally moving their weekly card to the Fairgrounds Coliseum. Their first event there took place on March 12, 1965, with Bruiser defending the WWA title against Johnny Valentine in the main event. Newspapers reported Valentine being transported to a local hospital after the match. They had a rematch on April 10, again at the Fairgrounds, with Snyder reportedly helping Dick win the match. Bruiser's creative booking included re-inventing wrestling cousins Dennis Hall and Roger Kirby, who became bleached-blond Dennis and Roger Dolly. Bruiser and Snyder also added Louisville, Kentucky, to their regular circuit of towns.

Bruiser held the WWA title until August 21, at which time he dropped it to Gene Kiniski in Indianapolis at Victory Field. Having Kiniski as the promotion's champion gave the business a boost. The most notorious confrontation between Bruiser and Kiniski took place on October 30, 1965. The "death match" drew a heated reaction from the fans and detailed coverage from local newspapers. Dr. L.J. Holladay, head of the Indiana Athletic Commission, stopped the match due to excessive bleeding on Bruiser's part. Dr. Holladay's son, Thomas Holladay, was a youngster sitting ringside that night and recalled the incident decades later:

> "Gene Kiniski was the champion at the time. The world championship belt was solid brass and had grooves in it with sharp edges. Kiniski had been introduced and they were introducing Dick. Well, Kiniski took the belt and he slammed the belt on Dick's head. That's how he [Bruiser] got cut. Blood was everywhere."

— Feud with the Funks

One of the most notable matches in Dory Funk, Jr.'s rookie year (1963) was against Dick the Bruiser in Indianapolis, and in St. Louis in 1965, Bruiser faced both Dory Funk, Sr. and Dory Funk, Jr. in handicap matches. Each team would win one match apiece at Kiel Auditorium, held on August 20 and November 5, respectively. Dory, Jr. remembers his father being upset about the booking and asked, *"Why are there two of us against Dick the Bruiser?"* Dory, Jr. lost the deciding fall in the second match when he was disqualified for slamming a chair over Bruiser's head. Dory Jr. recalled years later, *"That was a time when hitting with a chair meant something."*

Terry Funk made his St. Louis debut on February 4, 1966, teaming with brother Dory against Bruiser and "Bulldog" Lee Henning. Two weeks later, Bruiser would face and lose to Dory Sr. in a Texas death match before a sellout at the Kiel Auditorium on March 4, 1966, but win the rematch on April 16.

CHAMPIONSHIP WRESTLING
COLISEUM
Fairgrounds
Tonite 8:30

2 Championship Matches
Double Main Event
DICK The BRUISER vs. JOHNNY VALENTINE
(No Disqualification)

Tag Match
The VON BRAUNERS
(World's Tag Team Champs)
vs. WILBUR SNYDER and PAT O'CONNOR

—Special Attraction—
COWBOY BOB ELLIS vs. BLACK BART

ANGELO POFFO vs. JOE BLANCHARD

Midgets
ROCKY MONTERO vs. PRINCE PULLINS

Watch Championship Wrestling
Sat. 6-7 P.M. WTTV, Ch. 4

Advance Tickets Only at
Claypool Ticket Agcy., ME 5-7533

Chapter 13 • 117

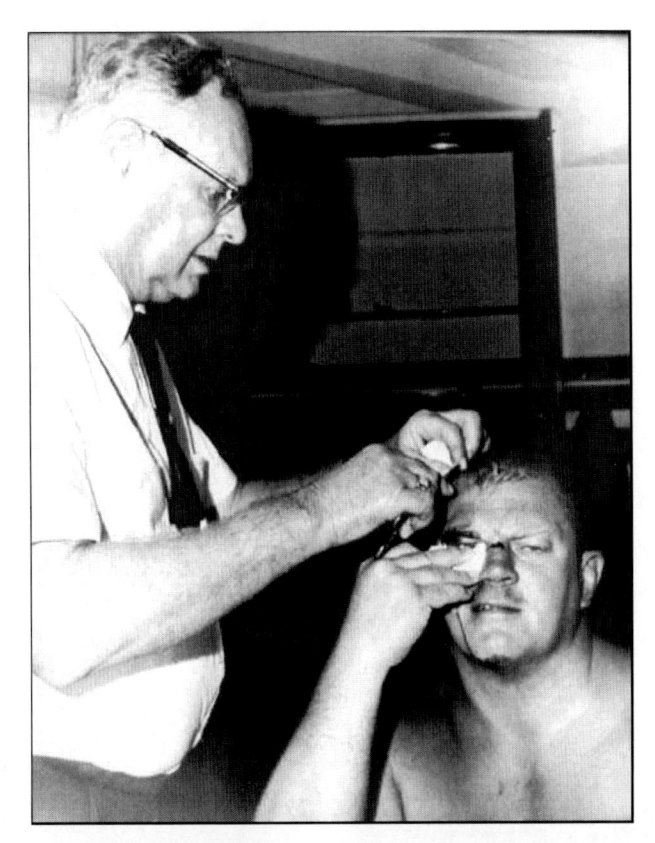

(above) Dr. L.J. Holladay sews up a cut on Bruiser's forehead
at the Fairgrounds Coliseum, October 1965
(below) Bruiser with Commissioner Dr. Holladay and son
Source: Holladay family

118 • BRUISER: The World's Most Dangerous Wrestler

Best In The Midwest
PARTS AND SERVICE OPEN TILL 2:00 A.M.
NEW AND USED CARS — NEW AND USED TRUCKS
JERRY ALDERMAN FORD SALES, INC.
5500 N. KEYSTONE AVE.   TEL. 251-1441

(above) "Pretty Boy" Bobby Heenan & his Assassins, 1966
(left) Heenan's employer in 1965
(below) "Pretty Boy" at ringside
Source: Rick Johnson

— Wrestling Giant Baba in Japan

It's interesting to note that, even with all the responsibility Bruiser had with running his own promotion, he still traveled extensively during this time. Throughout 1965, he found time to wrestle in places like Kansas City, Omaha, Des Moines, St. Louis, Nashville, Chicago, Atlanta, and San Diego. In most cases, he was featured in the main event.

Bruiser's ever-growing national reputation expanded to the international stage in November 1965. Bruiser was booked on a tour of Japan, specifically to wrestle Japanese icon Giant Baba. The International title, vacated when former champion Rikidozan died after being stabbed by a member of the Japanese Mafia, was to be awarded to the winner of the match. The primary way Japanese promoters got their top talent over was to have them score decisive victories over big-name American wrestlers. Bruiser fit that bill perfectly and he was imported to Japan specifically for the purpose of making Baba a champion in the eyes of the Japanese fans.

— Raymond Louis Heenan

One of Bruiser's most significant contributions to professional wrestling was the hiring and nurturing of a young employee of the Fairgrounds Coliseum named Raymond Louis Heenan. Heenan, born and raised in Chicago by his mother and grandmother, was exposed to pro wrestling at a time when Chicago was a mecca for the sport on national television. Heenan's family moved to Indianapolis in 1961, where he worked part-time at the Coliseum doing odd jobs for the promotion, such as taking ring jackets back to the dressing room, setting up the ring, and selling soft drinks. Heenan's regular job was that of a laborer at Gerry Alderman Ford dealership on Keystone Avenue in Indianapolis. In Heenan's book, *Bobby the Brain: Wrestling's Bad Boy Tells All*, Heenan explained how he got a telephone call from Bruiser telling him to report to WTTV-TV studios during his lunch break, which probably took place sometime in 1965. Heenan was puzzled when Bruiser kept referring to him as "Bobby." At the TV station, Heenan was told he was now "Bobby Heenan," and would be the manager of the new masked-villain tag team, the Assassins. Under the hoods were journeymen Joe Tomasso and John Steele Hill. Heenan described how Hill did all the talking on camera and how a mannequin with a mask and overcoat substituted for Tomasso. For the greater part of the eight years that followed, Heenan was the face of Bruiser's stable of bad guys. Heenan adopted the moniker "Pretty Boy" and became, by many accounts (including the author's opinion), the greatest pro-wrestling manager of all time. Heenan would later describe his modus operandi as "managing like a wrestler and wrestling like a manager."

CHAMPIONSHIP WRESTLING
TERRE HAUTE ARMORY
FRI., DEC. 17, 8:30 P.M.
GENE KINISKI vs.
WILBUR SNYDER
ASSASSINS 1 and 2 vs.
DICK THE BRUISER
and BOBBY MANAGOFF
CORA COMBS vs.
KATHY O'BRIEN
Adults $2.25, $1.50
Children 75c
Tax Included
Tickets on Sale at
RUST BROS. RECREATION
MECCA BAR, 1616 N. 13TH ST.
SARATOGA CAFE

Terre Haute, Indiana
December 17, 1965

Chapter 14
The Pfefer Experiment — 1963-1965

From January 8, 1960, through March 6, 1964, Dick the Bruiser didn't make a single appearance in Chicago rings. The trials and tribulations of Chicago promoter Fred Kohler have been thoroughly detailed in *The National Wrestling Alliance: The Untold Story* by Tim Hornbaker. Kohler gradually declined from being the leading wrestling promoter in the nation to a promoter with poor finances and an uncertain future.

— The Jack Pfefer Era

After several unsuccessful boxing-wrestling combination cards at the old Chicago Coliseum on south Wabash Avenue, Kohler made several changes in the hopes of bolstering sagging attendance. He pulled out of the National Wrestling Alliance, formed his own organization, which he called "International Wrestling Alliance," and created the International heavyweight title. He then brought in long-time wrestling promoter Jack Pfefer as his matchmaker to help turn things around and halt the decline.

From July 12, 1963, to December 13, 1963, Pfefer took control of seven wrestling cards at the International Amphitheatre, as well as cards in Milwaukee and Des Moines. Many decades later, Pfefer's profit

Chicago, Illinois
August 2, 1963
Source: Richard Vicek collection

and loss statements for each of these cards would become part of the special collections at the Theodore Hesburgh Library at the University of Notre Dame, South Bend, Indiana. The collection provides some of the most detailed records available on professional wrestling, a business that, traditionally, was kept private and secretive. Pfefer's profit and loss statements fully illustrate the financial difficulties Kohler and Pfefer faced in 1963. The wide range of operating expenses was meticulously detailed by Pfefer, down to a two-dollar cab fare. These rare, publicly available documents give insight into a very private and closely held industry. They are somewhat related to Dick the Bruiser because the financial failures of the Pfefer era led to Fred Kohler seeking out Bruiser as a new business partner to help turn around Chicago. The following financial table provides details of the income earned and expenses incurred from promoting a pro wrestling card in 1963 in a big city like Chicago. The details revealed illustrate all the expenses that went into staging a wrestling event. No wonder it was so hard to make money (and still is).

Professional Wrestling - Fred Kohler and Jack Pfefer
International Amphitheatre - Chicago, Illinois
Average of seven (7) cards in 1963
Selected Income Statement Accounts
Unaudited - In actual dollars $

REVENUES

Gross Ticket Receipts		$	8,271
Less: 16% Federal, State and City Taxes			(1,300)
Less: 21% payoffs to wrestlers			(1,707)
Net revenues		$	5,264

EXPENSES

International Amphitheatre

Rent	1,000	
Ushers and guards	490	
Ticket sellers	373	
Ring officials	180	
Electricians	120	
Burns Agency	70	
Chair rental	45	
	2,278	

Promotional

Newspaper and TV	1,602	
Circulars and postage	467	
Special promotions	234	
Press agent (Axman)	160	
	2,463	

Overhead

Office rent	986	
Telephone	216	
Liability insurance	98	
	1,300	

Other miscellanous expense	555		
Total Expenses			(6,596)
NET LOSS		$	(1,332)

In regards to the Chicago Amphitheatre during the Pfefer experiment, only two out of seven wrestling cards made any money ... the July 12, 1963, debut card and the follow-up card on August 2. Both of these shows had gross ticket sales of at least $10,000 (the equivalent of $75,527 in 2013 dollars), which was sufficient to cover operating expenses and allow profit to the owners. The next five cards had gross ticket sales ranging from $8,362 down to only $4,081. Each of these shows lost money in the range of $328 to a high of $3,736. Kohler and Pfefer each had to write checks to subsidize the operating losses. On each show, the gross ticket sales were hit with 16 percent taxes from federal, state, and city governments, and an average 21 percent distribution for wrestler payoffs. Except for one card with limited TV ads, Pfefer relied on newspaper ads to publicize his shows, including the black-owned *Chicago Defender*.

Many consider Pfefer's wrestling cards the lowest points for the professional wrestling business in Chicago since Kohler first began promoting in 1949. The first card, held on July 12, featured Johnny Valentine winning the newly created "world" championship from Moose Cholak. Unfortunately, before the second show, Valentine sent Kohler a telegram saying he was too ill to perform, so a virtually unknown wrestler named Ricky Ramirez took his place. For the third show on October 4, Pfefer brought in Buddy Fuller from Tennessee, and billed him as Cowboy George Valentine. Fuller, real name Edward Welch, was a member of the famous Welch family who promoted in Tennessee, Alabama, Kentucky, Arkansas, and Missouri. Pfefer also imported Jackie Fargo from Tennessee, and billed him as the "world heavyweight champion."

Jack Pfefer
Source: Scott Teal collection

Pfefer was famous for creating characters whose names sounded and looked a lot like those of famous, well-known wrestlers. One of the earliest was Bruno Nasartino, which led many fans to believe Bruno Sammartino, who was so popular in the Northeast, would be wrestling. Other knockoffs included Slugger Kowalski, Herman Schmidt, Texas Bruiser, Jumping Rococo, Angelo and Benito Sammartino, and Hillbilly Melby. The wholesale mockery of the existing professional wrestling establishment certainly didn't sit well with Chicago wrestling fans, and the low attendance at the Chicago Amphitheatre proved it. The overwhelmingly negative reaction by fans also prevented Kohler and Pfefer from attracting better wrestling talent. The only wrestlers of any significance appearing for Pfefer were Jackie Fargo and local resident Moose Cholak. Future NWA world heavyweight champion Harley Race appeared on the first Pfefer/Kohler card, but he used the ring name "The Great Mortimer." The payoffs were relatively dismal (as low as $15), while the highest payoff of the period ($300) went to special referee Jersey Joe Walcott for the card on September 13. That show lost money, as well.

The late wrestling historian, Ronald Dobratz, wrote extensively on this era saying, "Unfortunately, *1963 marked a year of rapid decline in the quality of its major wrestling 'extravaganzas,' reaching its lowest level as the year ended.*" He stressed that "*Chicago faded from the spotlight as a wrestling capital of the country.*" He closed with, "*Never so few superstars at the Amphitheatre meant more fan apathy in 1963, a year as disappointing as it was memorable.*"

— A New Partner for Kohler

It is believed that the continued red ink in Chicago and elsewhere led Fred Kohler to seek another business partner to help pump up business. While Kohler was looking for someone with ready cash who could help absorb potential losses on wrestling operations, he would benefit by being given an opportunity to buy a piece of Kohler's company.

That new partner turned out to be William F. Afflis, aka Dick the Bruiser. Mike Snyder remembers his father, Wilbur Snyder, also being a part of the revamping of Chicago.

After one final "Pfefer" card on January 10, 1964, Kohler moved in a different direction. He began using talent that worked for other Midwest territories. Main events featured familiar faces to Chicago such as former NWA world champion Pat O'Connor, who defeated Moose Cholak on March 6 and Seaman Art Thomas on April 3. However, on those two dates, gross receipts were only $3,000 and $3,460, respectively, according to the *Chicago Tribune* (which sometimes would compile results for a full calendar year), whereas the final "Pfefer" card on January 10 had pulled in a respectable $6,050. The box office take improved to $3,842 on April 24 for Johnny Valentine against Hans Schmidt.

The following week, Kohler pulled out all the stops.

Chicago, Illinois
May 15, 1964
Source: Robert Luce family

— **Bruiser Returns to the Amphitheatre**

In the *Chicago Sun Times* on May 14, 1964, sports columnist Dick Hackenberg interviewed Kohler, who made these new proclamations:

"Chicago is going square. We're concentrating on collegians. We're going highbrow, strictly intelligentsia. No more midgets. No more women rasslers. We're closing down the side show in favor of the big tent. From now on, it's nothing but class. No more carnival stuff."

Kohler's publicist Dick Axman pointed out those incoming collegians would be Dick the Bruiser from Purdue and Nevada, Wilbur Snyder from Utah, and Moose Cholak from Wisconsin. Kohler also admitted that he dropped around $40,000 "in recent years" in an attempt to develop new talent, so a change was in order. On May 15, Bruiser returned to the International Amphitheatre in the main event against Pat O'Connor. Once again, he played the role of heel and wore the WWA title belt he won the previous month in Los Angeles from Freddie Blassie. Johnny Valentine returned, as well, to face Moose Cholak, while Wilbur Snyder faced Jack Wilson. About 2,600 fans paid $4,026 to witness the initial installment, a box-office number well short of the $10,000 Kohler needed to be profitable.

It must be said that Bruiser didn't just show up in Chicago and immediately pack them into the rafters. The house on May 15 did increase by around two hundred dollars, but by the next Amphitheatre card, held September 12, the house jumped to $7,036, and it leveled off around $8,200 for the cards that followed. The houses were more than double what they had been during the first few weeks of the year. The increase in gate revenue also was credited to steady television exposure on the newly established WCIU-TV Channel 26.

The October 17 card was enhanced by wrestling's hippest gimmick performer of the times — George Ringo — when Chicago-based wrestler and photographer Bob Sabre attempted to capitalize on Beatlemania by wearing a wig and carrying a guitar to the ring. This appearance took place right after the first North American tour of The Beatles, who played the International Amphitheatre on September 5. Bruiser brought Ringo to Indianapolis for a TV appearance as well.

Ronald Dobratz reflected on the improving trend for wrestling in Chicago, saying, *"Considering the depths to which wrestling had sunk at the end of 1963, the recovery wrestling made in 1964 was cause for Chicago fans to rejoice."*

— Tag Team Titles in Minneapolis

While Kohler and Bruiser attempted to turn Chicago around, Bruiser also spent time in the Minneapolis territory for Verne Gagne's American Wrestling Association promotion. Bruiser and the Crusher went into 1964 as AWA tag team champions, but dropped them in February to Gagne and a young phenomenon named Moose Evans, who stood 6-foot-8 inches tall.

According to Minnesota wrestling historian, George Schire, the newly formed team of Larry Hennig and Harley Race were getting a big push in the AWA. Advance publicity for a match was written about that night in the Minneapolis wrestling program *Sports Facts*, which said Hennig and Race broke every rule in the book during the match with Gagne and Reggie Parks. Wilbur Snyder had wrestled earlier on the card and, sitting at ringside to cheer on his friend, Gagne, he called the referee's attention to rules being broken by the heels.

The following week on TV, Hennig and Race challenged Wilbur. *"If Wilbur Snyder wants to stick his nose in our business, why doesn't he just join Verne and Parks and we'll go out and find a partner of our own?"* Hennig and Race later announced their partner would be Dick the Bruiser and that Snyder would "... *be sorry he stuck his nose in our business."*

On December 26, 1964, the six-man tag team match was booked at the Minneapolis Auditorium. Schire, who was there for the match, tells the story:

> "They had the six-man tag and, throughout the entire match, Hennig and Race refused to tag off with Bruiser. They [Hennig and Race] would tag off to each other, but when the Bruiser would enter the ring, the referee would throw him out. Bruiser was prancing on the side of the ring apron. Finally, in the third fall, Bruiser was ticked, so he goes into the ring. The Bruiser takes the heads of Hennig and Race and smashes them together. Hennig flops outside of the ring and Wilbur pins Race ... one, two, three. This was the first time Hennig and Race lost, although it was a six-man tag match."

That match set up a long-running feud with Hennig and Race against Dick the Bruiser and his partner, the Crusher. On television, Bruiser promised to search every bar and honky-tonk in Milwaukee to

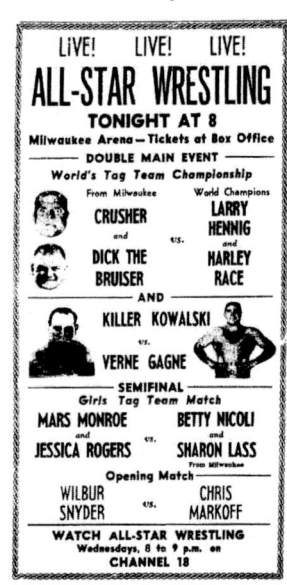

LiVE! LiVE! LiVE!
ALL-STAR WRESTLING
TONIGHT AT 8
Milwaukee Arena — Tickets at Box Office
— DOUBLE MAIN EVENT —
World's Tag Team Championship
From Milwaukee   World Champions
CRUSHER   LARRY
and   vs.   HENNIG
DICK THE   and
BRUISER   HARLEY RACE
— AND —
KILLER KOWALSKI
vs.
VERNE GAGNE
— SEMIFINAL —
Girls Tag Team Match
MARS MONROE   BETTY NICOLI
and   vs.   and
JESSICA ROGERS   SHARON LASS
— Opening Match —
WILBUR   CHRIS
SNYDER   vs.   MARKOFF
WATCH ALL-STAR WRESTLING
Wednesdays, 8 to 9 p.m. on
CHANNEL 18

Milwaukee, Wisconsin
February 16, 1967
Source: Milwaukee Sentinel

find the Crusher. When he did, the four kicked off one of the most heated, action-packed rivalries of the '60s.

When Hennig and Race first won the AWA tag team title, Harley pointed out that he and Larry, at ages 22 and 29, respectively, were the youngest AWA tag team champions ever. In 2009, Hennig said his most memorable matches were those tag-team matches at the International Amphitheatre in Chicago.

Bruiser and Crusher began referring to Hennig and Race as "The Dolly Sisters," a name taken from a 1945 film of the same name featuring Betty Grable. They were subsequently nicknamed "Pretty Boy" Larry Hennig and "Handsome" Harley Race. In his autobiography, *King of the Ring: The Harley Race Story*, Harley attributed the promotional angle to the Crusher, who "*portrayed Larry and me as cross-dressing sissies, but the angle kept the fans coming back for more.*" There was irony to the angle since neither Hennig nor Race would be considered to be "sissies."

Hennig also remembered, "*Bruiser and Crusher were very unpredictable, making them hard to work with. Neither one was a technical wrestler. Bruiser was a better athlete. Crusher did more punching and kicking.*" Race wrote in his autobiography that Bruiser "*might as well have gotten his technical wrestling degree from a Crackerjack box.*"

Other wrestlers there at the time remember how special the rivalry was. Eddie Sharkey loved being on a card with that tag team match-up because he knew his payday would be much better due to the big house. Sir Oliver Humperdink attended many of their matches, as well, and said, "*The people went ape-shit the minute either team hit the ring;* [they] *blew the roof off the joint.*"

Even a few years after the feud, the Bruiser occasionally reminded Chicago fans on television that "*Hennig and Race were a team that me and the Crusher had one big heck of a time defeating, and Hennig is probably, as a single wrestler, as good as anybody else in the world.*"

Milwaukee action (l) Harley Race on the attack; (r) Larry Hennig takes his lumps
Source: David Maciejewski

Former AWA television director and office official, Al DeRusha, had vivid memories of Hennig and Race:

> "They were something else. They were tough sons-of-guns, in the ring and out of the ring. They could go into a bar in downtown Minneapolis and clean it out in five minutes. They were a great tag team and had some fantastic matches with the Crusher and the Bruiser. That series ran for a long time. They hated each other."

— Action in Chicago

Promotional audio interviews, recorded starting in 1965 and preserved for posterity by Chicagoan Allan Fujara, demonstrate the Bruiser's uncanny ability to play the evil-heel role in the Chicago market. The wrestlers weren't the only targets of his jibes during interviews, either. Quite often, he mentioned the *"penny-pinching, chicken-liver promoter"* Fred Kohler in his diatribes (and later, he did the same thing for Bob Luce). Bruiser made fun of his real-life business partner, Wilbur Snyder, as well, calling him *"a goofy sissy with long ears."* The Bruiser mocked local attraction Yukon Moose Cholak, claiming "Cholak's tavern serves soup with cockroaches." By today's standards, some of Bruiser's rhetoric would have been considered politically incorrect, especially when he used the phrase "that blond-haired chimpanzee" during a television interview. (It was believed he was talking about a black wrestler.) It is acknowledged that Bruiser was playing the role of a ruffian wrestler at the time. During his lifetime, he had productive, real-life relationships with many black wrestlers, such as Bobo Brazil, Ernie Ladd, Sailor Art Thomas, and Prince Pullins

Other than a few cards in mid 1965, Bruiser headlined cards in Chicago for most of the year. After a summer hiatus, Kohler returned to the Amphitheatre on October 23 with Bruiser in the main event against Pat O'Connor. For the first time in many years, a wrestling card at the Amphitheatre grossed more than $10,000, which was the level of sales needed to generate a profit. Kohler was so proud of the accomplishment that he wrote a glowing letter to his old partner, Jack Pfefer, which has been preserved at the University of Notre Dame's library. Kohler attributed much of this success to his partner Dick the Bruiser.

— Chicago Wrestling Club, Inc.

In November, Kohler sold his remaining shares in the wrestling business to Verne Gagne and Wilbur Snyder. On November 12, "Fred Kohler Enterprises" was dissolved. In a detailed story in the *Chicago Tribune* dated December 14, 1965, it was announced that a new corporate entity had been formed; the Chicago Wrestling Club, Inc. The company had been registered on November 29 in the state of Illinois with an office in Planters Hotel at 19 N. Clark Street in downtown Chicago. The purchase price for the transaction was not announced by the Illinois Athletic Commission.

Source: Lake County Discovery Museum

"The Illinois Athletic Commission announces that the Chicago Wrestling Club, Inc., has purchased the mat interests of Fred Kohler, who is said to have promoted throughout the middle west 'for forty years.' The new group is headed by Buddy Lee Cliff, 26-year-old Rock Island policeman, and Robert Arden Luce, veteran Morton Grove promoter. Cliff is listed as promoter for the club and Luce as general manager and secretary. Richard (Dick) Axman, Kohler's longtime PR director, has been retained by the new combination to publicize its first show in the International Amphitheatre on January 8, 1966."

Fred Kohler

Buddy Lee Cliff had close ties to the Gagne family. His wife was the daughter of Donald Marxen, whose sister was Mary Gagne, the wife of Verne and mother of Greg Gagne. According to Greg Gagne, Cliff worked with Marxen promoting local AWA wrestling events in Rock Island and Moline (IL) and Davenport (IA).

The general manager and secretary of the organization was Robert (Bob) A. Luce, a long-time employee of Kohler's wrestling office, as well as writer, photographer, and eventually, publisher of *Wrestling Life* magazine. Luce's relationship with Bruiser and Snyder went back over ten years in Chicago.

The first wrestling event totally under the control of the new entity was scheduled for January 8, 1966. The trio of Gagne, Bruiser, and Snyder — a secret cabal, as it were — booked Chicago and the wrestling fans were none the wiser. For all the fans knew, the promoter was Bob Luce, which is what they were told. They had no idea Gagne, Bruiser and Snyder were calling the shots in the background. Bob actually was the promoter of record since one had to be an Illinois resident in order to get a promoter's license. From that point on, Luce was the front man for the organization.

A new chapter in Chicago professional wrestling was on the horizon.

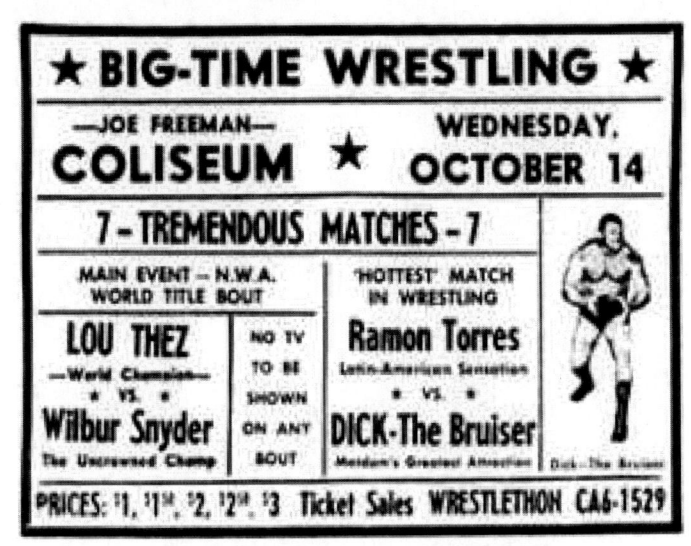

San Antonio, Texas • October 14, 1964

Chapter 15
Chicago Wrestling Club, Inc. — 1966-1968
— The Three Amigos

The Chicago Wrestling Club presented their first unified wrestling card on Saturday, January 8, 1966, at the Amphitheatre. The program lineup printed for the card called it *"A Sports Spectacular presented exclusively by the Chicago Wrestling Club, Inc."* Publicity written by Bob Luce promised *"1966 will see the greatest year of wrestling ever featured in Chicago."* Luce resurrected his *Wrestling Life* magazine after a two-year hiatus with volume ten. Decades later, Bob Luce's widow, Sharon Luce, said, *"Bob was not an owner, but the partners valued his input."* Somebody had to handle all the logistics, and Bob Luce was the perfect choice to fill that role. He made it possible for wrestling fans to buy tickets at the Amphitheatre box office or any Sears Roebuck & Company department store in Chicagoland.

All roads lead to the International Amphitheatre
Source: Rich Tito

Wrestling on TV aired on WCIU-TV, channel 26, on Monday, Wednesday, and Friday nights. At first, the program consisted of WWA tapes from Indianapolis, but later, tapes from Minneapolis were added, giving the Chicago fans a double dose of action and interviews ... and a big talent base.

The headlines in the arena program for the debut night screamed out — *"Congo Death Match! Kiniski vs. Bruiser!"* Luce also spelled out the conditions for the battle. "To a finish. No pin falls. No disqualification. No time limit." Concerned about the fans' health and well-being, Luce warned, *"Wrestling fans who watch the Bruiser-Kiniski match are urged to keep calm and cool. This match could bring on a heart attack to any fan who cannot control his nerves."*

Kiniski emerged victorious from the match and there were no reports of cardiac arrest taking place at the Amphitheatre that night.

Just one night before, at the Kiel Auditorium in St. Louis, Gene Kiniski won the NWA heavyweight title from the legendary Lou Thesz and began a highly respectable three-year run as champion.

This debut card for Gagne, Snyder, and Bruiser included two other main events — Wilbur Snyder vs. Johnny Valentine and Verne Gagne vs. Chris Markoff. Chicago fans were quick to welcome back Verne Gagne, as it had been more than six years since he had last wrestled in the Amphitheatre.

The partnership presented exciting opportunities for the three mat veterans. Not only would the three new partners be able to share in profits generated by the new corporation, but they could book themselves into the main events on those cards and secure the highest payoffs each night. To be fair, the owners were among the most talented scientific wrestlers (Gagne and Snyder) and explosive brawlers (Bruiser) in the professional wrestling business. They could capitalize on their talents without having to work for Barnett, McMahon, or any other promoters unless they chose to do so.

— AWA vs. WWA Titles

When the Chicago Wrestling Club presented their inaugural show in January 1966, the AWA heavyweight champion was Maurice "Mad Dog" Vachon (1929-2013), a four-time champion who won the belt from the Crusher in Denver on November 12, 1965. Like Verne, Vachon also was a true wrestler, having represented his native Canada in amateur wrestling at the 1948 Summer Olympics in London and the 1950 British Empire Games in New Zealand. The AWA tag team champions were Larry Hennig and Harley Race; although they had not yet appeared as AWA tag team champions in Chicago.

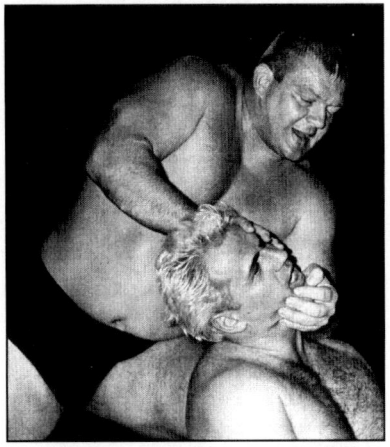

Typical Bruiser style of wrestling
Bruiser vs. Chris Markoff
Indianapolis, 1967
Source: Rick Johnson

At the same time, the WWA heavyweight champion was Dick the Bruiser, who won the title belt for the second time in Indianapolis on December 26, 1965, from Gene Kiniski. Wilbur Snyder and Moose Cholak won the WWA tag team titles from the Assassins that same night.

With Chicago now showcasing the talent roster of both the AWA and WWA, a natural question would be "which championships would be part of the storylines and bookings at the International Amphitheatre?" The owners decided to stage a showdown match between AWA champion Mad Dog Vachon and WWA champion Dick the Bruiser at the International Amphitheatre on February 26, 1966, and followed up on Saturday, March 26, with the net result of the AWA reigning supreme in Chicago. From that point going forward, the WWA championship belt, and later its tag team titles, would never again appear at the International Amphitheatre. Whatever happened in Indianapolis, stayed in Indianapolis as far as Verne Gagne and his AWA was concerned. For years after that, Bruiser's WWA television program would never show the WWA belts on the tapes sent to Chicago for broadcast. At the TV tapings in Indianapolis, wrestlers would sometimes wear the championship belts to the ring and show them off to the fans. However, they would take off the belts before the cameras started recording.

On May 21, a rematch between Bruiser and Mad Dog was booked ... a non-title Congo death match contest, the same stipulations as were in the January 8 Bruiser-Kiniski match. By this time, Bruiser was a fan-favorite, in spite of the fact that his in-ring brawler style did not change one iota from that of when he was a hated heel.

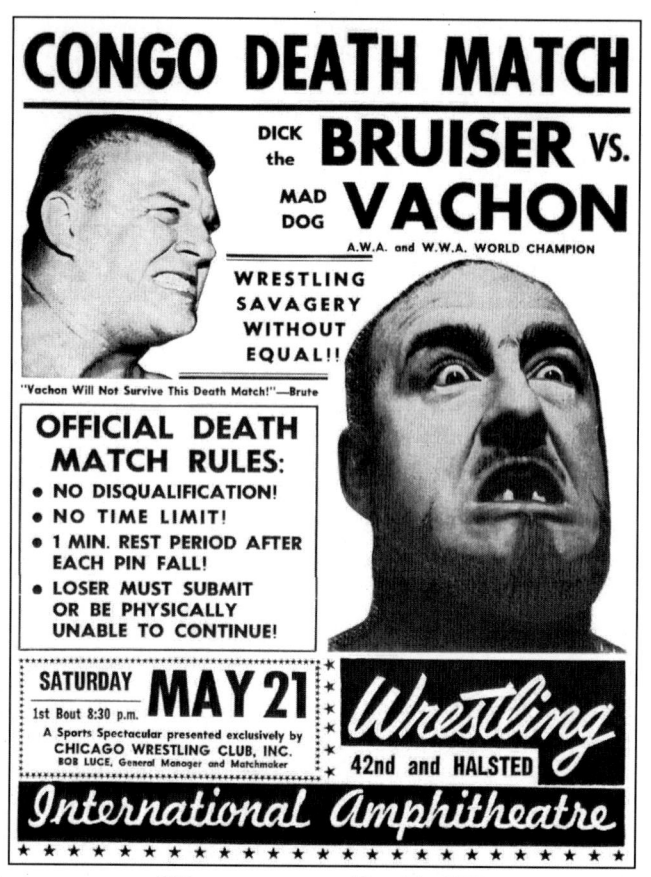

130 • BRUISER: The World's Most Dangerous Wrestler

CONGO DEATH MATCH

DICK the **BRUISER** VS.
MAD DOG **VACHON**
A.W.A. and W.W.A. WORLD CHAMPION

WRESTLING SAVAGERY WITHOUT EQUAL!!

"Vachon Will Not Survive This Death Match!"—Brute

OFFICIAL DEATH MATCH RULES:
- NO DISQUALIFICATION!
- NO TIME LIMIT!
- 1 MIN. REST PERIOD AFTER EACH PIN FALL!
- LOSER MUST SUBMIT OR BE PHYSICALLY UNABLE TO CONTINUE!

SATURDAY **MAY 21**
1st Bout 8:30 p.m.
A Sports Spectacular presented exclusively by
CHICAGO WRESTLING CLUB, INC.
BOB LUCE, General Manager and Matchmaker

Wrestling
42nd and HALSTED

International Amphitheatre

Chicago program, May 21, 1966
Source: Robert Luce family

Author's note: I attended this card when I was only nine years old, and it was this card that hooked this youngster onto professional wrestling.

Mad Dog, the first to enter the ring, proceeded with his customary jumping and stomping around the ring, almost like he was on a pogo stick. The hatred the fans in the building directed toward Mad Dog was fierce. On the other end of the scale was the ovation given Bruiser when he walked out. Up to this time, the author had only seen Mad Dog and Bruiser wrestle in separate single matches on TV, in so-called "squash matches" — bouts where a superstar wrestler like Mad Dog and Bruiser would dominate 95 percent of a match and never let their hapless opponent gain the upper hand. This May 21 rematch was reminiscent of two powerful express trains colliding, and the author does not remember much scientific wrestling. In the end, Dick the Bruiser prevailed, but both men were bleeding, something of which the fans and the young author approved.

Decades later, Mad Dog Vachon would tell the author about his recollections of this program: "*Those matches were the hardest of them all. The crowd could tell those kicks and punches were for real.*"

The matches between Bruiser and Mad Dog were, undoubtedly, one of the highlights of the new era in Chicago wrestling.

Chapter 15 • 131

— **Successful Momentum**

In 1966, the Chicago Wrestling Club would promote fifteen wrestling cards in the Windy City. Finances for the shows weren't always released. However, the April 16 card headlined by Verne Gagne vs. Johnny Valentine grossed a solid $10,500 before a crowd of 3,773. The average ticket price was $2.78. If that same average ticket price were applied to the March 26 card (7,564 fans attended), the box office receipts would have reached a whopping $21,000, an outstanding night for wrestlers and owners alike. Besides Gagne, Snyder, Bruiser, and Vachon, the talent pool in 1966 was loaded with other superstars, including AWA tag champions Larry Hennig and Harley Race, Pat O'Connor, The Crusher, Ernie Ladd, Killer Kowalski, Mitsu Arakawa, and Moose Cholak.

International Amphitheatre • First sellout • March 11, 1967
Source: Robert Luce family

The promotional momentum kept building into 1967 and the new owners had their first sellout on March 11, with attendance of 9,782 and a gross gate of $27,579. The first of two main events found Bruiser and Crusher facing Hennig and Race, while the second pitted Verne Gagne against Pat O'Connor. A second sellout followed the next month on April 15 with 10,735 rabid fans paying $32,092 to see another chapter in the Bruiser and Crusher vs. Hennig and Race saga. For each of these cards, the payoff for Bruiser was a whopping $1,600 and an additional $1,800 dividend from his ownership stake in the company. Happy days were here again, indeed.

Author's note: The payoff figures were taken from Bruiser's booking calendars. Tim Replogle, aka Dick the Bruiser, Jr., provided some of Bruiser's calendars for the years 1967 through 1984 for research purposes. They were moldy, faded, and smudged, but were fascinating to study.

— **Bruiser's Mother Dies**

Margaret Afflis Johnston, age 68, died on Monday, April 17, 1967, of a heart attack at her home, located at 5354 N. Meridian Street in Indianapolis. Mrs. Johnston lived an accomplished and distinguished career in politics, government, and charities. She was survived by her husband, Leroy O. Johnston Sr.; a son, William Franklin Afflis, a professional wrestler known as Dick the Bruiser; and a sister, Ethel Patterson of Delphi. Funeral arrangements were handled by Flanner and Buchanan Mortuary on Fall Creek Road. A funeral service was conducted on Thursday, April 20, 1967, at the Second Presbyterian Church at 7700 N. Meridian Street in Indianapolis, a church where Margaret was one of the original organizers. Margaret was then buried at Masonic Cemetery in Delphi next to her first husband, Walter William Afflis, and her parents. Her tombstone gives tribute and refers to three groups that she cherished — Democrat, Presbyterian, and Psi Iota Xi.

Margaret served as an alternate delegate to the 1956 Democratic National Convention in Chicago, which nominated Adlai Stevenson for President. She held the position of Indiana National Democratic Committeewoman from 1960 to 1964, was very active during the 1960 Presidential Campaign, and was part of the Indiana Delegation to the 1960 Democratic National Convention at the Los Angeles Sports Arena. Her archives at the Indiana State Library contain multiple telegrams of thanks from both President John F. Kennedy and Vice-President Lyndon B. Johnson. In 1965, she was elected president of the Indiana Democratic Women's Club, a position she held at the time of her death. The list of institutions she was associated with was endless, including the Booth Tarkington Civic Theater, Herron Art Museum, Kennedy Memorial Commission, and the American Legion Auxiliary.

Upon her death, Democratic state chairman Gordon St. Angelo said Margaret *"represented the very best qualities that had made the Democratic Party great — idealism, dedication, imagination, and tireless energy."* Mrs. Agnes Woolery, Democratic state vice-chairperson, called the death *"a great personal loss to me and a tremendous loss to her many friends in Indiana and across the country."* Mrs. Dorothy Elmore, current Democratic National Committeewoman said, *"Mrs. Johnston left a great tradition of zeal and love of the Democratic Party."* One of her home town newspapers, The *Journal Citizen of Delphi*, called Margaret a "pioneer" and noted that *"pioneers have always had a special place in the hearts of Americans."*

Margaret was a "pioneer in politics — a woman in a field predominantly populated by male citizens." The editorial continued:

> *"It took no small amount of courage to become an active politician in the era in which Mrs. Johnston was born. Woman's place was in the home and she chose to prove to the world that a woman can succeed in the political arena. Margaret made it, bringing not only acclaim to herself but to her home town. Her success was found in her genuine interest in people — all kinds of people from all walks of life. Yes, Mrs. Johnston was a pioneer and we shall revere her memory and treasure our friendship for years to come."*

Around 1990, her son, William Franklin Afflis, spoke candidly about his mother's influence in an interview with Indianapolis journalist Karen Grau:

"My mother was a very positive person and was way ahead of her time. She ran for Congress against Representative Halleck, who was the toughest, most ferocious and vicious Republican. My mother shaped my career by giving me this positive force to go ahead and don't be afraid of anything. I followed her footsteps; although, she never once told me what to do."

— Regular TV and Arena Work

It was unusual for a wrestler who was both an active wrestler and a co-owner of a promotion to spend steady and meaningful time working for somebody else, but Larry Matysik revealed the kind of money Bruiser was making as a headliner in St. Louis. The main event was a handicap tag-team match in which Bruiser and Edouard Carpentier faced NWA heavyweight champion Gene Kiniski. Matysik described the mathematics for that May 19, 1967, card at the Kiel. With an attendance of 10,659 fans, the gross box-office receipts approximated $43,000, less 17 percent in state and local taxes, for an after-tax gross of $36,000. The main-event participants would then split 16 percent of the after-tax gross, equal to a $1,920 payday each for Kiniski, Carpentier, and the Bruiser.

— Kansas City Chaos

On August 10, 1967, Bruiser and Crusher traveled together to Kansas City, Kansas. Bulldog Bob Brown told Scott Teal about that time:

> "Bob Geigel [in 1967] *called and said that he wanted me to take the place of Dutch Savage as his tag team partner. I came in and never believed what I saw for the first six or seven months. I remember seeing them lined up twenty deep in front of Memorial Hall to see me and Geigel wrestle Dick the Bruiser and The Crusher. When we had a big show lined up, we'd go over to the Municipal Auditorium in Kansas City, Missouri. It held a lot more people. When we really had a super doozer, we'd go into Kemper Arena. Things were wild.*
>
> *We had plenty [of riots] in Kansas City, which is a bad place, anyway. We had four matches, and every one, we couldn't get out."*

— Arrival of Dick Beyer

In the first half of the 1960s, most of wrestling veteran Dick Beyer's time had been spent wrestling in California and Japan under his "Destroyer" identity. From the mid to late '60s, he found himself in Indianapolis, Chicago, and Minneapolis quite frequently. Bruiser and Snyder brought Beyer into their territory for the bigger towns, like Indianapolis, Fort Wayne, or Elkhart, including summer ballpark shows at Victory Field. In Elkhart on February 3, 1967, the main event was the Bruiser and The Destroyer against the Devil's Duo, managed by Bobby Heenan while the semi-main event was Cowboy

---

WRESTLING TONIGHT 8:30
air conditioned
KIEL AUDITORIUM
A Handicap Tag Match
GENE KINISKI
(World Champion)
vs.
"DICK THE BRUISER
and
EDOUARD CARPENTIER
also
another tag match
and 5 other bouts.
TICKETS—Arcade Bldg.
and Kiel Auditorium
PRICES $1.50-$2.00-$3.00
Doors of Kiel Auditorium open 7 p.m. tonight when tickets will also be on sale.

Dick Beyer, The Destroyer
Tyndall Armory, Indianapolis
1966
Source: Rick Johnson

Jack Lanza vs. Mitsu Arakawa. Bruiser's 1967 calendar book indicates he paid "The Destroyer" $80 for the shot in Elkhart.

Payoffs for the performers that night in Elkhart reflected a typical hierarchy with the main-event performers and owners getting a bigger share of the pot. Bruiser received $220, the other main-event and semi-main guys got $80, while the remaining wrestlers and manager Heenan got either $35 or $40. Bruiser's cut likely included wrestler pay plus owner profit.

"Pretty Boy" Bobby Heenan • Indianapolis, 1966
Source: Rick Johnson

In Chicago, the Destroyer made one single appearance in 1966 using the Destroyer gimmick, but then changed his identity due to the insistence of Verne Gagne. For future appearances in the AWA and Chicago, Beyer adopted the new identity of Dr. X.

After a series of appearances on Minneapolis TV, in which Dr. X quietly sat at ringside with the studio audience, a decision was made to give Beyer a run as a serious contender for Gagne's title. Gagne had regained the AWA world title from Mad Dog Vachon on February 26, 1967, in St. Paul, Minnesota. The masterful build-up to the Gagne vs. Dr. X series involved Dr. X first getting past Crusher. Dr. X told TV interviewer Marty O'Neill:

> "If you want to hear a lot of confusion, you should have been in the dressing room after I beat the Crusher on the last show here in Chicago. The phones were buzzing. The cousin [Crusher] called Bruiser [and told him], 'I was robbed.' I got news for the Bruiser. I know you watch this here television show. The same thing is going to happen to you that happened to the Crusher. As far as I'm concerned, I want Gagne, and the Bruiser and the Crusher are just stepping stones because Gagne has the belt."

Bruiser and Dr. X wrestled twice in Amphitheatre main events — December 2 and December 30 — and those led to the early 1968 Gagne vs Dr. X title matches. Dr. X told his TV interviewers, "*The people here in Chicago don't have a hero to worship. The White Sox lose, the Bears lose, and the Cubs lose. They all went down the drain.*" Dr. X was a master at antagonizing Chicagoans.

— New Talent in Chicago and Indianapolis

In 1967, Cowboy Jack Lanza arrived in Indianapolis. Lanza, who initially was a babyface, frequently teamed up with Wilbur Snyder. Lanza would later admit,

"*I never wanted to be a babyface. It's more fun to be a heel.*" After getting Bruiser and Snyder's blessing, Lanza transformed himself into "Blackjack" Lanza. With Pretty Boy Bobby Heenan as his manager, Lanza became one of the true bad guys of the WWA and held the WWA heavyweight championship for 20 months, the longest continuous reign of any champion in the history of the promotion, which reflects the high regard Bruiser and Snyder had for him.

In the golden era of professional wrestling, standard fare among bad guy wrestlers included Japanese characters, the most prominent of which was Mitsu Arakawa who held several singles and tag team titles in the 1960s. Another prominent team was the Devil's Duo, Angelo Poffo and Chris Markoff. Leaping Lanny Poffo, son of Angelo, had vivid memories of the Devil's Duo days:

Crusher & Bruiser double-team Angelo Poffo • 1967
Source: Rick Johnson

> "My dad was semi-retired as he was teaching school. The Bruiser had an idea to make him a blonde, but Wilbur Snyder said, 'They'll never believe in an Italian with blonde hair.' The Bruiser wanted to prove that he [the Bruiser] was right."

Lanny also recalled that Markoff did not take orders well and that Bruiser would tell Angelo to remind Markoff of who owned the territory.

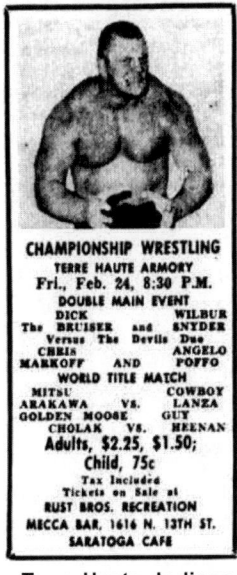

Terre Haute, Indiana
February 24, 1967

The Devil's Duo, Angelo Poffo & Chris Markoff, with manager Bobby Heenan
Source: Rick Johnson

Chapter 16
Yippies, Dippies, Hippies — 1969

— The Chain Gang

After Bruiser and Crusher's feuds with the Devil's Duo and Mitsu Arakawa & Dr. Moto had run their course, fresh talent was needed to revitalize the WWA roster. That new talent consisted of veteran wrestler Don Kalt and relative newcomer Kenny McMullen, who had previously been wrestling in Louisiana and Mississippi. Bruiser brought them into Indianapolis with a new identity, calling them Jack and Frank Dillinger, the Chain Gang.

John Dillinger, a legendary bank robber in the '30s, had actually been born in Indianapolis in 1903, and his notorious reputation was deeply engrained in Indiana folklore. The Chain Gang portrayed a modern-day motorcycle gang, complete with attire that reportedly resembled the real-life Hells Angels. Their ring jackets had the names "Fat Christ" or "Crazy Judas" embroidered on the front, along with skull-and-crossbones patches. Jack Dillinger (Don Kalt) sometimes wore a wristband with a swastika patch attached, a

The Chain Gang
Source: Robert Luce Family

symbol used in their publicity material, as well. They had long, dirty, unkempt hair and beards, similar to the 1960s cultural creation known as "the Hippie." Jack Dillinger recalled the origins of the team and credited Dick the Bruiser for his guidance:

> "We started riding motorcycles and got looking rough. Man, we got into a lot of trouble there in Indianapolis with the police, and some of it made pretty good publicity. We got busted in a restaurant. People wanted nothing to do with us as because they were scared of us ... too much trouble. Bruiser heard about this and he loved anything like that. He was a wild and crazy guy himself. At that time, we had a hearse and we stood out, you know. At that time, every [wrestling] gimmick that I had, I lived it twenty-four hours a day. I actually lived my gimmick. I lived it like a movie star doing his part."

Jack also remembers the first television interview taping in which the Chain Gang appeared:

> "We went up to Indianapolis after getting into trouble in Louisiana. We were driving the hearse to the TV station and the hearse broke down. Here we are with a broken down hearse, standing on the highway, our

boots held together with duct tape, and who comes by? The worst person to come by in the world — Wilbur Snyder. He stopped to see us. He couldn't believe what we looked like. He sent for help for us. We made it to the TV station, but we didn't know who the hell we were. We went in there, and Bobby Heenan is already on the air talking about us — Jack and Frank Dillinger. Kenny said, 'Who the hell is Jack and Frank Dillinger?' They built us up like crazy. Bruiser told us to hang out in bars and get into fights. He wanted publicity, so that's what we did."

The heat generated by the Chain Gang, whether on television or in the live shows, was extraordinary. This observation was seconded by mid-'70s WWA wrestler and manager Handsome Johnny Starr, who remembers being extremely impressed with the heat generated by the Chain Gang. Starr remarked:

"The greatest tag team that was ever in the business was the Chain Gang. They were outlaws and motorcycle guys. They were tough sons-of-guns. When they were working, I never saw a tag team get as much heat as those guys did."

On one telecast from one of the Indianapolis armories, the Chain Gang would take turns pounding their opponents down to the mat, yelling out before each hit, *"This one's for Dick the Bruiser,"* or *"This one's for Wilbur Snyder."* The Chain Gang took the WWA by storm, and even made appearances in Chicago, building up to a big feud with Bruiser and Crusher. Veteran ringside photographer William Ondecko still considers this tag match-up one of the best he ever saw. The Crusher had many classic rants in anticipation of the bouts with the Chain Gang:

"Yippies, hippies, and dippies. They never take a bath. They never comb their hair. They have earrings in their noses. You bums, we're gonna murder you. And then we're gonna take you down to Lake Michigan and scrub you and give you a bath, which you haven't had in ten years. The people will have to boil their water around Chicago for a month or two after that."

On September 13, 1969, the Chain Gang was booked in Milwaukee, where they defeated Man Mountain Mike and Moose Cholak. After the matches, they were lured to the Village Inn in Rochester, Wisconsin, where they were assaulted by a real-life gang of thugs. Jack Dillinger recalled, "*What happened was, I grabbed Kenny as they were hitting us with everything. I took off and I thought he was behind me, but he wasn't.*" Jack and Frank got separated, with Jack making his escape by wading across a nearby lake and, eventually, calling for help. The *Standard Press* newspaper reported that "*a witness said he watched through a window as a group of men beat one man on the street, apparently McMullen* [Frank]." The report said the witness turned away, heard gunshots, and then saw a man lying on the ground. Later, McMullen was dumped into an alley in nearby Burlington with gunshot wounds to both legs, plus lacerations to his head, face, and body. Police were called to the scene, and Frank was later taken to two hospitals for treatment. Robin Luce, daughter of Chicago wrestling promoter Bob Luce, said, "*My father actually did have my uncle* [a law enforcement officer] *guard Mr. McMullen while he was in the hospital.*" That was done in case the thugs decided to show up and finish the job. The *Standard Press* elaborated on the story:

Bruiser leaps off the top rope onto a helpless Frank Dillinger
Copyright Pro Wrestling Enterprises/ Arena Publishing

"*The sheriff's investigation has not turned up reasons for the brawl, but several theories have been advanced. Authorities said the two may have become involved in a quarrel with members of the "Outlaws," a Milwaukee motorcycle gang. A Waterford man told deputies that the Outlaws were mad because the wrestlers used their club name and may have set up the wrestlers for the beating. The wrestlers dressed in costumes resembling motorcycle gang members.*"

Steve Albright was a teenager back then and was hired to clean up the mess. The Village Inn was a mess inside, with windows broken and paint splattered around. There are no reports to indicate anyone having been brought to justice for the assaults. Jack Dillinger added, "*For a long time, Kenny and I didn't speak because Kenny thought I had something to do with it.*"

After the incident, Jack Dillinger had to call Bruiser and tell him what happened. Bruiser had wrestled that same night in Chicago against Dr. X. Jack recalled, "*Right away, I thought I had to change my gimmick. I got clean shaven and dressed up better.*"

Indianapolis, Indiana
June 20, 1969

Wrestler Chris Colt came into the territory the following week to play the role of "brother" Jim Dillinger. Jack told Bruiser about his idea for a "New Chain Gang," and Bruiser liked the idea. In pretty short time, the New Chain Gang made their debut in the WWA territory including some Chicago dates, and wrestled as a team into the next year. However, the New Chain Gang never duplicated the terror the original Chain Gang held for the fans. After a time, they faded away without fanfare.

— Tag Champions in Japan

By mid-1969, the team of Dick the Bruiser and the Crusher had developed quite a reputation in the wrestling world and were invited to wrestle in Japan as a tag team. On August 11, Bruiser and Crusher defeated Japanese icons Giant Baba and Antonio Inoki in Sapporo to win the NWA International tag team title, an officially sanctioned title of the Japanese Wrestling Association (JWA) promotion. Just two days later in Osaka, Baba and Inoki recaptured the belts when Inoki forced Crusher to concede to his signature octopus hold. American wrestlers Gerry Brisco and Art Michalik also were on that tour. Art remembers that Charlie Moto, who worked in the Los Angeles wrestling office, organized the trip, and all the American wrestlers traveled together in a tour bus. *"We were well taken care of,"* said Art, *"and they put us up in the best hotels."*

Gerry Brisco noted, *"That was my first tour of Japan, right out of college."* Brisco said the wrestlers, including Bruiser, played "high stakes" card games on the tour bus and *"the jackpots were more than I was making in a week."* Brisco had good memories of Bruiser. *"He was very kind to me, took me to dinner, and picked up the tab."* Brisco was impressed with Bruiser's kindness and generosity when Bruiser gave him advice. *"Here's what you got to do, kid."*

Bruiser & Crusher win International tag team title in Japan • 1969
Source: Dr. Mike Lano

Gerry added, "*Bruiser was a real source of knowledge*" and "*taught me to stand up for myself.*" From Brisco's viewpoint, Bruiser "*was sort of a mentor to me and I never will forget that.*"

— AWA Invasion in Los Angeles

Upon his return home from Japan, Bruiser had a new project on the front burner. His partner in Chicago, Verne Gagne, wanted to expand his AWA wrestling territory even further. This time, the target market was Los Angeles, almost 2,000 miles away from Minnesota.

The LA promotion was a firmly NWA-entrenched territory under the promotional leadership of Mike LeBell. Since LeBell promoted in the Olympic Auditorium, Gagne chose the Fabulous Forum in Inglewood, the same arena in which the Los Angeles Kings played professional hockey and the Los Angeles Lakers played professional basketball. The hockey team and the arena were owned by legendary sports entrepreneur, Jack Kent Cooke. Televised promotional pieces were shot in Minneapolis with legendary LA Lakers announcer Chick Hearn participating.

TONIGHT'S OFFICIAL LINE-UP
THE FABULOUS FORUM — SATURDAY, SEPTEMBER 6, 1969

MAIN EVENT FOR THE WORLD'S HEAVYWEIGHT CHAMPIONSHIP
VERNE GAGNE vs. DICK THE BRUISER
228 pounds, Mound, Minnesota — 260 pounds, Detroit

SEMI-FINAL MATCH
LOU THESZ vs. PRETTY BOY LARRY HENNIG
265 pounds, Phoenix, Arizona — 270 pounds, Minneapolis, Minnesota

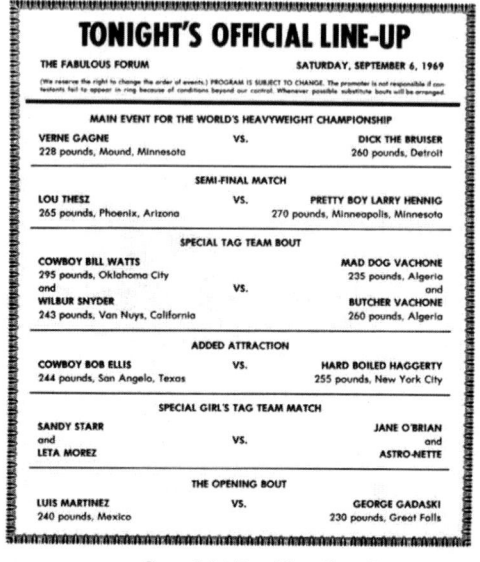

SPECIAL TAG TEAM BOUT
COWBOY BILL WATTS 295 pounds, Oklahoma City and WILBUR SNYDER 243 pounds, Van Nuys, California vs. MAD DOG VACHONE 235 pounds, Algeria and BUTCHER VACHONE 260 pounds, Algeria

ADDED ATTRACTION
COWBOY BOB ELLIS vs. HARD BOILED HAGGERTY
244 pounds, San Angelo, Texas — 255 pounds, New York City

SPECIAL GIRL'S TAG TEAM MATCH
SANDY STARR and LETA MOREZ vs. JANE O'BRIAN and ASTRO-NETTE

THE OPENING BOUT
LUIS MARTINEZ vs. GEORGE GADASKI
240 pounds, Mexico — 230 pounds, Great Falls

Copyright Pro Wrestling Enterprises/Arena Publishing

The card was booked for September 6, 1969, with Gagne defending his AWA championship against Bruiser in the main event. While Bruiser had a great run in Los Angeles in 1964, Gagne had not established such a reputation there. The lineup also had Wilbur Snyder and Cowboy Bill Watts against Mad Dog and Butcher Vachon, Lou Thesz vs. Pretty Boy Larry Hennig, Hardboiled Haggerty vs. Cowboy Bob Ellis, a ladies tag team match, and an opener between Luis Martinez and George Gadaski.

Jeff Walton, a publicist in the NWA office at the time, remembers a lot of what happened:

> "*Since we [NWA] could not run a wrestling card on the same night per state law, we decided to run a charity event the same night called 'Save Our Sport.' Other NWA promoters sent in talent for the event. There were weightlifting and arm-wrestling demonstrations. Admission was free, as were the hot dogs and beer. The idea was to stop Gagne. It cost Gagne a fortune to just put on a show in Los Angeles.*"

The night before the AWA card, the NWA ran a card stacked with eight wrestling matches, headlined by Dory Funk Jr. defending the NWA world heavyweight title against Buddy (Killer) Austin, plus Mexican sensation Mil Mascaras against Black Gordman in a mask vs. hair match. The Sheik flew in from Detroit to face Pedro Morales in a stretcher match, while the rest of the card was packed with talent like Pat Patterson, Bull Ramos, Ernie Ladd, Bobo Brazil, and a woman's tag match with the Fabulous Moolah. Few wrestling fans in Los Angeles were able to pass up that outstanding line-up.

The AWA show could not be labeled a success. According to Jeff Walton, he heard the event attracted somewhere around 1,500 fans. Payoffs weren't very good, especially for the time spent traveling back and forth, and there may not have been much left over due to the high cost of staging the show, transporting the wrestlers from Minnesota to LA, and television advertising. Gagne, of course, got the biggest payoff at $400. Bruiser's payout was only $300, while Snyder, Watts, the Vachons, Thesz, and Hennig each got $200.

Los Angeles wrestling photographer Dan Westbrook witnessed the card and remembered how events unfolded that night:

"*The Bruiser looked okay, but both* [Bruiser and Gagne] *were well beyond their peaks. Their ages took a toll. Bob Ellis was a 'no show.' Thesz wrestled a mismatch against Larry Hennig. The Vachons were pleasing, but not much else to remember, and worst of all, they drew less than three thousand. Many tickets were complimentary. The next show flopped.*"

Yes, indeed. Verne brought his crew back to LA on November 25 and he worked on the semi-final against Luke Graham, while the Vachons wrestled the Flying Redheads — Red Bastien and Billy Red Lyons — in the main event.

The AWA presence in Los Angeles was short-lived and wasn't repeated. Jeff Walton later remembers the Bruiser calling the Los Angeles NWA office and apologizing for being part of this intrusion, claiming it was Gagne's idea.

Bruiser and his cousin, The Crusher
Source: Robert Luce family

Chapter 17
Comiskey Cage Contest — 1970-1971

— Return to Comiskey Ballpark

The Bruiser and the Crusher were formidable AWA tag champions in the late 1960s. They would have memorable matches in 1969 with Bruiser's old nemesis from single competition, Mad Dog Vachon, and his younger brother, Paul (The Butcher) Vachon. The big showdown between the two teams was booked for August 30, 1969, at the International Amphitheatre.

The program for the event, produced by promoter Bob Luce, called it "The First Superworld Tag Title Match in Wrestling History." Minneapolis promoter Wally Karbo was interviewed and explained "Superworld" as the *"beginning of a new and more exciting era in modern wrestling than we have ever known."* The program posed the question to readers, "Will Bruiser and Crusher be able to withstand the powerful offensive weapons of the Vachons?" The program also quoted the Illinois State Athletic Commission as praising the promoters for not raising ticket prices for the event.

Mad Dog and the Butcher weren't expected to win the tag team title that night, but they did, both shocking and angering the fans present. The Vachon brothers would hold the title for the next year and eight months before dropping them to Red Bastien and Hercules Cortez.

However, in the meantime, fans clamored for a rematch between the champions and the former champions. The promoters booked the two teams against each only two times — July 11 (1970) in Milwaukee and July 13 in Denver — wisely keeping them apart in Chicago for almost a year before pitting them against each other again on August 14 in Comiskey Park. It would be the first time a wrestling match had been held in Comiskey Park since Buddy Rogers won the NWA world heavyweight title from Pat O'Connor on June 30, 1961.

In a television promo aired to promote the event, Mad Dog Vachon growled and roared at TV audiences:

> "We want no part of this whatsoever. They are trying to kill us in the city of Chicago. Yes, it is true that we signed to wrestling the Crusher and the Bruiser, but what's this I hear about wrestling in a cage? You must be kidding me? Look, my brother and I, Chicago is trying to kill us. I appeal to somebody. This is treating us like dogs, like animals. I want somebody, who still has their mind left, to stop this kind of butchery. We are wrestlers

by nature [and] *by profession. We are not sadists like the Crusher and the Bruiser. They never forgot we took the title from them in a clean and respectable match. Now they want to wrestle in a cage like animals. Let me tell you something, if you want us in a cage, it is going to cost you Mr. Luce and the city of Chicago — twenty thousand dollars for me and twenty thousand dollars for my brother."*

— Mad Dog and Butcher Vachon

It was announced the following week that promoters agreed to the $20,000 demand for both Mad Dog and Butcher, so the stage was set for what looked to be the biggest wrestling event in Chicago in many years. When Minneapolis TV announcer Marty O'Neill told the viewing audience that *"Mad Dog and Butcher want no part of this,"* Mad Dog barged into the set. *"Can you imagine making us live in the cage — to survive like animals? Are we going back to the Roman days?"*

Minneapolis promoter Wally Karbo joined the discussion and pointed out, *"You signed for the match, you got the $20,000 apiece for the match, and all the conditions have been met. You signed!"* hollered Wally.

Mad Dog appeared to backtrack. *"We made a mistake, so take the money back. We want no part of it."*

The Crusher also chimed in:

"They figure that Bob Luce would never come up with the twenty grand. I'm not saying that Bob Luce throws money around like a handful of glue, but he knows the people of Chicago want this match so bad. He'd do anything to give it to them, so he came up with the twenty thousand dollars apiece. The title we lost when they crippled me. I was out of wrestling for four months. I think of those guys knocking me out, making me sit at home for four months. I could hardly get out of a chair and had to have my beer brought to me. Me and the Bruiser will throw those goofy dogs through the fence."

Promoter Bob Luce issued a press release on July 22, claiming an expected "sellout crowd of 51,200 fans would gross a new, all-time U.S. record of $206,659." The document continued: *"The present record for a professional wrestling show held in the United States is $128,071, set by the late Fred Kohler in this same ballpark on June 30, 1961."*

On August 14, the wrestling ring was set up around second base with 1,200 ringside chairs priced at $12.50. That was expensive since Amphitheatre ticket prices for ringside seats at the time cost five dollars.

Wrestling fans knew Bruiser and the Crusher would get sweet revenge against the Vachons and win back the belts. The match that night was an epic battle. Butcher Vachon remembered, *"All four of us were bleeding."* Long-time Chicago wrestling aficionado, Richard Tito, said, *"This was the match everybody was talking about"* and *"the cage match was brutal."* Tito, who attended hundreds of Chicago Wrestling Club wrestling cards from 1966 to 1983, admitted, *"We were shocked when the Bruiser and the Crusher lost."*

144 • BRUISER: The World's Most Dangerous Wrestler

The Bruiser and The Crusher with the title belts they held one year ago when this photo was taken.

Butcher and Mad Dog Vachone now hold the title belts. Only one person in the building claps when Mad Dog is introduced.

CRUSHER AND BRUISER BACK TOGETHER

It was about a year ago that The Crusher and Dick the Bruiser lost the World's Tag Team Championship to the Vachone Brothers. Crusher was injured in that match and out of action for almost six months. When he returned, The Bruiser was no longer in the area, and so The Crusher has tried, with several partners, to regain the tag title.

The Vachones gave Bruiser and Crusher a terrific licking when they won the title, but the word is now that both are healthy and want a return shot at the title. While both men have had return shots with other partners, it must be said that they seem to be at their best as tag team wrestlers when they are partnering each other.

The return match between these two teams should be a real gem. It will be a match that should draw a SRO crowd into any arena in the United States. It might not be surprising if a new championship team should emerge. After all, Crusher and Bruiser had successfully defended the title several times against the Vachones before the match in which they lost the title.

From the previous encounters between The Crusher and Mad Dog Vachone this year, it can be said with a great amount of certainty that this tag team match will be one of the bloodiest brawls ever seen anywhere. All four of the grapplers—The Crusher, Dick the Bruiser, Mad Dog Vachone, and Butcher Vachone—have no regard at all for rules and regulations. The big job may be to come up with a referee who can handle the four and keep some semblance of order in the ring.

Both The Crusher and The Bruiser have sworn revenge. The Crusher says that he will pay the Vachones back by putting both of them out of action for a lot longer than six months. Mad Dog, on the other hand, says that since they want to wrestle them again, Crusher and Bruiser had better both be prepared to be out of action for a long time after this one.

The match has not been signed as we go to press with this part of this issue of **The Wrestling News**. We hope to be able to announce more of the details in our next issue.

PHOTOS ON THIS PAGE BY HARTLEY COOPER.

Blood seems to always color the match when The Crusher and Mad Dog Vachone are in the ring together.

Butcher Vachone seems to be suspended upside down as our photographer caught him in mid air.

From *The Wrestling News*, Volume 1970, Number 27
Copyright Pro Wrestling Enterprises / Arena Publishing

— Baron Von Raschke

While the fans were disappointed with the outcome of the tag team match, another big match also took place that night. Verne Gagne defended his title against Baron Von Raschke, billed in promotional material as "The Beast of Berlin." Raschke, a former collegiate wrestler at the University of Nebraska, was a school teacher who got into the wrestling business by setting up the ring, refereeing, and starting out as an entry-level wrestler.

Chris Parons talked about the days leading up to the match. *"Von Raschke carried the territory at that time, but he didn't know the bosses were slotting him against Gagne in the ballpark. While doing promos for Indianapolis TV, Raschke was surprised when Bruiser told him to talk for two minutes about facing Gagne at the ballpark. That was a huge surprise for Raschke, who was only 30 years old."*

Baron Von Raschke

On the photo in the arena program, Bob Luce blackened some of Raschke's teeth, giving him an air of menace.

Gagne was accompanied to the ring that night by long-time newspaper columnist David Condon of the *Chicago Tribune*, who had a long history of being friendly to and respectful of the wrestling business. As usual, Gagne successfully defended the AWA belt (that he owned) for the Chicago Wrestling Club (that he co-owned). A few days later, Condon devoted most of his newspaper column to that match:

"Gagne humiliated the Beast, Baron Chauncey Von Raschke ... as more than 20,000 cheered the Gagne triumph over probably the most dangerous opponent he ever has faced." Condon even played along with the storyline, writing *"The Baron vowed to take the coveted wrestling crown to Berlin and never give another American a chance to regain it."*

Bruiser promotion in Louisville, Kentucky January 8, 1964

— Business Story from Louisville

During the '60s and '70s, professional wrestling was a territorial business. Distinct borders for the individual territories could be drawn on the U.S. map and it was easy (in most cases) for promoters to know which towns were in their territory from those that weren't. During the first few years of their promotional efforts, Bruiser and Snyder booked regular shows in Louisville, Kentucky. A lack of ticket sales and audience interest resulted in them eventually abandoning the town. A few years later, wrestling promoter Jerry Jarrett, who worked for the wrestling promotion headquartered in Nashville under Nick Gulas, became interested in Louisville. Jarrett approached WLKY-TV Channel 32 in

Louisville about the possibility of showing the Tennessee program, then videotaped at WMC-TV in Memphis. Their first TV program aired in Louisville on June 21, 1970, and they held their first house show on July 7. A newspaper report said, *"The crowd at the Convention Center was small — about 1,000."* With the TV program promoting the Tennessee wrestling crew, they began promoting weekly cards in Louisville. Mike Snyder remembers that *"Bruiser was irate about that."* Snyder added, *"They (Dick and Wilbur) were not going to allow somebody to come in and start doing what they did to Balk Estes and (Jim) Barnett."*

In his autobiography, *The Best of Times*, Jarrett described how Bruiser and Snyder confronted him with a dressing-room visit one night, and how he believed this country was supposed to have a free market and competitive economy. Mike Snyder called the entire incident a big "brouhaha" and said, *"I tell people this whole thing is like the Mafia — people took care of themselves and looked out for themselves."* Top boss Nick Gulas was brought into the dispute and offered a resolution between Jarrett, Bruiser and Snyder. Steve Regal explained that Jarrett agreed to pay a certain percentage of the gross receipts for Louisville, as well as Evansville (IN), to Bruiser and Snyder. Jarrett's autobiography noted that, eventually, he quit making the payments and Bruiser agreed to let it go.

WATCH ALL-STAR
Professional Championship Wrestling
TODAY & EVERY SUNDAY
FROM 4 TO 5 P.M.
WLKY-TV CHANNEL 32
Nick Gulas & Roy Welsh, Promoters

— Bob Luce Wrestling

In the mid-'60s, wrestling fans in Chicago were able to watch the wrestling programs produced in both Indianapolis (WWA) and Minneapolis (AWA), with the local promotional interviews inserted between the matches. In October 1971, Bob Luce began airing a weekly TV program originating from WSNS-TV Channel 44 in Chicago. Bobby Heenan later recalled:

"He (Luce) was a guy who could get things done. He was a flashy guy. He was a writer and a photographer. He could do it all."

Luce aired both edited video from Indianapolis and film footage of the matches in Chicago. Eventually, Luce opened up a "Wrestling Hall of Fame" in the southeast corner of the International Amphitheatre building, paying tribute to the legendary wrestlers of the past with his photos from *Wrestling Life* magazine. Broadcast outlet WSNS-TV was the flagship station for the Chicago White Sox and former Chicago White Sox broadcaster and member of the Baseball Hall of Fame, Bob Elson, added an element of class and dignity to the wrestling program. The only minor flaw was the fact that Elson had trouble, at times, keeping a straight face when

Bob Luce, circa 1971
Source: Dave's Classic Wrestling Photos

menaced by villains like Ox Baker. Bob Luce also would video tape interview segments from WSNS-TV that served as publicity stunts for the upcoming live events. Those stunts included classic events like:

- Bobby Heenan slapping an unprepared Pepper Gomez in the face.
- Manager Saul Weingeroff clobbering a midget wrestler with a briefcase.
- Don Fargo breaking a two-by-four board over the head of Moose Cholak.
- Ox Baker administering his heart punch to a stunned Johnny Kace.

The most famous stunt occurred in December 1974 when Pepper Gomez allowed a Volkswagen automobile to be driven over his "cast-iron" stomach. Afterwards, a melee erupted in the studio involving troublemaker Ox Baker.

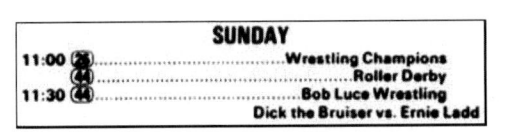

```
              SUNDAY
11:00 .................Wrestling Champions
      ..............................Roller Derby
11:30 ......................Bob Luce Wrestling
                 Dick the Bruiser vs. Ernie Ladd
```
August 26, 1973 TV listing for
Bob Luce Wrestling
Source: Wheeling (IL) Herald

Sponsors of Luce's program became cult figures, such as Ben's Auto Sales at 5959 S. Western Avenue, where every sales price ended in "59." Bobby Heenan made a cameo ad, warning consumers that all cars Ben sold were "klunkers." Another long-time sponsor was the One-Stop convenience store at 4301 S. Lake Park, whose TV spokesperson was Bobo Brazil. Bobo claimed he bought *"chitlins by the case"* and *"spareribs by the thirty-pound box"* at the retailer. Bob Luce would utilize telephone hotlines to promote his cards with area phone numbers (312) 729-4080 and 729-4866. Don't call them now because the wrestling office closed down more than 30 years ago.

— **Feud with Harley Race**

In mid-1971, the Bruiser began what would become a series of bouts in St. Louis against NWA legend Harley Race, a feud dating back to the mid-'60s in the AWA. Two months after the Central States title was introduced to St. Louis fans, Harley made his first defense of the belt in Kiel Auditorium against Bruiser. One year later, September 16, 1972 on *Wrestling at the Chase*, Race won a tournament to become the first Missouri state champion. Six nights later, Race defended the belt for the first time in Kiel ... once again, against Dick the Bruiser.

When author Roger Deem interviewed Harley for his book *The Strap*, Harley talked about working with Bruiser:

> *"Wrestling Bruiser was always work* (to make the match interesting to watch). *I couldn't do a lot of my flashier moves because he wouldn't sell worth* (anything). *Meanwhile, I had to make it look like he was kicking my butt all over the ring."*

— **Return to Detroit**

Throughout 1970 and into 1971, Bruiser and Snyder staffed their talent roster with many of the same workers who regularly worked in the Detroit territory for the Sheik.

WRESTLING TONIGHT 8:30
Air-Conditioned
KIEL AUDITORIUM

New Missouri Champion
HARLEY RACE
versus
DICK THE BRUISER

Texas "Death Match"
BLACK JACK LANZA
versus
RUFUS R. JONES

Four Other Top Bouts, Including Two Tag Team Matches

TICKETS: Arcade Bldg., Kiel Auditorium
Prices: $1.50, $2, $3, $4
TICKETS ON SALE AT THE DOOR
436-4400   231-7487

Wrestlers who worked in Detroit and Indianapolis concurrently included Luis Martinez, Bobo Brazil, Angelo Poffo, The Mighty Igor, as well as the prominent tag team known as the Fabulous Kangaroos — Al Costello and Don Kent, who were managed by Crybaby George Cannon. The sharing of talent afforded Indianapolis fans with a favorable transfusion of new and interesting talent.

Long-time Detroit wrestling historian and photographer Dave Burzynski pointed out that *"anytime a guy wasn't booked for the Sheik, they were free to go to work elsewhere."*

It looked like the Sheik and Bruiser were getting along in peaceful harmony until June 3, 1971, when a column by Michael O'Hara of the *Detroit News*, shocked Detroit wrestling fans. *"Well, get ready. The Bruiser is on his way back to wrestle again, as mean and tough as ever."*

Bruiser also was quoted. *"I'm looking forward to Detroit, and I'll be there in a couple of months to sign some contracts with* [the] *Olympia."*

O'Hara reported that the lawsuit settlements with the Detroit policemen (Andrew Meholic and James Carolan), who had been injured in the Bruiser-Karras brawl, had been settled the previous week. That freed up Bruiser for a return to Detroit without the possibility of having his payoffs being confiscated by a court order. Dave Burzynski recalls that *"when it was announced the Bruiser was coming to Detroit, it caught the Sheik completely off guard."*

The WWA invasion began on October 23, 1971, with Baron Von Raschke defending the WWA title against Bruiser. An interesting story behind this was that Bruiser had already won the title from Von Raschke in Indianapolis on October 14. In those days, most wrestling fans weren't privy to what went on in other territories, so, as a way to get Bruiser over in Detroit, they had him "win" the title from Von Raschke ... a title he already held.

The Sheik didn't sit idly by while Bruiser invaded his territory. He booked a spectacular card at Cobo Arena that same night with no less than eleven matches and 26 wrestlers appearing. The Sheik pulled out all the stops with NWA heavyweight champion Dory Funk Jr. wrestling Ernie Ladd on the top billing. He stacked the card with his bread-and-butter stalwarts, like Bobo Brazil, Lord Layton, Crybaby Cannon, Al Costello, Don Kent, Dewey Robertson, Wild Bull Curry, and Fred Curry, and promoters of other NWA territories sent in some of their top names, including Tiger Jeet Singh, Johnny Valentine, Rocky Johnson, Chris Tolos, Gorilla Monsoon, Crazy

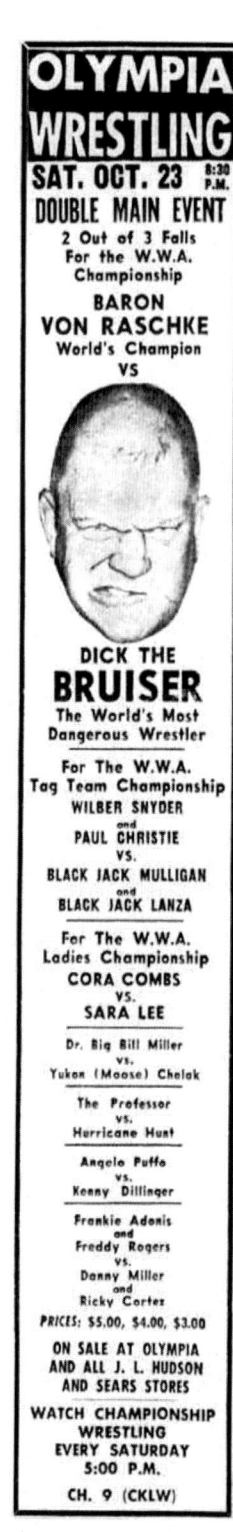

OLYMPIA WRESTLING
SAT. OCT. 23 8:30 P.M.
DOUBLE MAIN EVENT
2 Out of 3 Falls
For the W.W.A.
Championship
BARON VON RASCHKE
World's Champion
VS
DICK THE BRUISER
The World's Most
Dangerous Wrestler

For The W.W.A.
Tag Team Championship
WILBER SNYDER
and
PAUL CHRISTIE
VS.
BLACK JACK MULLIGAN
and
BLACK JACK LANZA

For The W.W.A.
Ladies Championship
CORA COMBS
VS.
SARA LEE

Dr. Big Bill Miller
vs.
Yukon (Moose) Chelak

The Professor
vs.
Hurricane Hunt

Angelo Puffo
vs.
Kenny Dillinger

Frankie Adonis
and
Freddy Rogers
vs.
Danny Miller
and
Ricky Cortez

PRICES: $5.00, $4.00, $3.00

ON SALE AT OLYMPIA
AND ALL J. L. HUDSON
AND SEARS STORES

WATCH CHAMPIONSHIP
WRESTLING
EVERY SATURDAY
5:00 P.M.
CH. 9 (CKLW)

Luke Graham, Pat O'Connor, Mil Mascaras, Fred Blassie, Eddie Graham, and Buddy Fuller. Dave Burzynski said, "It was NWA policy to strike down, wipe out, and eliminate competition to any of its members." The goal was to divert Detroit wrestling fans from the Olympia.

The first eight shows at the Olympia through February 28, 1972, were met by head-to-head competition from the Sheik with help from the NWA. That set the stage for a promotional war in Detroit that would last almost two years.

Detroit wrestling photographer/writer Brian Bukantis remembers that era for Detroit wrestling:

"If you were a wrestling fan, it was fantastic as every major wrestling star came through Detroit because of the two promotions. But the problem was, you couldn't decide where you wanted to go. That was the issue because, when the Bruiser would put up a date, the Sheik would automatically put a card on, regardless if he had anything or not. He would whip something up and [provide] direct competition. This sort of killed the town because, eventually, there was just too much. If you were a wrestling fan, this was the place to be in the early 1970s."

Detroit, Oct. 23, 1971

— Sam Menacker Arrives

When Bruiser moved into Detroit, changes were made on the Indianapolis TV program. Chuck Marlowe, the voice of wrestling in Indianapolis since 1957, stepped down from his wrestling duties. Marlowe's had so many other broadcast responsibilities: Indiana University basketball, Indianapolis 500 television and radio reporting, and anchoring the nightly sports news on WTTV-TV. Replacing Marlowe was a veteran of many wrestling roles, Sam Menacker. Ironically, Menacker had been the studio TV announcer at CKLW-TV in Windsor, Ontario, when Bruiser revitalized the Detroit promotion in 1959, leading one to believe Bruiser thought Menacker could contribute to another rebirth of Detroit in 1971.

Sam Menacker
Source: Scott Romer

5:00 ❾ Championship Wrestling
Four matches with such wrestling notables as Dick the Bruiser and Baron von Ratchke. Commentator Sam Menecher, ring announcer Chuck Marlow.

Detroit TV listing • October 17, 1971

Chapter 18
Making Money ... and Lots of It — 1

— Blackjacks Lanza and Mulligan

By 1972, Bruiser and Snyder boasted one of the strongest talent line-ups, from top to bottom, of any territory in the nation. At that time, Black Jack Lanza was teaming up with Bob Windham, who had recently adopted an identity in the Northeast as Blackjack Mulligan. No other heel tag team made such a thunderous impact in the Indianapolis wrestling market, and the combination was further strengthened by their manager — the inimitable Bobby Heenan. Chicago sports radio personality Mike North remembers vividly:

> "Heenan was one of the greatest wrestling managers who ever lived. Heenan would stand between [Black Jack] *Lanza* and *Blackjack Mulligan. Lanza and Mulligan would put their hands on their hips with the cowboy hats*, and looked at you while Heenan started talking. It was awesome."

Blackjacks Mulligan & Lanza with manager Bobby Heenan 1972
Source: Bill Ondecko

The Bruiser also assembled a "second string" tag team (behind the Blackjacks) called "The Graduates," who donned caps and gowns and proclaimed superior intelligence to the wrestling community. The team consisted of mat veteran Angelo Poffo and preliminary wrestler Ken Russell, who adopted the new ring name, Ken Dillinger. Bruiser recruited a former amateur weightlifter from South Bend, Indiana, named Mark Kroll to manage the Graduates. Kroll, who installed floor coverings as an everyday job, had extremely long hair and a beard. To put it politely, Mark had an uncanny resemblance to notorious mass murderer Charles Manson. Bruiser changed his name to Mark Manson and he became the second best bump-taker in the entire company, besides Bobby Heenan. Manson remembers this big break in his young wrestling career:

The Graduates
Ken Russell, Mark Manson & Angelo Poffo

"*I started out as a manager. They needed a second string tag team. You had the Blackjacks but you needed a second team heel tag team* — [Angelo] *Poffo and Ken Dillinger. Anytime I would see the Bruiser, I would say* 'Hey, Dick. I'm ready.' *The Bruiser said,* "We'll do something pretty soon." *I just kept hanging around and hanging around. I don't know if Poffo wanted the manager or if Bruiser wanted the manager. I remember the Bruiser telling me my name was going to be Mark Manson. He said,* 'Yeah, you look like that killer.' *Dick added,* 'Kenny Dillinger looks like that Sheppard guy — the doctor that killed somebody. We have a team of murderers.'"

— Talented Roster

Baron Von Raschke continued working for Bruiser and Snyder and held the WWA title on three occasions — two times in Indianapolis and once in Detroit. Raschke talked with a heavy German accent, replacing the consonant "W" with a hard "V," such as "*I vill vin da match against Vilbur Snyder.*" His finishing maneuver was a claw hold, which he applied by wrapping his fingers of his huge hand around the top of his opponent's head and squeezing. When introduced to the audience, Raschke would raise his right arm with the right hand clenched in a claw-like position. It became his trademark, one of the most enduring in the wrestling business.

In August 1999, the Baron shared the origins of the claw in Scott Teal's *Whatever Happened to ...?* magazine.

"*Eddie Farhat, the ... I call him the original Sheik, but I don't know if that's true or not. He came up to Quebec and saw me work a few shots. He asked me if I wanted to go work for him. Not knowing any better, I*

Letterhead for "Championship Wrestling, Inc."
Officials of the company included Louise Afflis & Shirlee Snyder
Source: Tim Replogle

said, 'Sure.' [laughs] *He did treat me all right. I was finishing up in Quebec, so we moved to Toledo. He was in the NWA, although he never used the champion. They needed cannon fodder or something, so they sent me one time. Actually, I think ... I don't know the story, but I'm sure there's some talk about me through the grapevine, among the different promoters. They flew me in from Toledo, or Detroit, or wherever. I wound up wrestling against Pat O'Connor at the Kiel Auditorium. He was a master, just excellent. During the match, he said,* 'Put the claw on me.'

I asked, [whispers] 'What's the claw?'

He guided me through it and it seemed to get over pretty good. We had a real good match."

Besides Bruiser, Snyder, and an occasional appearance by Bruiser's "cousin," the Crusher, the WWA's roster of talent included wholesome good guys like authentic Native-American Billy Red Cloud who, shortly after his arrival, found himself the victim of a sneak-attack when Bobby Heenan destroyed Red Cloud's Native-American ceremonial dress at the WTTV-TV studios. This event ignited a heated feud between Cloud and Heenan, and many say it helped kick off a wrestling boom in the territory. In mid-'72, Red Cloud was paired with veteran journeyman Bob Boyer, who had been given the new ring identity of Bobby Bold Eagle. The Bruiser sent Boyer to Oklahoma to obtain authentic Native-American headdress and outfit to complete the package. Eagle's self-administered face paint was so good that, on occasional spot shows, he would referee the opening bouts as Bob Boyer and then paint himself up backstage to wrestle as Bobby Bold Eagle later on the card. Veterans like Yukon Moose Cholak, Sailor Art Thomas (one of the first "ripped" bodybuilder types), Paul (Golden Boy) Christy (clean-cut to the core), and Calvin (Prince) Pullins (another black bodybuilder type and real-life trainer) rounded out the roster.

Billy Red Cloud
Source: David Maciejewski

— WRTV-TV, Channel 6

In early 1972, WRTV-TV Channel 6 began broadcasting the wrestling programming from the Tyndall Armory — also known as Northside Armory — at 711 N. Pennsylvania Street. The other venue where Bruiser and Snyder held their TV tapings was Southside Armory at 2015 S. Pennsylvania Street.

Chris Parsons remembered watching Bruiser's shows regularly. *"Competitive bouts were regularly featured on TV, replacing the standard TV lineup of squash matches."* Having more competitive matches on television went a long way to help popularize house (arena) shows in the territory,

Bobby Bold Eagle
Source: Scott Teal collection

including the weekly matches held at the Northside Armory in Indianapolis. Below is an example of ticket prices and revenue from a sample sold-out card:

Fans	Section	Price	Revenue
579	Ringside	$3.00	$1,737
424	Reserved	$2.50	$1,610
800	Bleachers	$2.00	$1,600
500	Upstairs	$2.00	$1,000
TOTAL 2,303		**TOTAL**	**$5,947**

The maximum number of people allowed in Northside Armory was 2,303, which capped the amount of revenue Bruiser and Snyder could make. For bigger shows, or the blowoff match of a particularly hot program, they would move to the Victory Field ballpark or the Fairgounds Coliseum.

However, in 1972, construction on a new venue — the Indianapolis Convention and Exposition Center, also known as the "Expo Center" — was completed. This large venue, located just south of the state capitol building, offered a large main-floor seating area and tall portable bleachers that would hold potential of crowds of 7,000 to 8,000. The Expo Center became the new home of WWA wrestling and they remained there for many years.

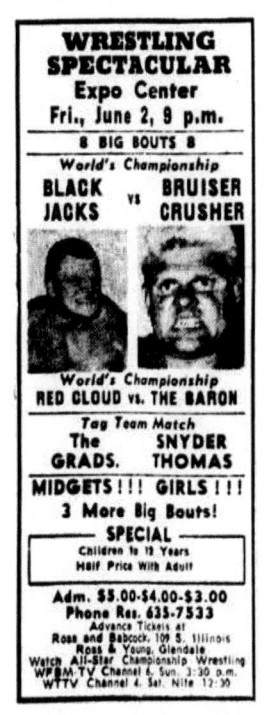

The debut event at the Expo Center took place on Friday, June 2, 1972. The main event featured the match Indianapolis fans had been clamoring to see — Dick the Bruiser and The Crusher vs. The Blackjacks, with their manager, Bobby Heenan.

— **First Expo Center Card**

The *Indianapolis Star* reported on this event:

> "The promoters were the big winners last night as thousands of pro wrestling addicts battled for tickets. Around 2,000 people were turned away from the show, and 7,000 successfully gained entrance to the arena."

The newspaper reported that only 1,000 tickets were sold in advance and thousands of walk-up customers were crammed into the box office windows due to limited ticket sellers. The only other problem of note was the main event being delayed due to fans tossing beer cups and popcorn into the ring.

The year 1972 would go on record as the best year ever for Bruiser and Snyder. Some financial records from Indiana Championship Wrestling, Inc., survive. Tim Replogle shared reports for the eight months ending August 31, 1972. Revenues overall for the Indianapolis and Detroit territories — not including Chicago — increased 2.4 times over the same eight-month period in 1971, while profitability increased 3.3 times. Those are financial results any business owner would die for. The increase cannot be explained merely by that fact that Detroit had been added to the circuit. The houses shot up across the board, especially at the Expo Center. The talent mix, a nice blend of veterans and new faces, was close

154 • BRUISER: The World's Most Dangerous Wrestler

to being perfect. There was minimal participation of AWA talent in Indianapolis, although AWA wrestlers would show up occasionally, usually to take the place of someone injured or unable to appear for whatever reason. Steve Regal, Snyder's son-in-law, would later comment, *"After they went on Channel 6 (WRTV-TV), the money they made was unbelievable."* Never before and never again will the Indianapolis wrestling fans experience the wrestling excitement generated in 1972.

— TV Taping from the Expo Center

In June 1972, the Bruiser and Snyder began shooting their TV program at the Expo Center, the main arena for Indianapolis. Here is an example of how the Bruiser edited (in his own handwriting) a live card into two 47-minute wrestling broadcasts. Thirteen minutes of each hour were allocated for commercials.

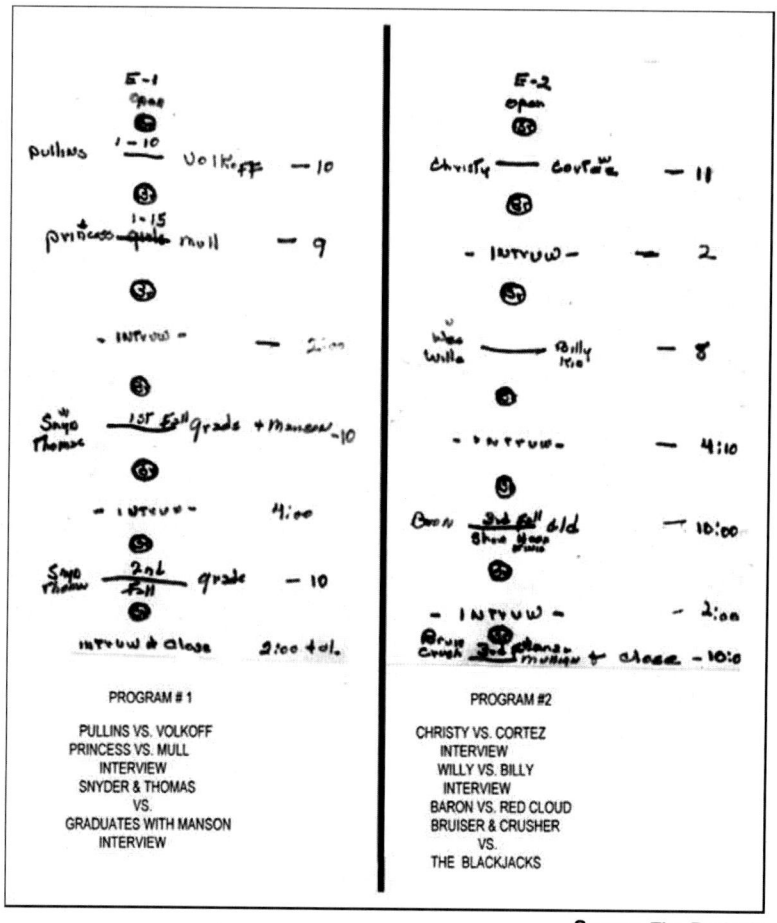

PROGRAM #1
PULLINS VS. VOLKOFF
PRINCESS VS. MULL
INTERVIEW
SNYDER & THOMAS
VS.
GRADUATES WITH MANSON
INTERVIEW

PROGRAM #2
CHRISTY VS. CORTEZ
INTERVIEW
WILLY VS. BILLY
INTERVIEW
BARON VS. RED CLOUD
BRUISER & CRUSHER
VS.
THE BLACKJACKS

Source: Tim Replogle

— Soldier Field Spectacular

Chicago also did well in 1972, with shows featuring the best talent from both Minnesota and Indianapolis. When the upcoming Summer Olympics became the focus of news reports, the Bruiser-Snyder-Gagne trio got together and hatched a plan to book a very special card to coincide with the Games. The date was set for Friday, September 1, at Soldier Field, the home field for the Chicago Bears football team.

Bob Luce put an Olympic spin on the card by having the prime seating areas designated as "Gold," "Silver," and "Bronze," just like the Olympic medals. Tickets for normal Amphitheatre events had traditionally been priced from two dollars for general admission to five dollars for ringside. However, the promoters packed the card with no less than ten bouts and, accordingly, raised ticket prices significantly. The author of this narrative would like to give readers a first-hand account of the card that night, but he was a teenager and didn't have the nerve to ask his parents to pay triple the normal fares. As a result, he wasn't able to go.

Author's note: I wanted badly to attend this card at Soldier Field, but I didn't have the nerve to ask my parents to pay the exorbitant ticket prices.

In an attempt to obtain publicity in mainstream print and broadcast media, the owners held a press party and luncheon on August 25 in downtown Chicago at Marina City Restaurant, which was owned by the former 1953 Heisman trophy winner, quarterback Johnny Lattner. Lattner played football for the University of Notre Dame and, in 1954, when Bruiser was playing for Green Bay, Lattner was playing for the Pittsburgh Steelers. Lattner later wrote a letter to the author of this book, explaining how wrestling influenced his life:

Soldier Fields press party • 1972
Source: William Ondecko

"As a young boy living on the west side of Chicago, I would go watch wrestling at the Keyman Club Hall. As a kid, we wrestled on the sidewalk and alleys. It definitely taught me how to compete in sports."

The dais at Johnny Latter's Marina City Restaurant was filled with Chicago's wrestling royalty — Bob Luce, Dick the Bruiser, Sam Menacker, Wilbur Snyder, Verne Gagne, Greg Gagne, Bobby Heenan, and Andre the Giant. Wrestling photographer Bill Ondecko was permitted by Bob Luce to take photographs that afternoon. The only restriction Luce made was that Ondecko must *not* take any pictures of Bruiser standing next to Andre the Giant. The author believed the promotion wanted to avoid diminishing Bruiser's larger-than-life image.

Andre had made appearances in 1971 in both Minneapolis and Milwaukee, but his booking at Soldier Field on September 1 was his first-ever appearance in

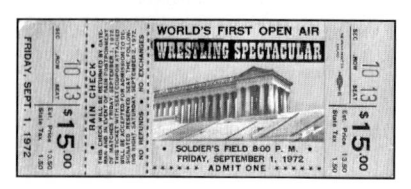

156 • BRUISER: The World's Most Dangerous Wrestler

Chicago. To reinforce Andre's colossal reputation, he was booked at Soldier Field against two very big men, Larry Hennig and Butcher Vachon, each of whom previously held one-half of the AWA tag team championship. The lineup at Soldier Field was as follows:

The first of the two main events at Soldier Field was an AWA heavyweight title match with champion Verne Gagne defending his title against Ivan (The Russian Bear) Koloff, managed by the Big K. Koloff briefly held the WWWF heavyweight title in early 1971 after defeating legend Bruno Sammartino at Madison Square Garden in New York City. Koloff scored AWA victories over Billy Robinson and Wilbur Snyder to earn the shot against Gagne. Gagne was seconded by wrestling-friendly newspaper columnist David Condon from the *Chicago Tribune*. Condon got involved at the end of Gagne's victory when he conked Koloff's manager, the Big K (Stan Kowalski) with the championship belt. It must have been tough for a rugged mat veteran like the Big K to take a bump from a newspaper reporter.

Replica poster of the Soldier Field card Created by Scott Teal

The second main event was a steel cage match with Bruiser and the Crusher facing Blackjacks Lanza and Mulligan, who were managed by Bobby Heenan. The special referee for the match was former world heavyweight boxing champion "Jersey Joe" Walcott, who had officiated some of Lanza's previous matches. Promoter Bob Luce helped publicize the match with a profile of Walcott in the African-American newspaper, the *Chicago Defender*.

In the weeks preceding the match, Heenan was at his belligerent best, insulting an absent Walcott on television. However, Heenan turned into a scared pussycat when Walcott confronted him in person at the WSNS-TV studios the night before the cage match. Walcott and Heenan both had important roles in the match.

During the heat of battle, Heenan took a swing at referee Walcott, but missed. Walcott retaliated with a big uppercut that sent Heenan reeling. Immediately, the Bruiser shook hands with Walcott (so much for impartiality). Less than a minute later, Bruiser pinned Mulligan to win the match. When all was said and done, Bruiser was the only participant who wasn't bleeding. The damage to Heenan's face was horrific and photos were later published in wrestling magazines. Wrestling magazines reported an attendance of 12,000 and a box office gross of $100,000. Throughout that year, that same feud would carry over into other cities in the Indiana territory.

Years later, promoter Bob Luce looked back on the match in his video production, *Caged Madness*. He said it was *"one of the greatest classics of all* time. Nobody who ever witnessed this will ever forget it. Dick the Bruiser and the Crusher were at the height of their career. They were never tougher than this night in 1972."

Blackjack Mulligan also looked back fondly at the Soldier Field event, telling Internet host Bob Brooks: "*I miss them both [Bruiser and Crusher]. The money was right. The promotion was right. Everything was done to perfection. What a night.*"

— **Blackjacks Depart WWA**

According to Chris Parsons, the biggest house at the Olympia Stadium in Detroit was 10,252 fans on December 2, 1972, with the same match on top. As the saying goes, though, all good things come to an end, as did that very successful program. Black Jack Lanza remembers several issues that took place behind the scenes. "*He [Bruiser] stiffed us on some payoffs and I had a talk with him. I told him, 'You know, you should rectify this or we're leaving.'*" Lanza and Mulligan gave their notice in Elkhart, Indiana, when Lanza told the Bruiser, "*You better change the finish because we're leaving.*" Lanza remembered another incident at an arena show towards the end of the Blackjacks' run in the WWA:

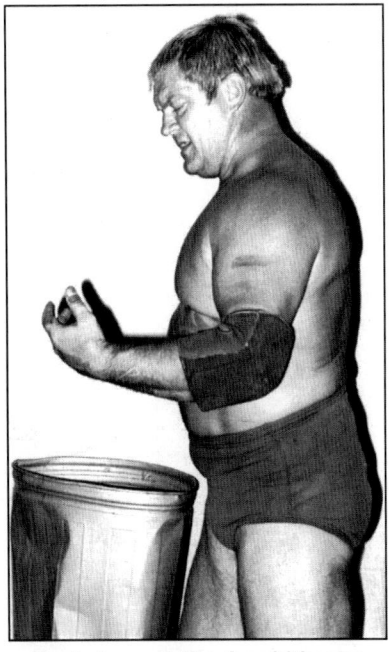

Backstage at the Amphitheatre
Source: William Ondecko

"*I remember one night, we were in there with the Bruiser to get heat on him. Here's the situation. We had Raschke, Mulligan, Ladd, and myself, all pounding on the Bruiser, and he [Bruiser] was holding onto the rope. That's how he was selling himself. I said, 'Bruiser, are you ever going to sell anything?'*

He said, 'I can't afford to sell.'

I said, 'Well, you can't afford us,' so we left. We could see the handwriting on the wall. When people see that, then they don't buy anything. If this was earlier in his career, he wouldn't have done that. You could see the senselessness of it all."

The best year Bruiser and Wilbur Snyder would ever see came to an end at that point. The standards they set during that boom period would never be achieved again.

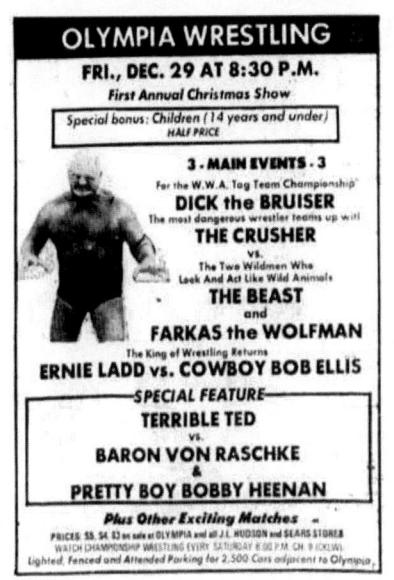

Christmas show in Detroit
December 29, 1972

Chapter 19
The Sheik vs. The Bruiser — 1973-1974

— **Wrestling War in Detroit**

Hoping to capitalize on the success he had in Detroit beginning in April 1959, Bruiser booked himself in the main event on 37 out of 39 Olympia wrestling cards. Wilbur Snyder wrestled occasionally, but preferred to keep himself off the cards so he could take care of box-office business.

The WWA television show in Detroit aired on CKLW-TV, Channel 9 out of Windsor, Ontario, the same outlet that helped kick off Bruiser's first Detroit run. Ed Farhat Jr., son of The Sheik, recalls, "*They* [Bruiser and Snyder] *had local TV on Channel 9 out of Windsor, and they couldn't do anything against us.*"

Dave Burzynski remembers, "*I attended and photographed for the Bruiser show, even though I worked for the Sheik at Cobo. They let me do* [that] *with their blessing because I could spy* [on Bruiser] *and report back to them* [The Sheik]."

The Sheik eventually emerged victorious. Ed Farhat Jr. recalls, "*We put our TV into Indianapolis on a major station.*" That station was WISH-TV Channel 8, the CBS-affiliated station in Indianapolis, and the program aired on Friday nights after the local late show. Farhat continued, saying, "*Dad got a phone call one afternoon from The Bruiser, who asked The Sheik, 'What are you doing?'*"

Dave Burzynski looked back at the promotional wars many decades later.

"*The Sheik drew great houses because of fan loyalty. Most had certain favorites and disliked the core top heels. Most of the Bruiser's following had to do with fans who had seen him back in the early '60s. Olympia Stadium was about seven miles outside downtown with only one bus line (that) ran along Grand River Avenue. It wasn't the safest part of town in those days.*"

Wrestler Big Jim Lancaster, who observed the Sheik's territory in person during the early '70s, offered his comments:

"*The Sheik was lucky. I'm telling you right now. There were two programs that popped in the territory — Killer Brooks vs. Tony Marino and The Kangaroos vs. The Stomper and Ben Justice. The Sheik needed to step up his product and he did.*"

Ed Farhat, Jr., also reflected on his father's victory:

Detroit advertisement April 7, 1959

"Big Time Wrestling was not threatened at any time by losing this war because the fans had decided who their wrestling company was the first time Big Time Wrestling opened their doors. Bruiser came in and tried everything under the sun, but he would draw twenty-five hundred people. Bruiser and Gagne were just bugs and, after putting up with the bugs and letting them wear out themselves, we hit them with a fly swatter and sent them to bug heaven."

Detroit wrestling photographer and writer Brian Bukantis remembered an incident at the Olympia Stadium towards the end of the promotional war:

"I remember the Bruiser and Bruno were walking down the hallway, and the TV show had run the night before at one-thirty a.m. I opened my yap, but shouldn't have done it. I said to the Bruiser, 'You know what time the TV show ran last night?'

He said, 'No.'

I said, 'One-thirty in the morning. No wonder nobody is here.'

Bruno gave me a look like, 'What?' I know I shouldn't have said anything, but that's how it was. It didn't last that much longer."

— **Banned from St. Louis**

During the time Bruiser was involved in a promotional war against The Sheik, Bruiser and his WWA talent weren't allowed to wrestle in St. Louis. Sheik was a member of the NWA, so Muchnick, as president of the NWA, told Bruiser that as long as he was involved in a promotional war against an NWA member, the NWA flagship office couldn't use him in St. Louis. This was mentioned during interviews with both Bobby Heenan and Larry Matysik. The prohibition ended a few years later when Bruiser and Sheik settled their differences and appeared on each others' promotions.

During their review of the manuscript for this book, both Chris Parsons and Scott Teal realized there was a gap of almost a year between when Bruiser began promoting Detroit and when his bookings in St. Louis ended. Bruiser invaded Detroit in October 1971, but continued to wrestle in St. Louis until September 1972, at which time he was out until February 1974. Why Muchnick continued to book Bruiser from October 1971 (when he first invaded Detroit) until September 1972 is a mystery we have been unable to solve. On the other end, Bruiser's last show in Detroit was February 22, 1974, so Bruiser's pulling out of Detroit and him wrestling in St. Louis coincides, so that rings true.

Barring Bruiser from wrestling in St. Louis, though, had been purely a business decision on Muchnick's part, and Bruiser understood that. His friendship with Muchnick was substantial and long-lasting. Some people even suggest that Sam Muchnick was like a father-figure for Bruiser, whose real father passed away in 1945. When Sam's wife, Helen Muchnick, passed away years later,

OLYMPIA STADIUM
FRI., FEB. 22
8:30 P.M.
For the WWA
Tag Team
Championship

BRUISER and ELLIS
vs.
THE VALIANT BROS.

MEXICAN DEATH MATCH
MARTINEZ
vs.
HEENAN

KOLOFF vs. CHOLAK
OTHER STAR BOUTS

Prices $5, $4, $3

Children 14 Years
And Under Half Price

On Sale at Olympia,
Sears, Grinnells, Hudsons

Watch Championship
Wrestling TV—Ch. 9
Sat. 5:00 p.m.

Detroit card
February 22, 1974

160 • BRUISER: The World's Most Dangerous Wrestler

the wrestling world flocked to Sam's side, including the Bruiser, who flew to St. Louis and attended the funeral services at Krieghauser Mortuary.

— Peace Treaty Between Bruiser and The Sheik

The Sheik and Bruiser eventually buried the hatchet and ended the war once and for all. Farhat Jr. pointed out that "*He* [Dick] *came to the Sheik's house and felt proud to be on the same team as my dad. He also seemed to be really happy my dad let him back inside our house.*"

It is believed Bruiser and Snyder ended their promotional activities in Detroit because they realized they couldn't compete profitably against the Sheik. They also had unsuccessfully attempted to promote shows in other Michigan cities, such as Grand Rapids and Kalamazoo.

But that wouldn't be the end of the story of Dick the Bruiser and the Sheik.

— Handsome Jimmy Valiant

With the departure of Blackjacks Lanza and Mulligan, the ever-evolving cast of characters at Indiana Championship Wrestling moved forward. Former WWA preliminary wrestler and Indiana native Jim Valen returned to Indiana as "Handsome Jimmy Valiant." Valiant now was a conceited, bleached-blond bodybuilder who became an easy target of Cowboy Bob Ellis' sense of humor. Ellis coined the nicknames "Jimmy Sue" for Valiant and "Bobby Ann" for manager Heenan. Heenan retaliated by regularly referring to Ellis as a "dirt farmer" and "hayseed hillbilly." Valiant gave the speech of his life on his first appearance on the WWA TV show.

Jimmy Valiant vs. Bruiser
1973
Source: William Ondecko

"*I have the body that women love and men fear. I'm the woman's pet and the men's regret. I'm the diamond ring and Cadillac man. Every time Handsome Jimmy steps into the ring, he has problems with all the women fans out there. They all keep throwing their house keys into the center of the ring. They all want to take Handsome Jimmy home with them. At this time, I want to say something to all my women fans out there ... 'Don't bother me, I'm busy.'*"

Editor's note: Jimmy Valiant was one of the great interview subjects, but credit for the first three sentences of the above promo must be given to Sputnik Monroe, who created and used those exact words for promos he did back in the '50s.

Cowboy Bob Ellis & Bruiser
Source: William Ondecko

— The Texas Outlaws

One of the most explosive, albeit short-lived, tag team feuds for Bruiser and Crusher involved The Outlaws, Dick Murdoch and Dusty Rhodes. Their matches were limited to Green Bay and Chicago, but Bob Luce had the foresight to have the Chicago battles filmed for posterity. Their first confrontation took place on March 9, 1973 and the follow-up battle on March 24th.

For the first clash, Rhodes and Murdoch entered the ring and awaited Bruiser and Crusher, who jogged to the ring surrounded by Andy Frain security men. Murdoch and Rhodes attacked their foes as soon as they entered the ring, but quickly retreated to safety. The match, if it could be called such, was a complete brawl and little tag-team protocol took

Dusty Rhodes vs Bruiser
1973
Source: Dave Maciejewski

place. Close-up footage revealed the combatants having a good time entertaining the sold-out crowd. Bruiser and Crusher got carried away and were eventually disqualified during that first encounter. Dick and Reggie sent the crowd away happy, though, by doing a test of strength demonstration whereby they repeatedly exchanged powerful forearm smashes to each others' chests and shook hands afterwards. The rematch was a no-disqualification event won by Bruiser and Crusher. The chemistry between the four performers in that match was exemplary, but in many ways, their talents were underutilized. Other than the two Chicago matches, Bruiser and Crusher wrestled Murdoch and Rhodes just one other time (Green Bay, February 4, 1973) and never went to Indianapolis.

— Ernie Ladd

A former AFL football player, Ernie (The Big Cat) Ladd returned to the WWA in 1973 after scattered appearances during the first few years of the promotion's existence. Ladd played defensive tackle in the AFL from 1961 to 1968 for the San Diego Chargers, Houston Oilers, and Kansas City Chiefs. Standing 6-foot-9 and weighing more than 300 pounds, he was one of the most agile giants ever to appear in a wrestling ring. This go-around, Ladd wore a jeweled crown into the ring and proclaimed himself to be the "King of Wrestling." Ladd towered over his opponents and generated controversy with his taped right thumb. Ladd claimed the tape was needed to support an old injury, but fans saw the thumb as an offensive weapon in his wrestling arsenal. Ladd intimidated Sam Menacker, Bruiser's play-by-play man, by yelling at him — "*Let me tell you something, Mr. TV announcer*" — and poking his finger into Sam's chest. Ladd demanded the fans be silent when he removed his crown, which only motivated wrestling fans to make even more noise. Of all the wrestlers Bruiser feuded with over the years, some of his most competitive matches were with Ernie Ladd. The two had no less than four

162 • BRUISER: The World's Most Dangerous Wrestler

main events in Indianapolis in 1973, including a cage match at the Fairgrounds Coliseum on September 22, 1973. Longtime Chicago wrestling observer Glen Rylko summarized the program:

"I remember seeing Ladd selling for Bruiser, even though Dick seemed to be at least a foot shorter. Dick was looking older in 1973-74, but his opponents made him look good and helped him maintain his unbeatable persona. Dick was strong enough to 'block' a thumb thrust to his throat by Ladd, and turn it around so Ladd would hit himself."

**Ernie Ladd has Bruiser on the ropes
Detroit • 1973**

Source: Brian Bukantis
Copyright Arena Publishing

— The Valiant Brothers

During this period, some of Bruiser's wrestlers would moonlight outside of the territory, going across the border into Canada to work for Ontario promoter Dave McKigney, known in wrestling circles as the "Bear Man" due to his stable of wrestling bears. Quite regularly, Raschke, Valiant, and Heenan would wrestle for McKigney on days when the WWA didn't have a show scheduled. Heenan had worked the better part of seven years for the Bruiser and now wanted to move onto another territory. In Handsome Jimmy Valiant's book, "*Woo ... Mercy Daddy!,*" the story was retold firsthand:

"*Bobby came to me with a proposal to substitute himself with another main-event wrestler. Who came to our minds was a big, young, good-looking, blond-headed kid that we met during the summer working for the Bear Man in Ontario, named John L. Sullivan. Heenan's idea was to make Sullivan a Valiant brother and tag partner for me. We came up with a finished plan to present to Bruiser.*"

Sullivan was no stranger to Dick the Bruiser. On August 8, 1967, on *Wrestling at the Chase*, a young Pittsburgh native named John L. Sullivan was booked against Dick the Bruiser on St. Louis television. Bruiser threw Sullivan over the top rope, but Sullivan didn't know how to hold onto the rope and brace his fall. Sullivan, who landed head-first on the studio floor, remembers, "*There was blood all over the place.*" Sullivan was able to recover enough to get back into the ring, where he was promptly pinned by Bruiser. Afterwards, in the dressing room, Bruiser came over to Sullivan with the antiseptic Phisohex and helped clean out Sullivan's wound. Sullivan responded, "*Thank you, sir.*"

Sullivan eventually became Luscious Johnny Valiant, but first had to pass a formal audition for Dick the Bruiser. On Saturday, September 7, 1973, at the Pittsburgh Civic Arena, John L. Sullivan was teamed up with Handsome Jimmy Valiant. Bruiser flew to Pittsburgh, not only to wrestle, but to assess the tag team's chemistry. The audition was a resounding success and the newly formed Valiant Brothers became destined for the WWA tag team championship.

Johnny Valiant remembers the start of the team under the Bruiser and Snyder:

"*There was no formal meeting. They [directed] by the way they handled us. It was always business. They [directed] by the way they pushed us. Not a lot of money changed hands. I was never in it for the money. There was no sit-down meeting. There was no contract signed. There were no promises made.*"

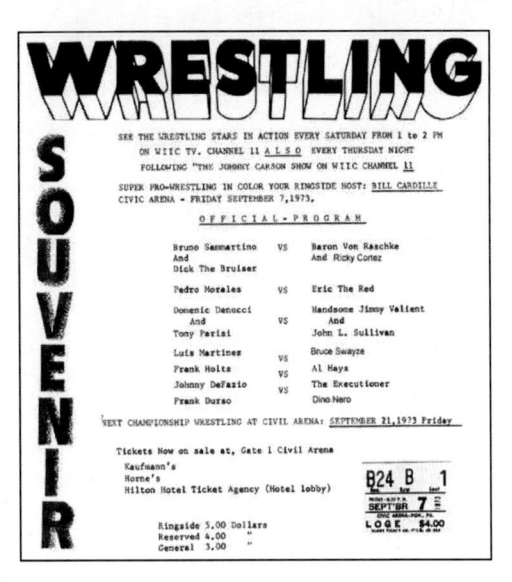

164 • BRUISER: The World's Most Dangerous Wrestler

— **Bruno Sammartino**

The next superstar to be brought into the WWA was a monumental addition ... former WWWF heavyweight champion, Bruno Sammartino, who held that title for a seven-year period between May 1963 and January 1971. Bruno, who wrestled in the WWA in May 1973, was reported to be a favorite of Bruiser's wife, Louise Iacomo Afflis. Wrestling photographer Dr. Mike Lano interviewed Bruno Sammartino about his days with the Bruiser: "*I'd stay in touch with Dick a little bit before going to work for his promotion, every now and then. We were always on a friendly basis, a very personable guy that I liked. I enjoyed working for and with Dick. He and Wilbur were very personable guys and did right by me.*"

It was Bruno who first teamed with Bruiser in the WWA against the Valiant Brothers, not Crusher, Dick's most frequent tag partner. They teamed primarily in the largest cities — Fort Wayne, Indianapolis, Chicago, and even Detroit during the final days of the Detroit incursion. The feud was extremely successful. However, like the Blackjacks before them, in February 1974, the Valiant Brothers left the WWA territory for the much greener pastures on the East coast, working for the WWWF and headlining at their showplace venue, Madison Square Garden, in New York City.

Bruno Sammartino visits Olympia
Source: Gary Kamensack

— **Bruiser and Sheik Make Peace, Outside the Ring**

From July 1974 through December 1974, the Bruiser and The Sheik wrestled each other in Chicago, Detroit, Fort Wayne, and Indianapolis, usually in singles matches, but occasionally in tag team bouts. Most matches ended without a decisive victory on the part of either man, although they both were victors in terms of the money they made with their program. The standard formula had the two playing cat and mouse with each other, Bruiser being the cat and Sheik being the mouse in the Indianapolis territory, and with the roles reversed in Detroit.

On Saturday September 7, 1974, The Sheik teamed with Bobby Heenan against Bruiser and Bobo Brazil at Comiskey Park in Chicago. Bruiser teased the match by airing an August 1974 Indianapolis match in which he pursued Sheik all over the ring, but was unable to get his hands on the madman from Syria. It was designed to instill Chicago wrestling fans with the notion that The Sheik feared The Bruiser, and the only way they could see the feud settled would be to attend the card at the ballpark. Once again, though, nothing was settled as Sheik burned Brazil with a ball of fire and pinned him.

MAIN EVENT: THE SHEIK, U.S. CHAMP vs. DICK THE BRUISER
WRESTLING
TOMORROW
SAT. 1st Bout 8 P.M.
Olympic
A Complete Big Card
SEE TV 20 | 50 | 9
THURSDAY 8-9 P.M. | 11-12 | 5-6
SATURDAY 5-6 P.M. | SATURDAY
For Res. 895-7000 #4,#5,#6,#7 #10
Olympia, Sears, Hudson's, Grinnell's

Detroit • August 31, 1974

In his first autobiography, Bobby Heenan said he considered that tag match to be "one of the biggest thrills of my life."

Payoff records from the card have survived (see below), showing this event to have one of the best box-office grosses for the Chicago Wrestling Club, Inc. The biggest payoffs of the night went to the wrestler/owners Dick the Bruiser, Verne Gagne, and Wilbur Snyder, reflecting their financial control in the organization and their position on the card line-up. The second tier of payroll consisted of Robinson, Sheik and Heenan. The next tier of payoffs belonged to the six men in the six-man tag team match. Here is a listing of the payoffs for this event, details of which had been a highly guarded subject.

— Charity Softball Game

On September 8, 1974, Bruiser and several WWA wrestlers — Cowboy Bob Ellis, Mike Snyder, Pepper Gomez, Mitsu Arakawa, Chief Bold Eagle, Sgt. Jacques Goulet, Don Fargo, Kim Duk, and "Gorgeous" Johnny Starr — played a charity softball game against reporters, editors, and photographers of the Indianapolis Star at Municipal Stadium in Indianapolis. Sam Menacker and pro boxer Marvin Johnson were umpires. The *Indianapolis Star* reported the wrestlers losing 14-11. *"A crowd of about 600, cheering enthusiastically for the wrestlers, watched the see-saw battle — which featured players running the bases backwards, among other oddities."*

CHICAGO WRESTLING CLUB, INC.
(an Illinois Corporation)

SCHEDULE OF TALENT PAYOUTS AND SHOW STATISTICS

Exhibition
(White Sox Park)
September 7, 1974

Payments to Wrestlers:	
Dick Bruiser	$ 3,500.00
Verne Gagne	3,300.00
Wilbur Snyder	3,500.00
Ray Stevens	1,100.00
Mike Snyder	100.00
Jim Brunzell	350.00
Chris Taylor	400.00
Bobby Heenan	1,500.00
Kim Duk	350.00
Pepper Gomez	600.00
Rene Goulet	600.00
Buddy Wolff	400.00
Walter Karbo	500.00
Larry Hennig	1,100.00
Ivan Putski	1,100.00
Nick Bockwinkle	1,100.00
Sam Menacker	300.00
Baron Von Raschke	600.00
Billy Robinson	2,750.00
R. Lisowski (Crusher)	1,100.00
Greg Gagne	400.00
Bobo Brazil	1,000.00
The Sheik	2,000.00
Superstar Billy Graham	1,100.00
Vivian Vachon	450.00
Lucille Dupree	300.00
E. Creechman	500.00
Ox Baker	500.00
Total Talent Payments	**$30,500.00**
Gross Admissions	$108,363.00
Percent of Talent to Gross Admissions	28.15%
Total Paid Attendance	16,989
Average Single Admission	$ 6.38

PREPARED WITHOUT AUDIT
CERTIFIED PUBLIC ACCOUNTANTS

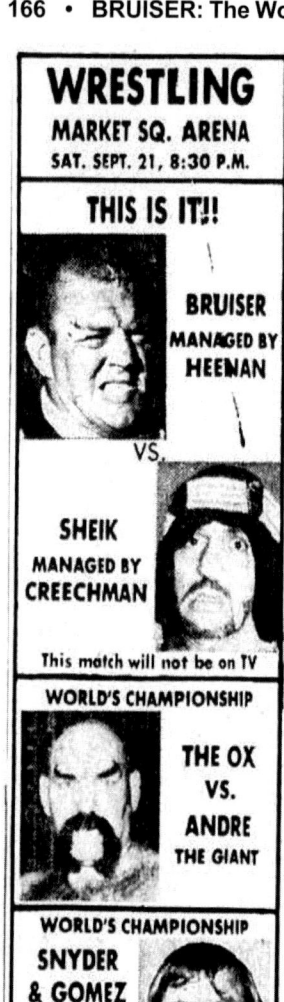

— Bobby Heenan Leaves

The second most important match-up in the Bruiser-Sheik program took place two weeks later — September 21, 1974 — at the newly built Market Square Arena in downtown Indianapolis. Bruiser and Snyder did great business two years earlier at the Expo Center and thought they might be able to catch lightning in a bottle once again.

The main event that night featured Dick the Bruiser and his perennial nemesis, "Pretty Boy" Bobby Heenan, against the Sheik and his manager, Eddie Creachman. Most wrestling fans would be quick to conclude that Heenan would wind up turning on Bruiser and joining forces with their opponents. Webmaster Chris Parsons attended that match and remembered, "*Heenan turned on the Bruiser, causing a near riot, the most heat I've ever seen.*"

A more interesting finish to the match took place in the dressing room. In Heenan's first book, *Bobby the Brain: Wrestling's Bad Boy Tells All*, Heenan said his main-event payoff was a mere $600, while The Sheik received $2,000. Considering Heenan's drawing ability, which no doubt helped draw the sellout crowd, he thought he deserved a payoff equal to that of The Sheik. Heenan quoted the Bruiser saying, "*If you can make more someplace else, you can go do it.*" Heenan added "*I gave notice on a few Indianapolis wrestling cards under the ownership of Bruiser and Snyder and finished up to go back to the AWA.*"

Heenan made sporadic Christmas season appearances during the '70s when he returned to Indianapolis during the holidays to visit his mother, but the author and many long-time fans of the WWA believe the loss of Heenan was the first step of a ten-year gradual decline of the promotion. No other villain was able to elicit the steady and intensive animosity from WWA wrestling fans. The follow-up cast of managers couldn't come close to matching Heenan's skills on the microphone. Wilbur's son, Mike Snyder, who was still wrestling in Indianapolis in 1974, looked back at Heenan's importance in the WWA:

"*I remember him carrying towels to the ring and he was nothing. Then, before you knew it, they made him this manager-type. He had a way with words and knew how to make it work. And then, he was unbelievably one hell of a performer in the ring. Heenan trained me and showed me how to do it. Unfortunately, he was Dick's whipping boy. He was treated like hell by Dick, but treated like a king by Wilbur. He was upfront with me about that."*

Heenan was not the only wrestler with payoff issues after the spectacular at Market Square Arena. Veteran Bobby Bold Eagle had his own dispute:

"He [the Bruiser] paid me. He gave me a check and I didn't like the payoff. The whole deal was we had a sellout [at Market Square Arena]. When he gave me the check, I went back to him and said 'Here,' *and put the check back in his pocket. I wouldn't cash it. I said,* 'Here you are. Go buy yourself something from me ... a night out.' *I then walked away. He [the Bruiser] would send the money with one of the other wrestlers. The Bruiser said,* 'If you don't take it, you are fired.' *He fired me ten times. When the time came at the TV station, he came up to me and said,* 'I'm going to give you this check for the last time, and if you don't take it, you can pack your bags and get out.' *By that time, I needed the money, anyway. He picked up the check and wrote underneath,* 'overpaid for talent.'"

— The Business of Professional Wrestling

While wrestling fans think of professional wrestling as "sports entertainment" or an "athletic exhibition," or even a "real sport," professional wrestling is, first and foremost, a business enterprise that provides services to a consumer base in exchange for cash payments. Promoters hope (and still do today) that the money generated from tickets sales and other revenue streams will exceed the production costs. Like any other business, the enterprise must be profitable to provide dividends to the owners and generate positive cash flow.

— Private Finances

Promoters never divulged many details regarding finances of their promotions. For the most part, true numbers were private affairs of the company owners. The owners had to reveal details to the state athletic commissions, who took a percentage of the gross receipts, but owners didn't reveal as much detail to their workers — those wrestlers who were compensated based on a percentage of the adjusted gross receipts. Some promoters adjusted the gross receipts for the taxes paid to various government entities, and occasionally adjusted for the expense of producing the local television programing. The local wrestling TV program was vital to help draw wrestling fans into the "live" venues. Research by legendary pro-wrestling historian J. Michael Kenyon revealed a sampling of how much money could be made for both promoters and their star performers.

— Cutting up the Pie

A good example would be the card held Thursday, February 11, 1960, at the Fairgrounds Coliseum in Indianapolis. At the time, the promotion was owned and operated by Jim Barnett and Balk Estes. In the main event, Dick the Bruiser teamed with Gene Kiniski against Roy Shire and Ray Shire (Ray Stevens) and 11,824 fans paid $26,312 with an average ticket price of $2.23. The gross receipts were adjusted downward by 13 percent for federal and state taxes of $3,444 and by another $4,568 for televisions costs, leaving adjusted gross receipts of $18,300.

The fifteen wrestlers on the card in aggregate were paid $6,405, or 35 percent of the adjusted gross receipts. The main event participants each received a $1,000 payoff, while the other wrestlers on the card received either $200 or $300, depending on their placement on the card. To keep the Bruiser's earnings capacity in perspective, the average personal annual income for a male worker in 1960 was $4,080. As for the bosses, Estes received a $500 payoff and Barnett got $1,250. After those expenses, a net profit of $2,523 remained.

A song in Irving Berlin's 1945 musical, *Annie Get Your Gun*, was titled "There's No Business Like Show Business." That certainly was true in the world of professional wrestling during the early 1960s.

— Payoff Formula

Bob Luce's television program lasted into the '80s and helped promote the wrestling cards at the International Amphitheatre, and occasionally, at Comiskey Park and Soldier Field. Financial records of payoffs made to wrestlers who appeared on many of those Chicago cards give great insights into the business of professional wrestling.

The author, whose real-life work duties include financial analysis, reviewed payoff schedules for ten wrestling events at the International Amphitheatre during the time span of 1974 to 1977. Two unusual cards were excluded from the survey; one at a ballpark and one with a two-ring battle royal, both in 1974.

It is now commonly understood that wrestlers were allocated an approximate 30 percent of the gross revenues or after-tax revenues, depending on the town. From this pool of monies, wrestlers were traditionally paid on a graduated scale, beginning with the preliminary wrestlers being paid the least and ending with a main event star being paid the most. The following table summarizes the payoff hierarchy during one of the most successful periods for the Chicago Wrestling Club, Inc. These percentages, based on the payoffs as believed to be reported to the Illinois State Athletic Commission, are rounded up and are approximate.

Owner / Wrestler Category	Percent of Revenue
Owner who is the only owner wrestling on the card	6.00 percent
Owner who is not on the card	1.50 percent
Owner with other owners on the card	3.00 percent
Non-owner main-event wrestler	2.50 percent
Non-owner main-event manager	1.50 percent
Non-owner semi-final wrestler	2.00 percent
Non-owner mid-card wrestler	1.25 percent
Non-owner lower-card wrestler	0.70 percent
Non-owner opening-match wrestler	0.50 percent
Non-owner opening-match manager	0.25 percent

The actual dollar payoffs appear to be rounded up to the nearest $50 or $100 increment, and the percentages approximate the mid-point of the ranges surveyed. Wrestlers who worked more than one match were granted both payoffs, such as Heenan wrestling one match and managing in another match. Sometimes, selected non-owner main-event wrestlers, such as experienced

Chapter 19 • 169

veterans like The Sheik or Ray Stevens, would get payoffs closer to four percent when they were booked against Bruiser in the main event on cards when no other owners wrestled. Wrestlers who were on standby (in case somebody did not show up) were paid somewhat less than a non-owner opening-match wrestler for just waiting around the dressing room that night. Obviously, the biggest share of the monies went to the owners who wrestled, although the owners reduced their payoff percentages when the box-office receipts were relatively low. These figures probably do not include dividends paid to the owners based on the operational results of the company. Wrestling veteran Baron Von Raschke pointed out, "*They* [owners] *have the first count and get most of the money.*"

The Sheik vs. Dick the Bruiser • Chicago White Sox Park • September 7, 1974
Source: William Ondecko

PART IV
SLOW FALL FROM GRACE

Chapter 20
Ten Year Decline Begins — 1975-1976

ALL-STAR CHAMPIONSHIP WRESTLING
Wed., Nov. 26, 8 p.m.
DICK the BRUISER
Plus Many Others
Delphi Community High School
Tickets available from Delphi Jaycees

Hometown spot show
Delphi, Indiana
November 26, 1975

Even though business was good in 1974, Bruiser and Snyder were conscious of the need to recruit new talent. Bruiser and Snyder went back to the drawing board for their new cast and brought in new players.

— Sgt. Jacques Goulet and the Legionnaires

In June 1974, long-time veteran Rene Goulet was brought in to play the role of a sadistic drill sergeant from the French Foreign Legion. Goulet, who had previously portrayed a handsome and sophisticated Frenchman in the AWA, had new instructions from Dick the Bruiser:

"*I came back from a trip to Japan and went to the TV studio* [in Indianapolis]. *Bruiser put the* [Legionnaire] *hat in my hand and said I was going to be Sgt. Jacques Goulet.* [Bruiser] *told me to talk like Mad Dog Vachon and Chris Markoff, and handed me a broken horsewhip.*"

It is believed the creation of the character could have been inspired by feature films released in 1926 and 1939, both called *Beau Geste*. The French Foreign Legion, a military unit known for training that was both physically challenging and psychologically stressful, was the perfect subject for a heel wrestler.

As an officer in the Legion, Goulet needed a subordinate. That role was filled by another wrestling veteran, Don Kalt, who had wrestled in Indianapolis earlier as Jack Dillinger. Fargo returned to the territory as Private Don Fargo.

Fargo was enthusiastic about the Foreign Legion role and enhanced the costumes with puffy plume pants over wrestling trunks with French flag colors of red, white, and blue. In his autobiography, *The Hard Way*, Fargo relates several hilarious stories about his time with Goulet, including smashing the grill of Goulet's car in a parking lot and leaving the scene of the accident, forgetting to put on his wrestling trunks and accidentally exposing the audience to his

The Legionnaires • 1974
Source: William Ondecko

red speedos when taking off the plume pants, and smearing limburger cheese over his body to hide the smell of alcohol on his breath from Wilbur Snyder.

The Legionnaires had a gimmick series of matches with Bruiser and various partners, one of which was an Algerian hood death match, in which each wrestler wore a cloth sack over his head. Supposedly, this was what people wore when sentenced to death via the guillotine during the French Revolution of 1789. When Fargo left the territory in March 1975, he was replaced by French-Canadian wrestler Pierre Lafleur, who later wrestled in the WWA as Igor Volkoff. Lafleur came in as Private Zarinoff LeBeouf. LeBeouf would later wrestle for the WWF with Scott Irwin as Pierre and Eric, the Yukon Lumberjacks.

— Ox Baker

The next wrestling personality arrived in Indianapolis in June 1974 after making wrestling headlines in the early '70s. Douglas (Ox) Baker, a former amateur wrestler in Iowa, made his professional debut in the Central States territory. On June 13, 1971, Ox and his tag-team partner, The Claw (Tom Andrews), faced Alberto Torres and Bob Ellis in Verdigre, Nebraska. After the match, Torres complained of pain, was admitted to the hospital, and died a few days later. On August 1, 1972, Ox was wrestling in Savannah, Georgia, against promotion co-owner Ray Gunkel. In the dressing room after the match, Gunkel suffered a massive heart attack and died. In the aftermath of both of these tragedies, local wrestling promoters

Ox Baker

exploited the situation and suggested that Ox Baker had been responsible for the deaths. For years afterwards, Ox claimed his signature wrestling maneuver, the heart punch, could permanently maim an opponent. Baker's famous saying was, "*I love to hurt people.*"

Ox Baker was involved in one of the worst riots to take place at a wrestling card in the United States. In January 1974, during a match at the Cleveland Arena in Ohio, Ox repeatedly administered his "deadly" heart punch to a prone and helpless Ernie Ladd. The crowd went berserk, storming ringside and throwing folding chairs into the ring. With security personnel unable to protect him, Ox ran for the dressing room. Along the way, he was hit in the head by a flying chair and had to get stitches. A silent home movie captured the mayhem. Dick the Bruiser likely appreciated explosive events like that because they generated a lot of publicity.

Ox remembered an important call he received in 1974:

"*Sam Menacker called me and said,* 'Dick the Bruiser wants you up here right away [as] you wore out your welcome in Atlanta.' *That was a new world with Dick the Bruiser. When you talk about the stars I had over the years, Dick the Bruiser was probably the best and biggest star I became associated with. He was a legend everywhere.*"

Ox recalled that Bruiser anticipated a long drawn-out program between them and told him they would "knock down commissioners, beat up referees, and fight back to the dressing room." Bruiser told Ox they would face each other 60 to 70 times. Promoter Bob Luce repeatedly ran the Cleveland riot footage to build up Ox's arrival. Bruiser and Snyder decided to put the WWA heavyweight belt on Ox, who won the title from Cowboy Bob Ellis in Indianapolis at the Expo Center on Saturday, August 10, 1974. After the match, Sam Menacker handed the microphone to Ox, who told the crowd:

> "I didn't come here to make friends. I didn't come here to kiss babies. I came here to show you the greatest wrestling machine in the world today. You people have got to believe it's Ox Baker because I believe it's Ox Baker. Every person in the audience knows. Ladies and gentlemen, I did you a favor. He [Ellis] has run his last race. He's roped his last horse. And now all he can do is go in the back yard and milk a few cows. He doesn't belong in wrestling. He doesn't belong in the same ring as Ox Baker."

Ox spent the better part of three years feuding with Dick the Bruiser and remembered:

> "In the ring, he (Bruiser) was as tough as he wanted to be. You had to stay on Dick the Bruiser and pound on him or he would gobble you up. All the matches, I jumped him right away. When he was ready, Dick the Bruiser knew when he would make a comeback. If you potatoed [really connected with a punch] Dick the Bruiser when he made his comeback, he would put a knot on the top of your head."

Dick the Bruiser's pre-match oratory was relatively limited. However, Ox Baker's pre-match orations were major events on WSNS-TV in Chicago:

> "Dick the Bruiser, you've had that ugly mug around long enough in Chicago. It's been ten years. These people are tired of you. They've had enough of you, Bruiser. So I have put it on myself to get rid of you to really show the people the number-one man, the class of Chicago, is Ox Baker. I'm going to beat you like I own you. I'm going to run you out of Chicago. You don't belong here. Bruiser, Chicago doesn't need you anymore. They need Ox Baker. All I can tell these people is I've got a secret to hurt you. You're going to retire after this match tonight because I know how to stomp you. I'm going to prove it tonight, Bruiser. I'm going to hurt you ... and I'm going to hurt you bad."

In a September 1995 interview with Scott Teal, Ox gave credit to Bruiser for teaching him more than he already knew about getting heat.

> "Dick the Bruiser taught me that all you had to do was argue that your shoulder was raised up on three ... argue with the old fat woman in the front row ... and you got your heat right back. I see all these prima donnas today. 'I can't get beat. People would hate me.' And that's probably true because they don't know how to use that psychology, and that thinking. Dick told me once, 'Put a stick in your trunks at the start of the match, and the whole match, reach for that stick. Plan never to take that stick out of your trunks.' He got more heat out of that then if he took the stick out and wiped out six people. You and I both know, the audience wants to participate and anticipate. They want to be part of the action. That's why tag team matches are so popular. The guy didn't tag in ... he cheated behind the referee's back. If you can get the audience involved, yelling and frothing at the mouth, they stay with you."

Later in the interview, Ox talked about his final days in the promotion:

I did very good with Dick, but he only wanted to run a couple of nights a week. He had millions and millions of dollars, and didn't need it. He treated me real good. I made four or five hundred a week, but I never had a six-hundred-dollar week. We filled up the Amphitheatre in Chicago eight straight times, but in three years, that was probably the eight best payoffs that I had. So, after a while, I said, "Bruiser, I have rent and a family in Missouri. I can't do it on just five hundred dollars a week." Dick started sending me to other places, but by the time I drove around, I was eating up what extra money I was making.

— Handsome Johnny Starr

Around the same time that Ox Baker was being groomed for his long-running program with Bruiser, a young, undergraduate English major at Indiana University was breaking into the business in Kentucky, and then attempting to get a wrestling promoter's license in Indiana. Since their start-up in 1964, Bruiser and Snyder had been the only ones allowed to have a promoter's license in Indiana. This newcomer, John B. Davis, of nearby Greenfield, Indiana, had been a standout scholar/athlete in high school. He used to watch Bruiser and Snyder on local television. The head of the Indiana Athletic Commission, Kelse McClure, talked Davis out of pursuing his promoter's license and introduced him to Bruiser and Snyder. In

Ox Baker & Johnny Starr
Source: William Ondecko

the same year Bobby Heenan left the promotion, Davis became "Handsome Johnny Starr," replete with a pink, glittering jumpsuit. Starr, assigned to be Ox Baker's manager and occasional tag-team partner, remembered Bruiser saying he could take anybody and train them to replace Heenan. "*I guess I was anybody,*" said Starr.

— Challenger to Jack Brisco

Bruiser would have some prominent challenges for the NWA world heavyweight title against Jack Brisco in the mid-'70s. Jack Brisco defeated Harley Race for the NWA crown on July 20, 1973, in Houston. While he held the title, he defended the title twice in St. Louis against Bruiser (January 3 and June 20, 1975). Jack's brother, Gerald Brisco, had many memories about their matches, particularly the first go-around:

"*It was a total contrast of styles. My brother was really concerned about the match. My brother was a pure wrestler and, of course, Dick was a brawler and a fighter, a completely unorthodox and different style than my brother. Sam Muchnick came to my brother and suggested the match would be a tremendous draw. At the time, St. Louis was based on pure clean wrestling* [in] *the tradition of the Funks, Race, Thesz, and O'Connor*

Jack Brisco vs. Dick the Bruiser
St. Louis • 1975
Source: William Ondecko

... guys like that. Sam and Dick were buddies, and he [Sam] figured that if anybody could handle the match if it got out of control, Jack could, and pull it back together. They went out [and] it was a pretty damned good match. It didn't get out of hand. I think my brother was proud of it, and he was a big fan of Dick the Bruiser, also. We grew up reading those wrestling magazines."

— Gunshots at the Amphitheatre

On January 25, 1975, while Bruiser was teaming with Yukon Moose Cholak in Indianapolis against Sgt. Jacques Goulet and Private Don Fargo, a card in the Chicago Amphitheatre featured a main event between Verne Gagne and Nick Bockwinkel.

After Verne pinned Bockwinkel, five gunshots rang out. They came from the mezzanine and were aimed at the ring. The headline on the front page of the *Chicago Sun Times* the next day read, "Gunman Shoots 5 at Amphitheatre." The paper reported, "...A man suddenly stood up and fired into the crowd." The shooter was described as having "shoulder length wavy hair, about 5-foot-10 inches, and weighed about 250 lbs," but escaped amidst the panic and pandemonium. Photos of the wounded victims and a composite sketch of the alleged shooter appeared in the newspaper on Monday January 27. The paper noted that the shooter "was annoyed by a referee's call in a wrestling match," in which Heenan interfered, setting up Gagne for a pin by Bockwinkel. The referee, however, saw through the subterfuge and ordered the match to continue. That was verified by another witness, who believed the shooter was outraged with the first decision in which Bockwinkel was awarded the match. John Husar of the *Chicago Tribune* headlined his column with a quote from an up-close witness: *"I saw the orange fire ... then the gun."* The witness's shoulder was used as an "aiming platform" by the shooter, and with the barrel of the gun so close to his ear, he thought his head was going to explode.

Bob Luce took the situation seriously and, at the next Amphitheatre card in February, everyone entering the Amphitheatre had to pass through metal detectors.

— More New Faces

Joining the WWA ranks in March 1975 was former NWA world heavyweight champion Lou Thesz, then 59 years old. Chris Parsons remembers the Indiana State Athletic Commission being concerned about Thesz' age and insisted on a physical exam, which he passed easily. In one of several interviews with Thesz conducted by Scott Teal, Thesz told him:

"Many years ago, at the Schroeder Hotel in Milwaukee, there was what you might call a shoot before the matches. Verne Gagne and the Bruiser were in the main event, and they had a professional disagreement while still at the hotel. Dick, who believed his own publicity and fancied himself

a brawler, decided to settle the dispute with his fists. Verne knocked him out cold. It's a credit to the Bruiser that he admitted to all of us in the dressing room what had happened. Of course, most of us already knew it — and, I must add, those of us who knew Verne were not at all surprised at the outcome."

In June 1975, Chuck O'Connor made his first appearance in the WWA, wrestling twice on a TV taping. O'Connor, who stood 6-foot-10, would change his name to Big John Studd in the '80s and go on to have legendary matches with Andre the Giant in the WWF.

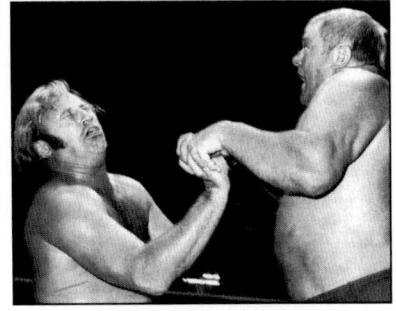

Nick Bockwinkel vs. The Bruiser Milwaukee
Source: Dave Maciejewski

— Last AWA Tag Title Reign

In 1975, Nick Bockwinkel and Ray Stevens were in their third run as AWA tag team champions. Bobby Heenan, their manager, said the following about The Crusher during that time:

"You know what I'm laughing about? All those beautiful holds the Crusher is putting on — the punches, the slaps, the chops, the kicks — everything illegal. And what do the idiot people do in this town? They applaud a man like that."

Bruiser and Crusher held the AWA tag team championship on four previous occasions. On Saturday, August 16, 1975, at Chicago's International Amphitheatre, they defeated Bockwinkel and Stevens to become five-time champions. Bruiser and Crusher held the title for eleven months before dropping the straps to Black Jack Lanza and "Bad Boy" Bobby Duncum.

Crusher & Bruiser in Winnipeg, Manitoba • 1976
Source: Terrance Machalek

— Challenger to Terry Funk

On December 10, 1975, Jack Brisco dropped the NWA crown to Terry Funk in Miami, and Bruiser was a natural challenger. As with Brisco, Bruiser received two shots at the title in the Kiel (April 23, 1976 & January 3, 1977). Terry wrote to the author during the compilation of this biography and said:

> "Dick was a great character in the business. [I] loved wrestling him. [He was] a great box office attraction. You always went to the bank with a smile on your face after a match with him."

In Terry autobiography, *Terry Funk: More Than Just Hardcore*, Funk noticed Bruiser's occasional aversion to bleeding, or "getting color" as it's known in the wrestling business. Funk said he remembered Bruiser refusing to get blood when requested by a booker or promoter, claiming he couldn't do it because he was scheduled to go to a wedding. That excuse came from the same guy who made tons of money having Bobby Heenan, Jimmy Valiant, or Baron Von Raschke bleed buckets in Indianapolis.

— Muhammad Ali vs. Antonio Inoki

On June 25, 1976, former world heavyweight boxing champion Muhammad Ali faced Japanese heavyweight wrestler Antonio Inoki in a "boxer vs. wrestler" exhibition. The event, which took place in Tokyo's Budokan Hall, was broadcast worldwide via closed-circuit television. Many pro wrestling promoters got behind the event and booked theaters in their territory for closed-circuit showings. Each promoter also booked matches featuring their local talent as warm-up bouts. In Indianapolis, Wilbur Snyder headlined in a non-title main event against The Masked Strangler (John Steele Hill, who wrestled as Guy Mitchell). In Chicago, the main events were Verne Gagne vs. Nick Bockwinkel and Bruiser & Crusher against Lanza & Duncum. Those two matches were broadcast into several other AWA cities, as well. All venues saw the Ali-Inoki bout, as well as another special event from Shea Stadium in New York City pitting Andre the Giant against boxer Chuck Wepner.

Bruiser, Kenny Jay, Muhammad Ali & Verne Gagne
Source: Frederic Stein

An event of such proportions was given much more publicity than would normally be given to a pro-wrestling event. On June 10, 1976, a publicity event was staged at the International Amphitheatre for ABC-TV's *Wide World of Sports*. The inimitable Howard Cosell handled the commentary as Muhammed Ali took part in "exhibitions" against AWA wrestlers Kenny "Sodbuster" Jay and "Beautiful" Buddy Wolfe. Verne Gagne served as the referee and Bruiser seconded Jay and Wolfe. Kenny Jay says he "got a telephone call from Wally Karbo and was told to go to the airport," where he learned he was flying to Chicago to face Ali. Jay was eventually "knocked out" by Ali, of which the *Chicago Daily News* wrote, "Kenny Jay was just a hunk of cannon fodder offered to Ali."

Next up was Buddy Wolfe, who recalled *"they wanted someone who could take care of himself in the ring."* Wolfe remembers Bruiser "continually shouting very helpful instructions throughout the entire match." As the match unfolded, Wolfe gave Ali two backbreakers, only to see him kick out both times. Cosell complimented Wolfe's "beautiful performance" and added, *"They must have good dramatic classes at St. Cloud."* St. Cloud State was Wolfe's alma mater. Cosell warned, *"However fictional the scene, Ali could get hurt."* Ali won the three-round exhibition as Wolfe bled from the forehead from obviously self-inflicted cuts. After the third round, the defeated Wolfe charged across the ring to sneak attack Ali. Bruiser and Blassie helped pull Wolfe away and stood him up, allowing Ali to deliver an unobstructed right uppercut, which sent Wolfe flying. Cosell blurted out, *"That was a two-and-a-half back flip."* Afterwards, Ali was interviewed at ringside by a very young Vincent K. McMahon of the WWWF. Ali said, *"I am the Lord of the Ring. Not only the wrestling ring, but the boxing ring."*

The actual match on June 25, 1976, between Ali and Inoki was universally panned as Inoki spent almost the entire match sitting on the mat and kicking at Ali's legs with his feet. It seems the two superstars couldn't agree on a finish for the match, so they both stayed on defense. It was a sad chapter in the attempt to merge boxing and wrestling. Larry Matysik later quoted St. Louis promoter Sam Muchnick, who said, *"I'm glad that's over with."*

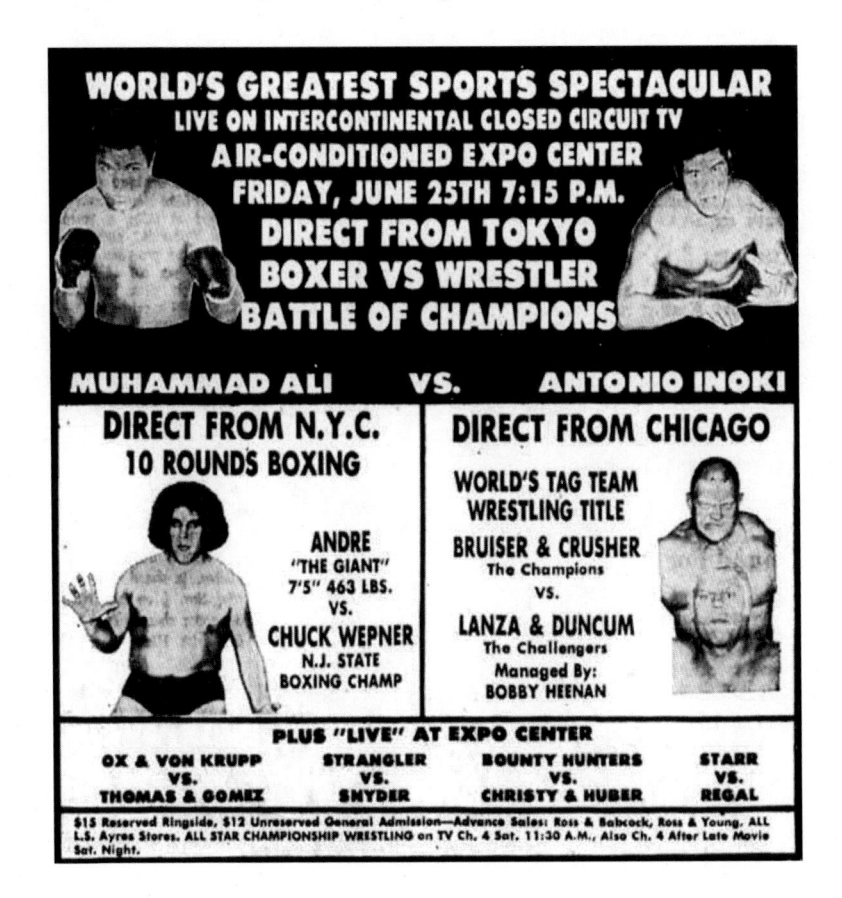

WORLD'S GREATEST SPORTS SPECTACULAR
LIVE ON INTERCONTINENTAL CLOSED CIRCUIT TV
AIR-CONDITIONED EXPO CENTER
FRIDAY, JUNE 25TH 7:15 P.M.
DIRECT FROM TOKYO
BOXER VS WRESTLER
BATTLE OF CHAMPIONS

MUHAMMAD ALI VS. **ANTONIO INOKI**

DIRECT FROM N.Y.C.
10 ROUNDS BOXING

ANDRE
"THE GIANT"
7'5" 463 LBS.
VS.
CHUCK WEPNER
N.J. STATE
BOXING CHAMP

DIRECT FROM CHICAGO
WORLD'S TAG TEAM
WRESTLING TITLE
BRUISER & CRUSHER
The Champions
VS.
LANZA & DUNCUM
The Challengers
Managed By:
BOBBY HEENAN

PLUS "LIVE" AT EXPO CENTER

OX & VON KRUPP	STRANGLER	BOUNTY HUNTERS	STARR
VS.	VS.	VS.	VS.
THOMAS & GOMEZ	SNYDER	CHRISTY & HUBER	REGAL

$15 Reserved Ringside, $12 Unreserved General Admission—Advance Sales: Ross & Babcock, Ross & Young, ALL L.S. Ayres Stores. ALL STAR CHAMPIONSHIP WRESTLING on TV Ch. 4 Sat. 11:30 A.M., Also Ch. 4 After Late Movie Sat. Night.

Chapter 21
Another Bruiser Arrives — 1977-1979

— The Masked Strangler

In mid-1975, veteran wrestler Guy Mitchell returned to the WWA territory, this time under a mask as The Masked Strangler. The Strangler provided competent and reliable lead competition for Bruiser and other top babyfaces. Also joining the roster on a steady basis was youngster Michael (Spike) Huber, an Indianapolis native who had married Bruiser's daughter, Michelle.

Going into 1976, a new heel tag team arrived in the form of the Bounty Hunters, David and Jerry Novak, managed by their spokesman Cashbox Jim Kent. While this new group stirred decent interest among fans, they never came close to replicating the tag team tradition of the recent WWA past — the Blackjacks, the Valiants, or the Legionnaires.

— Ivan Koloff

The real bright spot that enhanced the Indianapolis territory in spring 1977 was the arrival of former WWWF heavyweight champion Ivan (The Russian Bear) Koloff. Koloff recalled:

> "Dick wanted me in Indiana right after a short Japan trip. Dick the Bruiser was his own boss, and he went out of his way to help me. The Bruiser said, 'You cooperate with me, and I won't hurt you.' Bruiser was an idol to me as I saw him on TV before I started wrestling."

The chemistry between Koloff and the Bruiser was somewhere between excellent and outstanding. Ivan noted:

> "Dick respected me because he knew I would make a good accounting of myself. The Bruiser and I were both short and stocky. Fans knew about my successful run in the WWWF, so I had both credibility and ability."

WRESTLING EXPO CENTER
SAT., OCT. 9TH
8:30 P.M.

BRUISER VS THE STRANGLER
(THIS BOUT WILL NOT BE ON TV)

BOUNTY HUNTERS VS SNYDER & MILLER

6 MORE BIG BOUTS

Indianapolis, Indiana
Oct. 9, 1976

In one of Ivan's first matches in the territory, he won a 16-man battle royal in Indianapolis on March 5, 1977. Koloff went on to headline Indianapolis six times against Bruiser, including a cage match finale on December 26, 1977. Koloff remembered, "*I had the idea of jumping off the cage onto a prone Dick the Bruiser, who rolled away. Our objective always was to draw a full house and make it interesting enough to bring the people back the next week.*" Bruiser and Koloff also had two main events at the Amphitheatre. Ivan joked, "*I even rode back from Chicago with Dick once, sneaking out the back to avoid fans'* views." In Ivan's book, "*Is That Wrestling Fake?,*" he wrote about an experience he had with Bruiser:

> "*Bruiser loved to drink champagne. He always had two or three bottles with him. After leaving Chicago one night, he was driving 100 mph. Dick always did off-the-wall things, but this time, he even scared me. I was yelling, 'Stop the car and let me out!'*
>
> *He just looked at me and grinned, then turned the steering wheel and drove down into a ditch ... still at 100 mph. When he pulled back up onto the road, he said, 'Did I scare ya?'*
>
> *'What do you think?' I asked.*
>
> *That was the only time I can remember riding with one of my opponents. I had flown into Chicago from Florida and I needed a ride, so we waited until the fans left and I snuck out to Bruiser's car.*"

— **Angelo Mosca**

Ivan Koloff vs. Bruiser • 1977
Source: Scott Romer

During the second half of 1977, Bruiser took on various tag team partners to face the team of Super Destroyer and Angelo Mosca. Mosca had played football at the University of Notre Dame and was a veteran of the Hamilton Tiger Cats of the Canadian Football League. Both Bruiser and Mosca were interior linemen and had made smooth transitions from the gridiron to the wrestling ring. One could speculate that a match-up between Dick the Bruiser and Angelo Mosca would be a natural fit — an all-out brawl with no scientific maneuvers. On May 20, 1978, the city of Chicago hosted the first of three match-ups between the two. One month later, they faced off in a chain match, with the blow-off match taking place in a cage on July 15. Mosca considered the Bruiser to be one of the top brawlers in wrestling, along with King Kong Brody and The Crusher. He later pointed out that *"we're show biz and we're entertainers."* He doesn't remember how the Chicago-only bouts came about, but admitted, "*We got kind of lucky.*" In 2010, when he recalled the series with Bruiser, and said:

> "*I wasn't scared at all. I had confidence that I could handle myself. We never really conversed, Dick and I* [before the matches]. [It was] *just one of those things; we got matched up and it worked and clicked. We never really talked to each other about our football profession.*"

Jasper, Indiana
October 28, 1977

— Pepper Gomez

One of the big names who came to Indianapolis three times was Pepper Gomez, The Man with the Cast Iron Stomach. Pepper did well the first two times in (1971 and 1973-74), but wasn't happy with his payoffs the third time around:

> "The last time [July 1978] I went to Indianapolis, it was the shits. Then Bruiser screwed me on my payoff. I asked him, 'Why are you giving these guys more money than me?'
> He said, 'Well, they're all world champions.'
> I said, 'Come on, Dick. It's a work.'
> He stole my money from me. He had me booked in main events in all these different towns that week, so I packed my car and came home ... left him holding the bag."

(from *Wrestling Archive Project: Classic 20th Century Mat Memories*, volume 1, Crowbar Press, 2015)

— Missouri State Title

Back in St. Louis, Dick the Bruiser won the Missouri state title on three occasions, the first being July 14, 1978, when he defeated Dick Murdoch. The promotion that followed was leading towards a showdown between Bruiser and Frank "King Kong" Brody.

— Lawsuit by International Championship Wrestling

In August 1979, Bruiser and Snyder had an out-of-the ring courtroom conflict with the Poffo family — Angelo, Lanny, and Randy. Angelo, the patriarch of the family, had worked for Bruiser and Snyder many times, while his sons would achieve notable success as pro wrestlers years later as Randy "Macho Man" Savage and Leaping Lanny Poffo. The Poffos, who owned a wrestling promotion called International Championship Wrestling, Inc., sued nine territorial wrestling promoters in the U.S. The defendants included Nick Gulas, George Gulas and Tom Renesto (Nashville, TN); Eddie Graham (Tampa, FL); James E. Barnett (Atlanta, GA); Ed Farhat (Williamston, MI); Verne Gagne (Minneapolis, MN); Jerry Jarrett and Jerry Lawler (Memphis, TN); Buddy Fuller (Knoxville, TN); Robert Geigel (Kansas City, MO): and Wilbur Snyder and Dick Aflis (Indianapolis, IN). The promoters were charged with establishing an illegal monopoly in the professional wrestling industry. In addition, the plantiffs claimed the group of promoters prevented them from appearing on any of the established promoters' wrestling events. They sought $2.4 million in damages, a temporary restraining order, and payment of all court costs.

In 2015, Leaping Lanny Poffo told the author "the case was thrown out." Internet sources reported that original witnesses or deposition sources failed to stick with their statements supporting the plaintiffs.

— King Kong Brody

As significant as the feuds with Ivan Koloff and Angelo Mosca were in the late '70s, the most high-profile feud for Bruiser in both Chicago and Indianapolis was with King Kong Brody, aka Bruiser Brody. Before he got into wrestling, Brody played football at West Texas State and with the Washington Redskins. He even had a stint as a sports writer with the *San Antonio Express-News*. Brody had a legendary run against Bruno Sammartino in the WWWF in the mid-'70s and would become one of the biggest wrestling stars in Japan. Brody stood at around 6-feet-8 inches tall, towered over most opponents, and became one of the best brawlers in wrestling history. Two biographies have been written about Brody: *Bruiser Brody* by Emerson Murray and *Brody: The Triumph and Tragedy of Wrestling's Rebel* by Larry Matysik and Barbara Goodish.

It is said that Brody changed his identity to "King Kong" from "Bruiser" when he arrived in territories where Dick the Bruiser had a long-established identity. Dick the Bruiser and King Kong Brody first faced each other in fall 1978 in the Central States (Kansas City) territory and afterwards in St. Louis. The feud migrated to Indianapolis and Chicago throughout 1979 and 1980, and their battles were witnessed in places like Fort Wayne, Indiana, and Springfield, Illinois. The battle of the "Bruisers" over the years included Texas death matches, lumberjack matches, chain matches, and cage matches. Rarely did the fans see a scientific hold or move during one of the set-tos.

In the book *Bruiser Brody*, author Emerson Murray wrote the following:

"Brody actually beat Dick the Bruiser in a match on April 1, 1979 to win exclusive use of the name "Bruiser." Dick the Bruiser, for a short time, called himself Dick the Loser during interviews, while announcer Sam Menacker called him, "Just plain Dick." Later that month, Dick the Bruiser's WWA title was also held up when Brody defeated him via disqualification. On June 9, 1979, Dick the Bruiser got revenge when he defeated Brody by countout to regain the vacated WWA title.

"Since Dick owned the WWA, he could call himself anything he wanted, so even though Dick never won back the title of "Bruiser," on August 4, 1979, "King Kong" Brody defeated Dick the "Bruiser" for his WWA title in a Texas Death Match. Brody held the belt for over nine months until Dick the Bruiser regained the title on May 31, 1980."

Both combatants had massive egos and it is believed neither man liked "selling" for the other guy — wrestling defensively and letting the opponent have sizable offensive advantages. By the time their feud began, Brody had established himself as a free-agent persona who marched to his own drummer, which could make for a potential conflict with Dick the Bruiser, who was the dominating co-owner and top dog of the promotion. Their "in-the-ring" feud spilled over into an "out-of-the-ring" feud over the never-ending dispute of payoffs. Author Larry Matysik, one of Brody's best personal friends, noted that "*always sensitive about money, Brody felt that the Bruiser had shorted him.*" Verbal negotiations didn't seem to resolve the disputes. Their disagreements came to a head at a January 27, 1981, spot show in Peoria, Illinois. Dick and Brody were opponents in the main event that night. However, the two "Bruisers" also went at it for real in the locker room. As Matysik wrote, "*Frank [Brody] cracked Dick's head open, knocking him goofy, and a row of lockers was demolished.*" On Friday

February 6, 1981, both wrestlers were scheduled to appear on Sam Muchnick's wrestling card at the Kiel Auditorium in St. Louis. Matysik described their reunion in his Brody biography:

> "*Brody stomped up the steps. Dick came around the corner. He held out his hand with thumb cocked and forefinger and middle finger extended like a gun. Between the fingers was a check. 'Here,' snapped Dick. Dick nodded. 'We're square then.' Brody examined the check and said, 'That's fine. Thanks.'*"

Dick the Bruiser and King Kong Brody would never face each other in a singles match again. Brody later told Matysik that Dick put up a respectable fight in Peoria and "*must have been something when he was thirty.*" Never again would Dick the Bruiser have a steady opponent in the ring of the same imposing stature as King Kong Brody. Tragically, Brody was fatally stabbed in another locker room incident on Saturday, July 16, 1988, at Juan Loubriel Stadium in Bayamon, Puerto Rico.

— Another "Bruiser" Contender

Two weeks after Bruiser's initial match in St. Louis against Brody, Bruiser faced "Bruiser" Bob Sweetan at Kiel Auditorium with the Bruiser nickname at stake. Bruiser won with an atomic drop in 11 minutes, 21 seconds.

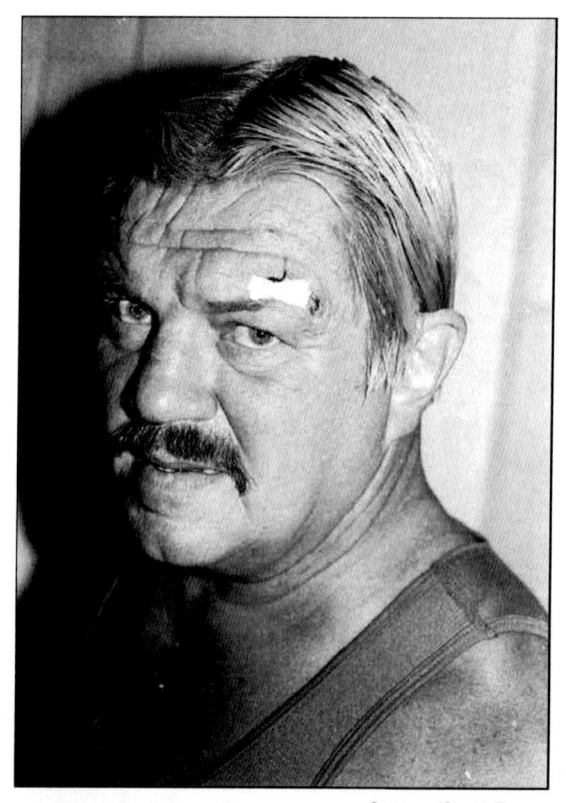

Source: Scott Romer

Chapter 22
Continued Lethargy — 1980-1983

— Decline in Business

As the new decade rolled in, the WWA roster of grapplers had a stable of heels that included Luscious Johnny Valiant (without Handsome Jimmy), Paul Christy with his valet and manager (and future wife) Miss Bunny Love, Dr. Jerry Graham Jr., and the heel manager Reverend Tiny Hampton. The cards were filled out by a steady stream of rotating talent, such as "Nature Boy" Roger Kirby and Guy Mitchell. Bruiser continued the Masked Strangler gimmick that Mitchell used earlier, only this time with journeymen Bobby Vann, Jim Grabmire, and his son Karl alternating in the role. The roster of WWA babyfaces (good guys) at this time included Dick the Bruiser (50 years old), Wilbur Snyder (50 years old), Bobo Brazil (55 years old), and Yukon Moose Cholak (49 years old). The only younger talents in a prominent position were Bruiser's son-in-law, Spike Huber, and Steve Regal, Wilbur Snyder's son-in-law.

Dr. Jerry Graham, Jr.
Indianapolis, early '80s
Source: Scott Romer

It can be safely said that no other wrestling promotion in the United States relied so heavily on a core of older good guys. Professional wrestling is a physical exhibition that traditionally reveres youth and athleticism. This situation of older stars in the WWA surely contributed to a decline of public interest. Veteran photographer Scott Romer reluctantly pointed out, "*Who wanted to see fat Moose Cholak and fifty-year-old Bruiser anymore?*" The author vividly remembers how the cable television wrestling originating from WTBS-TV in Atlanta and WOR-TV in New Jersey offered compelling storylines featuring young and exciting talent. Wrestler Greg Lake pointed out, "*I think Bruiser thought that as long as he was around, WWA would do well without any really younger talent, other than Spike Huber and Steve Regal.*" Veteran ring general Black Jack Lanza, who had decades of in-the-ring and out-of-ring experience, reflected on the decline of the Bruiser's territory:

> "*The thing with Bruiser was, they get older, but they don't want to admit it. Their work suffers, but they don't want to admit it. Instead of grooming people up to replenish the supply of talent, the problem was the promoters were wrestling. All decisions on the business side were made by people who were still wrestling. You don't get an objective view of anything. They never did. If Bruiser was eighty years old, he would still want to work like Dick the Bruiser.*"

Handsome Johnny Starr worked many years in the Indianapolis territory and saw the entire decline:

> "They wouldn't promote young talent. I mean, your babyfaces were, all of a sudden, sixty years old, and the young people don't want to see it. The Bruiser would just not let that go. When Vince McMahon got ahold of the business, he realized bringing young and hot talent, good-looking girls and good-looking guys. That's the key. You got to have good-looking athletes and he (Bruiser) didn't. We were doing the same old finishes over and over. It was horrible. Dick was afraid and, like a lot of the promoters who made themselves the top babyface, did that because they didn't want anybody to steal the territory. The problem was, they did that for too long. That being said, Dick the Bruiser, still, in my opinion, was the greatest talent the professional wrestling business has ever seen."

Veteran Paul Christy summed it up about the owner/main event wrestlers:

> "You get carried away with your power and don't want to step away from the spotlight."

It is acknowledged that the owners of any wrestling promotion had the undisputed final say on all aspects of their business. That would include the practice of booking themselves into the main events and receiving the highest payoffs. Bruiser and Snyder had worked hard since 1964 to build and grow their wrestling business in Indianapolis. Nobody can take away the decades of distinguished and unforgettable service they contributed to the wrestling industry. However, the rhetorical question should be, was that the best decision for the long-term viability of their business?

Bruiser vs. Paul Christy • 1979
Source: Scott Romer

The results of those business decisions are best illustrated by comparing Dick the Bruiser's payoffs from the zenith in 1972 to the lackluster year of 1980. For nineteen matches in Indianapolis and Chicago in 1972, Bruiser earned nightly payoffs of more than $1,000, and he was paid more than $2,000 for seven of those bouts. At the end of 1980, there were only six payoffs over $1,000, not counting one series in Japan for which he was paid $3,000.

Bruiser's son-in-law, Tim Replogle, points out that Bruiser saved his money and invested wisely during the earlier and most-profitable years. He owned several rental condominiums near Tampa, Florida, that provided years of supplemental income during the '80s. The same can be said of Wilbur Snyder, who had invested in undeveloped real estate in Hawaii with an uncle, a former music executive. Mike Snyder points out that "they made millions of dollars" on the deals.

While Bruiser and Wilbur were well-set financially in spite of the modest wrestling revenue, times were leaner for many of their employees. With so many of the main events featuring Dick and Wilbur, opportunities for other wrestlers to make a decent living in Indianapolis were somewhat limited. If a younger, experienced wrestler with big upside potential wanted to migrate to a robust and exciting territory, Indianapolis was not the place to go. For one thing, the WWA did not run shows every week in the same town, like so many other territories where there were many opportunities to perform. The WWA did not have that many arenas to draw huge indoor audiences like the WWF did on the East coast. Bobby Heenan referred to Indianapolis as *"a place you started and a place you finished."* True enough, the Indianapolis talent roster was full of starters and finishers.

— **David Letterman Connection**

There was a personal bright spot for Bruiser in 1980 as he received exposure on national television. On July 2, Bruiser was the guest on David Letterman's newly launched program on the NBC television network in New York City, which at the time was slotted in mid-morning. Letterman and Bruiser were no strangers. Letterman worked as a radio and television personality in Indianapolis in the late '60s after graduating from Ball State University in nearby Muncie. Letterman reportedly did some ring announcing at live wrestling events for Bruiser and Snyder during those days. Letterman would later tell Bob Costas in 1989 that he loved professional wrestling in his home of Indianapolis and said, *"You couldn't get a better known wrestler than Dick the Bruiser."* Letterman remembered that *"we would go to the matches periodically, and they would always have a big Thanksgiving card — ha, ha, ha."*

Costas retorted, *"That's the thing you want to do to top off a family day."*

Letterman also said, *"Dick the Bruiser was from Indianapolis but was always introduced as being from Reno, Nevada,* [and as] *the world's most dangerous wrestler."* Letterman wished he *"could become known as the world's most dangerous anything,"* and then added, *"How do you prove that?"*

— **Sam Muchnick Farewell**

January 1, 1982, was a sad date in St. Louis wrestling history as long-time promoter Sam Muchnick retired from the business. On that night, a spectacular "farewell" wrestling card was held at the Arena (also known as the Checkerdome), where the St. Louis political, sports, media, and business community turned out to honor Muchnick. NWA heavyweight champion Ric Flair defeated Dusty Rhodes with Gene Kiniski as the special referee, while Dick the Bruiser won the Missouri State heavyweight title from Ken Patera before a crowd of 19,819, the largest wrestling crowd ever to see a defense of the Missouri state title. This was the third time Bruiser held the prestigious title. Photographer Roger Deem remembers the finish of the title match:

> *"Patera swung a chair at the Bruiser and Dick ducked. The chair bounced off the ropes and whacked Patera in the face. The Bruiser covered for the win and his third reign as Missouri ruler. Dick was a good friend of Sam Muchnick, and Larry* [Matysik] *said the win was a final gift for Sam upon his retirement."*

Ken Patera's wrestling career began in the AWA and he frequently appeared in Chicago when both AWA and WWA appeared. In late 2011, he shared his memories of Bruiser:

186 • BRUISER: The World's Most Dangerous Wrestler

"I liked Dick and enjoyed working for him. Hell, when I wrestled him in the Checkerdome, it was sold out with an attendance record. While the Bruiser probably potatoed people in the past, by the time I wrestled him, he was so old it didn't hurt me. (laughs) I enjoyed working with Dick. I took care of him. I didn't hurt him or nothing. He knew if he got in the ring with me, I wouldn't beat him up."

— **"Curiouser and curiouser!"**

On February 19, 1982, in St. Louis, Bruiser won an 18-man battle royal and defended the Missouri heavyweight title against Greg Valentine. The payoff sheet for that night recently surfaced, showing Bruiser was paid $624.50. The participants in the main-event tag team match all were paid more — Harley Race ($1,403.50) & Crusher Blackwell ($1,403.50) vs. Andre the Giant ($1,754.38) & Terry Funk (not shown on sheet).

Several other interesting items on the sheet include:
- Gene Kiniski, who worked two matches below Bruiser, was paid $710.50.
- Ken Patera, who worked the match before Bruiser, was paid $662.00.
- Greg Valentine, Bruiser's opponent, was paid $862.00 ($237.50 more than Bruiser, the champion).
- Vince McMahon (Sr.) was paid $708.84 as Andre's booking agent.

— **Challenger to Ric Flair**

In his e-Book titled *From the Golden Era*, Larry Matysik gave Dick the Bruiser credit as one of the best challengers for the NWA heavyweight title in decades. Larry pointed out that, "It always took two to tango and no champion drew in a vacuum." In St. Louis, Bruiser wrestled for the NWA title 18 times, drawing 198,992 fans for an average of 11,055 per show. The second-largest drawing card of this era, 19,027 fans, was on June 12, 1982, at the Arena where NWA world champion Ric Flair won two out of three falls from Bruiser. The Bruiser generated memorable pre-match publicity on KPLR-TV for his challenge to Ric Flair. Matysik remembers that Bruiser "*stole Flair's robe and belt and paraded around the ring.*" The author remembers seeing video tapes of the publicity with Bruiser appealing to the blue-collar fans, screaming, "*I'm Union and I'm for you people.*" Payoff figures given for that night show Bruiser's take to be $5,841 for that night, the same as Flair's. The author believes this was likely the biggest payoff of the Bruiser's entire wrestling career.

Long time St. Louis wrestling photographer Roger Deem remembers:

"As he [Bruiser] aged, perhaps it became more that people still wanted to believe, the same way that John Wayne still held that machismo even into his later years. Dick still knew how to put on a good show, and though he finally went down to defeat in

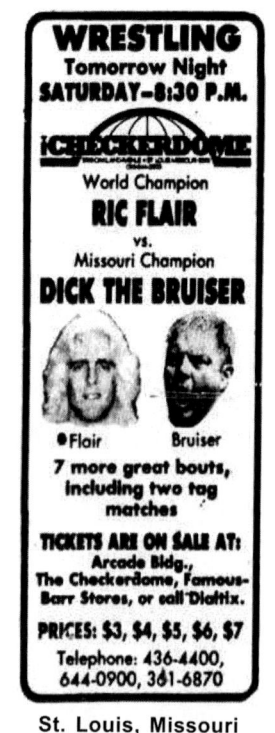

**WRESTLING
Tomorrow Night
SATURDAY – 8:30 P.M.
CHECKERDOME**

World Champion
RIC FLAIR
vs.
Missouri Champion
DICK THE BRUISER

● Flair   Bruiser

7 more great bouts,
including two tag
matches

TICKETS ARE ON SALE AT:
Arcade Bldg.,
The Checkerdome, Famous-
Barr Stores, or call Dialtix.

PRICES: $3, $4, $5, $6, $7

Telephone: 436-4400,
644-0900, 361-6870

St. Louis, Missouri
June 12, 1982

dignity, he gave Flair a beating for the ages. Dick had an aura about him, and I think his greatest strength was the unpredictability of his predictability. You knew he was going to explode, you just never knew how that would happen. People loved the Bruiser because he was an action star. You never saw him holding a guy in a headlock or arm bar. Dick was a man on the move, and you either moved with him or were moved by him. Nobody ever went away from a Bruiser match thinking it was boring. He held your attention."

Other than two high-profile main events against Harley Race in August and September, with Harley winning the Missouri title in the September encounter, the match with Flair would be Bruiser's last hurrah in St. Louis. Larry Matysik pointed out that, *"In the summer of 1982, Dick the Bruiser had worked before 28,000 people in just two shows* [June 12 and September 17]. *I grant you, he was nothing like he used to be, but he could put butts into seats."*

Sam Muchnick, Dave Burzynski & Dick the Bruiser in Indianapolis
Source: Dave Burzynski

Matysik added:

"The Bruiser got over because down deep, especially in his prime, he could scare people because of the way he looked, something in his eyes and body language and personal dynamics. Now that I got older, I recognize now that the look he had in his eyes was a sense of humor. It was almost like, 'I can scare these people and this is fun.' I think he enjoyed it."

Modern-day independent wrestling promoter Herb Simmons (Central Illinois-Eastern Missouri) remembers Bruiser as an "all-time great" in St. Louis. *"The Bruiser was part of a cast of characters — Pat O'Connor, Ric Flair, Fritz Von Erich, Dory Funk, Jr., and Ted DiBiase — who were larger than life."* If Dick the Bruiser was on a card in St. Louis, Herb Simmons was there. Simmons insisted that, *"Dick never lost a step, even when he got older."* Years after Bruiser's in-ring involvement ended, he would supply talent for Simmons' events. However, he always reminded Simmons that he (Simmons) was operating in his (Bruiser's) old territory.

Bob Geigel, a St. Louis Wrestling Club minority owner under Sam Muchnick's stewardship, had a very high regard for the Bruiser: *"Dick the Bruiser could go to St. Louis anytime his little heart desired, and we liked him."* Geigel and his long-time associate, Bulldog Bob Brown, had many legendary matches against Bruiser and Crusher in Kansas City.

— The Escapist

Also in 1982, Bruiser became involved in an independent film project headed up by a local disc jockey named Bill Shirk, now the owner of several radio stations in Indianapolis. Shirk's other vocation was that of an escape artist, and the film was aptly titled *The Escapist*. Bruiser, Bob Luce, Ox Baker, Guy Mitchell, and Spike Huber were written into the plot of the movie. Shirk had made guest appearances on several WWA wrestling events in Indianapolis

188 • BRUISER: The World's Most Dangerous Wrestler

years earlier. Shirk learned a lesson on the staging of live entertainment events from Bruiser:

"*I was teamed up with Spike Huber for wrestling matches as he protected me while I was doing escapes. I told Spike Huber about a match that I thought would be a good idea. About an hour later, the Bruiser called me into his office and he said, 'I come up with the matches and you don't come up with the matches.' I told him what I planned and, after I was done, he looked at me and said, 'That would work if you spread it over about five matches.'* Bruiser warned, 'Never give them the whole show in one match; always milk and stretch it out for the finale'"

Dick the Bruiser & actress Cynthia Johns on the set of *The Escapist*.
Source: Bill Shirk

— **Memphis Experiment**

In fall 1982, Bruiser and Memphis promoter Jerry Jarrett agreed to jointly promote some wrestling cards. Spike Huber and Steve Regal both appeared on WMC-TV Channel 5 and at the Mid-South Coliseum in Memphis, feuding with the New York Dolls — Rick McGraw and Troy Graham — a heel team managed by Jimmy Hart. Years later, Jerry Jarrett discussed that short-lived relationship in his autobiography, *The Best of Times*:

"*In 1982, the Bruiser called me and asked if I would put my tape in all his towns and split the gates with him. I agreed, but the partnership lasted only one tour. Kamala was a hot ticket for us at the time, and I discovered that Dick was taking our tape and editing it so that Kamala would be his opponent when the show ran. The towns did not draw, and the reason was fans thought this promotion was just more of the same. I pulled my tape and never returned.*"

By January 1983, the Bruiser would resume his WWA shows with his Indianapolis crew, and that year would bring some significant developments in his wrestling world.

— Menacker Leaves

Since 1971, Sam Menacker worked for Bruiser in the role of television play-by-play man, as well as general manager of the company. He performed many administrative functions for Dick and Wilbur. Something happened between Bruiser and Sam that caused Dick to terminate Sam's employment. Scott Romer, then a ringside photographer, and later Dick's son-in-law, told the author the dismissal was money-related. It was believed Dick fired Sam unilaterally without any consultation with Wilbur Snyder. Wilbur's son, Mike Snyder, also commented on the subject:

> "*Sam became a dear friend of mine as he was with Wilbur. Dick treated Sam like shit. He [Sam] was very instrumental in that whole deal. This was the epitome of the partnership, and it sent Wilbur up a tree. Sam was his [Wilbur's] guy, and I recall Wilbur taking a stand saying, 'Sam had been our right hand man.' If Dick made a decision to go sideways on somebody, that guy was going to go sideways. There were times when Wilbur would throw his hands up, and that was one of them.*"

Sam Menacker & Bruiser, 1977
Source: Scott Romer

— David McLane Arrives

At that time, ringside photographers for the WWA included Scott Romer and his long-time friend David McLane, who was an undergraduate at Indiana University. McLane recalls that his ringside presence helped him "*become exposed to the inside nuances of the business.*" McLane remembers what happened to him after Menacker left:

> "*I was called by Spike Huber, who told me to expect a call around twelve noon from the Bruiser. I said, 'For what?' and Spike said, 'Sam Menacker is out as the announcer and the Bruiser wants you to do it.'*
>
> *Then Bruiser called me and asked, 'What are you doing tomorrow?'*
>
> *I said, 'I got a math exam.'*
>
> *Bruiser said, 'Skip it, we're doing TV tapings and I want you to be the new announcer.'*"

McLane initially expressed three television-related concerns to the Bruiser. McLane said he "*didn't know a thing about it, never did it, and had a southern accent.*" Bruiser responded to McLane, "*Don't worry. You'll be a natural.*" McLane did skip math class that afternoon and drove to Indianapolis for the TV interview tapings. McLane remembers, "*Clearly, I was nervous*" as many of the wrestlers came up to him with all sorts of advice. McLane remembers Bruiser yelling, "*Time out,*" after seeing everyone advising McLane. Bruiser told McLane to "*take a breath. Everybody's telling you what to do. Who signs your checks?*"

"*You do,*" said McLane.

Bruiser asked, "*Who are you going to listen to?*"

McLane responded, "*I guess the guy who signs the checks.*"

Bruiser agreed. "*Exactly! Don't listen to anything they have to say.*" Bruiser pointed out, "*If they were smart, they wouldn't be working for me.*" Bruiser finished by saying, "*Don't do anything other than just be yourself.*"

Initially, McLane was disappointed when he read fan mail that said "*the kid stinks.*" However, Bruiser told McLane not to worry as "*you'll grow on them.*" Eventually, the fan mail turned positive as McLane did both television and general manager duties. McLane's prior experience promoting concerts and working as a wrestling photographer gave him many insights into various aspects of running an entertainment company like the WWA. McLane expanded the normal circuit to cities and towns that had not been run in several years. McLane's greatest education in the wrestling business was taking car trips to and from those out-of-town cards with Bruiser himself. McLane remembers, "*I wish I had a video camera or tape recorder to preserve all those great stories about wrestling. It would have been a great documentary.*"

McLane would later go on to produce three successful syndicated television wrestling programs featuring an all-girl wrestler roster: Gorgeous Ladies of Wrestling (GLOW), Powerful Women of Wrestling (POW), and Women of Wrestling (WOW).

First program by David McLane 1982
Source: David McLane

— **Divorce in Chicago**

By 1982, very few WWA personnel were getting bookings in Chicago. Bruiser, Spike Huber and Steve Regal would be booked now and then, but the vast majority of the talent came from Verne Gagne's AWA roster. On February 12, 1983, the final wrestling card under the auspices of the Chicago Wrestling Club, Inc., was held at the International Amphitheatre. The card featured all the big names in the AWA — tag team champs Greg Gagne and Jim Brunzell, Hulk Hogan, Jesse Ventura, Ken Patera, Wahoo McDaniel, Jerry Blackwell, Bobby Heenan, and even TV comedy star Andy Kaufman. No WWA talent was booked on the card. From that point on, each wrestling card in Chicago consisted almost solely of AWA talent and was held at the Pavilion at the University of Illinois. On AWA television, Verne Gagne thanked Bob Luce for his years of service and the author distinctly remembers seeing Bob Luce in person at the inaugural card at the Pavilion.

Larry Lisowski, AWA referee and son of the Crusher, pointed out to the author that "*the AWA was a global organization and the Bruiser's territory was not.*" Gagne's territory had a great talent line-up, a widespread TV syndication, and a vast territory covering hundreds of cities across the United

States and Canada. Lisowski added, "*To draw the biggest crowds at the University of Illinois at Chicago Pavilion and the 19,000 seat suburban Rosemont Horizon, you had to have the best TV and talent.*" Gagne was still one of the most powerful wrestling promoters, and "*he used that money and power to take over Chicago and buy out Dick the Bruiser.*" Lisowski believes "*Bruiser had enough and sold back his percentage.*" David McLane, who worked with Bruiser daily in Indianapolis at that time, recalls the situation being purely a business move and that Bruiser and Gagne remained friends. Gagne would later use Bruiser on many of his Rosemont Horizon cards in 1984 and 1985, resulting in some of the Bruiser's best payoffs during those years.

— **Wilbur Snyder Retires**

In May 1983, Bruiser's long-time partner, Wilbur Snyder, would wrestle in his final series of matches as a full-time wrestler. David McLane commented on what he understood of the situation at the time:

"*Wilbur saw that the market place was shifting and that Vince McMahon was growing. I don't think that he* (Wilbur) *was up for the traveling. The timing was right. The Bruiser wanted to continue, and Wilbur sold his shares of the promotion to the Bruiser. Even though he had sold out* (his shares), *Wilbur might wrestle on occasion or be there to collect the receipts.*"

Wrestler Steve Regal, who was married to Snyder's daughter Cindy, pointed out that, during his retirement years, Wilbur would spend half of his time in Pompano Beach, Florida, and the other half in Indiana. Regal recalled that "*Wilbur loved to play tennis. He drank and smoked and partied.*" In 1991, Snyder was diagnosed with acute lymphatic leukemia. He was 62 years old on December 25, 1991, when he died in a Florida hospital of a heart attack. His legacy in professional wrestling was sterling, and he did it all with enduring class and athleticism.

— **State Tax Lawsuit**

In August 1983, Bruiser and his company, Championship Wrestling, Inc., became embroiled in a legal dispute with the state boxing commission and the Treasury department of the State of Indiana. The *Pharos Tribune* of Logansport reported the wrestling company owed $28,676 in taxes due on the sale of admissions to professional wrestling matches, equal to ten percent of the gross receipts. Bruiser was represented by prominent attorney and former Indiana Bar Association president Douglass R. Shortridge. Mr. Shortridge (now deceased) declined to be interviewed for this biography citing attorney-client privilege. Mr. Shortridge's lawsuit against the two State of Indiana entities does survive and gives good insight into their grievances as plaintiff versus the State as defendant. Shortridge maintained, "*This purported tax upon wrestling has no relationship to the current act* [applicable state statutes], *which is the regulation of boxing only.*" Shortridge deemed the tax as "an occupational tax" that should be considered "discriminatory and unequal." The case was heard by Judge Kenneth R. Johnson of the Marion (County) Superior Court — civil division; although, he never met the Bruiser or Shortridge in person. Judge Johnson then issued the opinion of the court:

"The Court, having considered the said compliant, and having heard the evidence supporting it at the trial of the case, and having entered its written findings of Fact and Conclusions of Law, hereby ordered, adjudges, and decreed that judgment be entered for the defendant [State] and against the plaintiff [the Bruiser] on the plaintiff's complaint.

Author's note: After our first printing, Tim Tassler sent an article that showed Bruiser won his case on appeal in 1985.

```
STATE OF INDIANA     )              MARION SUPERIOR COURT
                     ) SS:
COUNTY OF MARION     )              CIVIL DIVISION, ROOM 2
                                    CAUSE NUMBER S282-1141

CHAMPIONSHIP WRESTLING, INC.
A Corporation,
           Plaintiff                      FILED
     vs.
                                        S-2  AUG 05 1983
STATE BOXING COMMISSION OF THE
STATE OF INDIANA AND TREASURER
OF INDIANA,
           Defendants

                        JUDGMENT

     Comes now the Plaintiff, Championship Wrestling, Inc., and
having filed its Complaint in this cause against the Defendants,
State Boxing Commission of the State of Indiana and the Treasurer
of Indiana, in the following words and figures to-wit:
                           (H.I.)
     And the Court having considered said Complaint and having
heard the evidence supporting it at the trial of this cause, and
having entered its written Findings of Fact and Conclusions of Law,
it is hereby:
     ORDERED, ADJUDGED AND DECREED that judgment be entered for
the Defendants herein and against the Plaintiff on Plaintiff's
Complaint.
     ALL OF WHICH IS ORDERED, ADJUDGED AND DECREED by the Court on
this 5th day of August, 1983 at Indianapolis, Indiana.

                                JUDGE KENNETH H. JOHNSON
                                MARION SUPERIOR COURT
                                CIVIL DIVISION, ROOM 2
```

1983 judgment against Championship Wrestling, Inc.
Source: Marion County Clerk of Court - Indianapolis, Indiana

As you can see, more noteworthy events happened outside the ring during these years than what transpired inside the ring. The days of drawing 10,000 paying customers or earning $1,000 paydays were long gone. Things had certainly changed from the '60s and '70s when Bruiser and Snyder made wrestling history in Indianapolis. Now, Dick the Bruiser remained the sole owner and operator with significant challenges facing him. Wrestler Sonny Rogers remembers this period:

"I worked for the Bruiser in 1983 for about six months, and it was a great experience. But, in all honesty, having watched Dick the Bruiser work with a young Bob Orton was kind of sad because Dick was a ghost of what he once was."

— The WWF Invades St. Louis

In 1983, internal disputes developed among the surviving principals of the St. Louis Wrestling Club, which led to the establishment of a rival wrestling promotion in St. Louis operated by Muchnick's right-hand man, Larry Matysik. The Bruiser stayed loyal to the old group, while son-in-law Spike Huber occasionally headlined for the new promotion.

In 1984, the unthinkable happened when Vince Kennedy McMahon (Jr.) brought his WWF into St. Louis. He took over the KPLR-TV, Channel 11 time slot and held a TV taping at the Chase Park Hotel on January 16. The WWF debut card at the Kiel took place on February 10, where they taped three weeks of television. The long-running NWA promotion in St. Louis just faded away, a victim of the wrestling revolution that began with the WWF expansion. Almost all the old-school independent wrestling promotions fell by the wayside, as well, including Dick the Bruiser's promotion in Indianapolis.

No matter what happened to the old-school wrestling promotions, though, Dick the Bruiser's legacy in St. Louis can never be erased. Bruiser's longevity in St. Louis was amazing and his importance cannot be overlooked. Unlike Chicago and Indianapolis, two cities in which he had influential ownership, he earned his spot in St. Louis solely on ability and drawing power. His first appearance in a main event at the Kiel was March 1, 1963. As best we can determine, between that date and June 10, 1983, he was featured in 84 main events, 63 of which were singles matches (handicap matches are included in that figure). His last match there was September 14, 1984 when he teamed with Black Jack Lanza to face The Road Warriors.

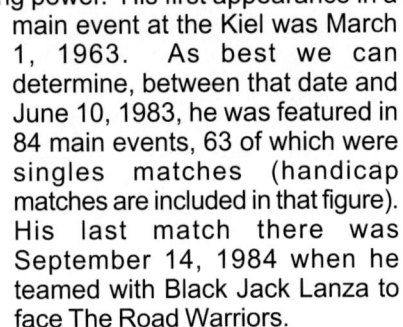

— There's Only One Bruiser

In June 1984, Verne Gagne brought Bruiser Brody into the AWA, but out of respect to his old friend Dick the Bruiser, Gagne had Brody come in as King Kong Brody.

(left) St. Louis • February 10, 1985

Chapter 23
Bruiser's Last Stand — 1984-1990

— The Road Warriors

Some of the most controversial matches the Bruiser ever had in Chicago during this period of a Gagne-dominated AWA franchise were when he teamed with the Crusher against the up-and-coming phenomenon tag team of the Road Warriors — Michael (Hawk) Hegstrand and Joseph (Animal) Laurinaitis. The Road Warriors were former weightlifters and bouncers from Minneapolis and were trained by Eddie Sharkey. They gained national recognition from their appearances on cable Superstation WTBS-TV in Atlanta where they utilized a bulldozer-like and ultra-aggressive wrestling style that rarely allowed their opponents any offensive advantage.

At the time, the Road Warriors were in their mid-20s, wore spiked shoulder pads and painted faces, and were billed from Chicago. Their in-ring manager, Paul Ellering, a former wrestler, also was their real-life manager. At the same time, Bruiser and Crusher were, on average, 30 years older than their young musclebound opponents. It was said that the Road Warriors would be a formidable challenge to the long-standing reputation of Bruiser and Crusher. This all took place during the second year of the Road Warrior's run in the national spotlight.

The foursome had two matches; the first on August 19, 1984, at the Auditorium in Milwaukee, and the final on September 15, 1984, at the Rosemont Horizon in suburban Chicago. AWA and WWF veteran "Jumping" Jim Brunzell appeared on the Milwaukee card and had bad memories:

> "I didn't like that match. What I didn't like was the Road Warriors really did not respect anybody in the ring. They actually made Bruiser and Crusher airborne, and I didn't think it was right."

Milwaukee wrestling historian and foremost expert on the Crusher, George Lentz, recalled the Milwaukee bout:

> "I do remember the end of the match as the Crusher had a chair while Animal and Hawk were out of the ring. The match got out of control. It only lasted seven minutes and the fans were disappointed. It was a pretty good match. I remember the Crusher had a chair and he threw it at Hawk, who was outside the ring. Hawk didn't pay attention as the [chair] caught him in the legs, and he didn't like that. So they [Road Warriors] started throwing any chair they could get a hold of and just flipping them into the ring. The Crusher and the Bruiser were ducking them. I think the Road Warriors were pissed when a chair hit Hawk. He looked like he was pretty mad. It was pretty brutal."

Son of the Crusher, Larry Lisowski, who also served as an AWA referee and sometimes promoter, commented on the second match-up at Rosemont:

"I know what happened that night at the Rosemont Horizon. [The] Bruiser never got his revenge. They [Road Warriors] were trying, in front of their home wrestling fans, to prove they were as strong, tough, and powerful, as Bruiser and Crusher."

Greg Gagne also was not happy with this situation and pointed out years later that the *"Road Warriors had huge egos and were most concerned with putting themselves over."* Gagne explained, *"The Crusher told the Warriors he had a bad back, and the Warriors slammed the Crusher on his back anyway."* Warrior manager Ellering recalled one of those bouts:

"Hawk held him [Bruiser] and he pressed him over his head. I remember the Bruiser looking out over the ring ropes right at me and he's saying, 'What are you doing to me?' Hawk slammed him down and responded, 'Anything I want.'"

AWA road agent Black Jack Lanza had argued with the Road Warriors about the practice of systematically destroying all opposition saying:

"You can't keep working like this and chewing up talent. You've got to make your opponents look good before you beat them. You can't just chew them up and beat them, you have nothing left. Who are you going to work with — each other? I never approved how they worked. In this case, they really kind of hurt the Crusher — hurt his back."

— Final Run for the WWA

Dick the Bruiser continued with the WWA with a core of loyalists who made one more big push to turn around the promotion. This full-time talent roster included family members Spike Huber, Dick's son-in-law, and Leroy Redbone, Dick's son Karl Afflis. For a short time, Huber was the WWA heavyweight champion. Since 1975, Spike Huber appeared hundreds and hundreds of times for the WWA and became the number-two babyface ... right behind Dick the Bruiser. Photographer Scott Romer remembers *"when David McLane was general manager and Dick the Bruiser was in Florida, David did a video of Spike Huber working out that was accompanied by modern music; Dick the Bruiser got mad at them when he heard they were using music."*

Nobody would have predicted the next development in February 1984 when it was learned that Spike was breaking up with his wife Michelle, the Bruiser's daughter. Spike was a highly admired wrestler on the team, but his bookings ceased immediately. The Great Wojo, himself an Olympic caliber amateur wrestler, said Huber *"was a good athlete and well-built guy,"* and even though Huber was the son-in-law of the owner, Wojo claimed *"you wouldn't know that Spike was the son-in-law as he was one of the boys."* Huber would never work for the WWA again. The following year, however, he attempted to promote opposition to his long-time employer at an antique barn in Zionsville, Indiana.

LIVE N' NEW SUPERSTARS OF
PRO WRESTLING
Logansport National Guard Armory
THRUSDAY, APRIL 11, 8:10 PM
POWERFUL, AWESOME TAG TEAM MATCH!
DICK THE BRUISER & YUKON MOOSE CHOLAK
VS.
BULLDOG DON KENT & DR. JERRY GRAHAM

Super Destroyer vs. Bobo Brock

Monster Murdock vs. Calyso Jim

Tickets on Sale NOW!
All Seats Ringside Reserved $6.00
Insure Best Seats
Buy Advance Tickets at...

Popular Tag-Team of Stormy Glanzig & Chris Carter
vs.
Mad Max & Abdullah

VAN'S SPORTING GOODS COMPANY
Day of Show Door Sales after 7 PM

Logansport, Indiana
April 11, 1985

Before the year was finished, the Bruiser's new son-in-law, Scott Romer, was brought into the WWA. Romer, considered to be one of the finest wrestling photographers of the '70s and '80s, adopted the name "Saul Creechman" in a managerial role. The name was a combination of old-school wrestling managers Gentleman Saul Weingeroff and Eddie Creachman.

— Wrestlers Remember

One steady performer for the WWA was the Hooded Hangman, who previously wrestled for the WWA in the '70s as The Big Whiz (Robin Whisman). The wrestler wore a mask because he worked in law enforcement in real life and preferred the anonymity. The Hooded Hangman was major competition for Dick the Bruiser and remembers a big main event at Market Square Arena:

"I had a huge flower wreath sent to the arena with a card that said 'Rest In Peace Bruiser — Sincerely, The Hangman.' *During that match, I accidentally kicked the Bruiser in the nuts. When he got me in a headlock, he said,* 'Big boy. That wasn't nice.' *He paid me back and then some."*

As 1984 progressed, wrestler Craig Carson worked in the WWA and remembered the advice Bruiser gave him upon being hired. *"Stay out of trouble and don't hang out with Karl [Afflis]."* Craig Carson ignored the advice and remembers:

"One story that stands out was the second week that I'm booked to wrestle in Indianapolis. I'm standing in downtown Indianapolis on a Saturday morning among the shoppers when I hear, 'Carson, my man. Ha Ha.' *I turn and Da Bone [Karl] is sitting on one of the sweetest bikes I ever saw chromed out. Bone kept hollering* 'Suzuki baby.' *A girl friend of mine pulls up [on a Suzuki motorcycle]. Bone says,* 'Will that thing run?' *She says,* 'We can find out,' *and she asks me,* 'You wanna race him?' *Young and full of testosterone, we go off zooming through downtown Indianapolis at high noon, streets packed. Later that night at the Armory, I hear the Bruiser ripping Da Bone down the hall. Bruiser screamed,* '%#@&#*, Karl, you and Carson are trying to kill my town.' *Later, the Bruiser was screaming my name.* 'Carson, get in here, man.' *He ripped me up one side and down the other."*

— Lean Times for the WWA

These were lean financial times for the WWA as the WWF was already in the midst of their national expansion — saturating the airwaves both on national cable and local television and snatching the top talent from the remaining independent wrestling territories. There just wasn't the widespread fan interest in the current crop of WWA talent like there was for many previous line-ups. Earlier in the '80s, top line performers like Harley Race or Cowboy Bob Orton would be brought into the WWA for quick shots, but even they couldn't turn the tide. Bruiser did give some younger talent opportunities to share main events with him and boost the box office, such as a country-boy character named J.R. Hogg, or playboy-type Bobby Colt, or the amateur standout Great Wojo. In everyday life, Wojo actually was a full-time teacher. He later said ring payoffs were so nominal that he could never give up his regular job. Dr. Jerry Graham, Jr. worked in his family's retail meat business in Toledo during those years.

Super Maxx, whose real name was Sam DeCero, would later form his own independent wrestling company called Windy City Wrestling. He looks back fondly at the wrestling crew he worked with during the closing days of the WWA.

"Nobody pissed and moaned about their egos because we all were on the same playing field. We all got to perform and all got to be on the big shows. We all got decent little paydays. You got to remember that if you are in it for the love of the game, it almost didn't matter if you got paid. I remember many times where there was a small house and I thought I would be lucky to get gas money."

The overwhelming majority of Bruiser's bouts in 1984 were tag team matches which would allow periodic down-time. To be fair, the Bruiser did his best to draw crowds and create excitement in an increasingly more-difficult environment. Historically, the only thing the Indiana territory needed for a decent turnout was to have Dick the Bruiser on the card, but times were slowly changing. According to Tim Replogle, many times during the '80s, Bruiser had to utilize personal resources to subsidize the costs of television production and airtime. Television was now relegated solely to Indianapolis, Fort Wayne and Terre Haute, and by 1984, the interview tapings no longer took place weekly.

On average, the promotion ran two shows a month in the armories in Fort Wayne, Indianapolis, and Terre Haute, occasionally shifting to larger venues. Schedules were stepped up for Hammond and Lafayette in 1984 and a few shows were staged at the Odeum in Villa Park, a suburb of Chicago. Spot shows were also promoted in dozens of Indiana cities and towns that year, including Marion, Frankfort, Logansport, Michigan City, Kokomo, Muncie, Hartford City, Peru, Boswell, and Warsaw. The WWA began utilizing "knock-off" wrestlers with names and physiques that looked similar to established wrestling personalities. There was a Jerry Lawler look-a-like named Gary Lawler, as well as a clone of the Road Warriors known as the World Warriors — Maxx and Super Maxx.

— **The Vogue**

Crowds continued to dwindle and lose interest, though, whereby the Bruiser eventually booked a May 16, 1985, date at a nightclub called "The Vogue" on College Avenue in the Broad Ripple neighborhood of Indianapolis. The main event of the evening involved an audience-participation challenge. The idea was that if a member of the audience could legitimately pin the

World Warriors with mgr. Saul Creechmann
Source: Scott Romer

shoulders of the Great Wojo to the mat within ten minutes, that person would win $1,000 cash. During that short run, nobody was able to pin Wojo. It would have been interesting to know what would have happened if someone had won the challenge. Can you imagine trying to collect $1,000 from Dick the Bruiser? As things wound down in Indianapolis, Bruiser made one last appearance in Chicago.

— Super Clash I

On September 28, 1985, Bruiser and Crusher made their final appearance together as a tag team at the Super Clash I Spectacular at Comiskey Park. The introduction to this book mentions this match, which represents the proverbial "swan song" for the legendary tag team. On that night, Bruiser, Crusher and Baron Von Raschke faced Ivan Koloff, Nikita Koloff and Krusher Khrushchev. Ivan Koloff remembered, "*It was great to be in the ring with all those guys — both partners and opponents.*" Koloff also admitted, "*Bruiser and Crusher were both up there in years, and so was I.*"

Nikita Koloff today says he looks back fondly on that match and has "*gained a whole new level of respect for those legends.*" At one point in the match, Bruiser trapped Nikita in the corner and hit him with multiple blows to the midsection, which Nikita said, "*looked good and couldn't break an egg.*" When finished, Bruiser whispered to Nikita, "*Rat-a-tat-tat.*"

When Raschke thought back to that match, he realized it was the last time in his life that he ever talked to or spent time with Dick the Bruiser.

Even though the Russians were victorious, the match was a fitting ending to the tag-team run of those two icons, and in a city where they became legends. The son of the Crusher, Larry Lisowski, retold his memories of the Bruiser-Crusher relationship for this biography:

> "*Bruiser and Crusher were really close, in and out of wrestling. They were there for good times and the lowest times. When the Crusher had his open heart surgery in 1990, Dick called him every day. My father told me that at the end of each phone call, the Bruiser told him that he loved him. My father at first didn't know what to think of that, or how to respond back. He had spent thirty-five years traveling around the world with this man, and he never saw that type of emotion from him, except when his mother died.*"

— Bruiser Bedlam

In the 1980s, Bruiser enjoyed new notoriety in the Detroit market as popular radio personality, George Baier, incorporated the Bruiser's personality and likeness into his programming. Baier worked for WRIF-FM and then WLLZ-FM radio stations, where the Bruiser appeared in print promotional ads. Baier did very good vocal impressions of the Bruiser on his programs, including a segment called "Meet The Bruiser," in which Baier would jokingly comment on current events in the gruff voice of the Bruiser. There was even a rock 'n' roll cover band named Dick the Bruiser that put its own spin on top 40 hits. The hit single, "We're An American Band," by Grand Funk Railroad become "It's Jack Kevorkian's Van," all about the infamous assisted suicide physician from Michigan.

BRUISER BEDLAM
WRESTLING
Thursday, April 10, 7:30 pm
Premier Center
Tickets: $10.75 and $8.75

Special Offer
Order your tickets by phone, by April 7, and receive $2.00 in discount drink coupons
Tickets at Ticket World and the Premier Center Box Office

Call **PASS** at 583-7600

Detroit was always a special city to the Bruiser, and another wrestling opportunity soon came about. After Bruiser closed down the Indiana territory, he entered into a handshake agreement with one of his associates, Jerry Jaffee (who

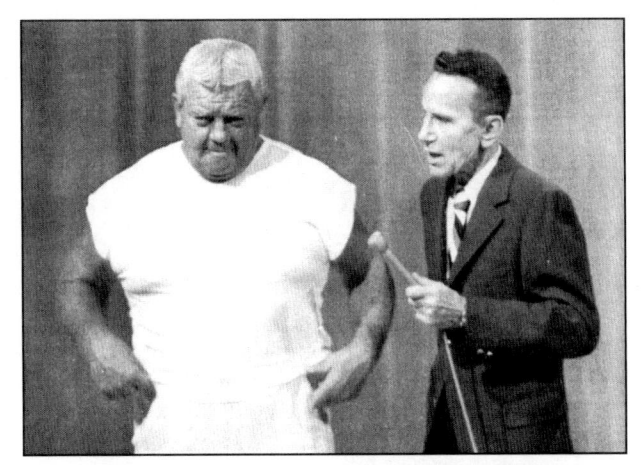

Bruiser during his "Bruiser Bedlam" days
Source: Scott Romer

wrestled as Dr. Jerry Graham, Jr.), to form a new promotion, appropriately entitled *Bruiser Bedlam*. Jaffee had been approached by a regional sports network to run and broadcast in the Detroit area with the Bruiser serving as color commentator. Jaffee suggested to Bruiser that he would like his former son-in-law, Spike Huber, to be part of the roster. He told Bruiser he thought there was money to be made with Huber, and added, *"It would be good to keep him employed in order to pay child support and alimony."* The Bruiser wanted nothing to do with Spike in the new endeavor. The eventual roster included Bulldog Don Kent, Calypso Jim, The Great Wojo, The Russian Brute, The Dark Angel, The Golden Lion, and a youngster named Scott Rechsteiner, who would later attain legendary status as Scott Steiner.

The TV show was taped at the Premier Center in suburban Detroit, a former theatre and concert hall. Long-time Detroit wrestling fan Rob Bauer recalls the crowds being decent at times, but the shows weren't run regularly. The events offered a rare opportunity for fans to talk directly to Dick the Bruiser in person, who had been aloof with fans for many years, reflecting his wrestling persona. The production later moved to Toledo, Ohio, when a sponsorship was granted by a major beer company. The Bruiser Bedlam promotion ran out of the Grand Ballroom of the Sofitel Hotel with the tape syndicated to Indianapolis, Chicago, Ann Arbor, Detroit, and even Windsor, Ontario, Canada. Jaffee recalled, *"After nine to ten shows in Toledo, the hotel started getting pressure from its mortgage holder who thought wrestling was too lowbrow and unsophisticated."* The hotel reluctantly shut down the wrestling operation even though Jaffee believed they were making money.

The Golden Lion, 1988
Source: Tim Replogle

| P A S S | **Bruiser Bedlam Wrestling:** Host Dick the Bruiser presents recent World Wrestling Association matches. (From 7:30) (Repeat) |

March 24, 1986 TV listing for *Bruiser Bedlam* in Detroit

Jaffee admitted, "*We never could recover from that and it was never the same.*" The group promoted spot shows all over the Midwest, but never could get a stronghold on the Midwest wrestling fans who were now exposed to live WWF events in their own towns. Ironically, on Friday, February 5, 1988, the WWF broadcast its first prime-time television event on NBC-TV from Indianapolis at Market Square Arena ... the Bruiser's hometown and former base of operations. The show featured Hulk Hogan, Andre the Giant, Bobby (The Brain) Heenan, Ted DiBiase, Randy Savage, Honky Tonk Man, and others. What local wrestling promoter anywhere could compete with that level of talent?

Jaffee looks back with some pride at Bruiser Bedlam and proclaims:

"*Bruiser Bedlam always made money. All that stuff on the Internet about what a flop we were, that is absolute bullshit. We made money every year, and I never had to stick a penny in that place.*"

Bruiser & Hard Boiled Haggerty
Minneapolis, Minnesota • 1988
Source: George Schire

— Final Twin Cities Visit

On February 4, 1988, Dick the Bruiser traveled to the Twin Cities to appear on the final wrestling card at the old Minneapolis Auditorium. Many of the old veterans — Leo Nomellini, Ray Stevens, Wahoo McDaniel, and Hard Boiled Haggerty — appeared on the card. Dick the Bruiser won his match when referee Haggerty disqualified Sheik Adnan El-Kaisee. In some ways, it was a special moment for Bruiser because Haggerty, a fellow teammate on the Green Bay football team, had been headlining in the Twin Cities in the '50s when Bruiser began wrestling full time.

Wrestling historian and author George Schire also had bittersweet memories as he was present that evening. Schire remembered it being the same venue where Bruiser made his Twin Cities debut on January 11, 1955. Bruiser was 58 years old in 1988 and Schire remembers thinking "*it was sad when I saw the match as Bruiser was living off his past laurels and past reputation*" and "*Bruiser was a lot slower and more methodical.*" He also added, "*Sheik Adnan was actually carrying the match and taking care of the Bruiser.*" Schire concluded by saying, "*Having followed him for 33 years, it was kind of tough.*" Schire's photographs from that night survive.

— Leon Spinks

In his final years, Dick the Bruiser got involved with some sporadic promotional efforts with former heavyweight boxing champion Leon Spinks, co-managing Leon along with Betty Spinks, Leon's wife. In Betty's own book, she praised Bruiser's efforts to promote the program. On June 25, 1989, at the Gateway Center in Toledo, Leon Spinks faced The Great Wojo in a "clash for ten rounds of boxing and wrestling." Independent wrestler Denny Kass was asked to be the color commentator for that event. He remembered the match came under the "$10,000 Wojo Challenge" series for members of the audience with Spinks being the challenger. Denny recalled the four-minute encounter:

> "In the beginning, Spinks danced around, came in, and punched Wojo in the face. Wojo then did a leg sweep and took Spinks' legs out from underneath him. Wojo picked Spinks up and body-slammed him. By this time, Betty Spinks had entered the ring and started hitting Wojo with her purse. The match was over."

Bruiser in Chicago with Rich Tito at Mike Ditka's 1990 fundraiser
Source: Rich Tito

— Starrcade 1990

One of Bruiser's final nationwide appearances in professional wrestling was on Sunday, December 16, 1990, at a wrestling pay-per-view event called "Starrcade 1990," held at the Kiel Auditorium in St. Louis. The card was promoted by World Championship Wrestling, the successor to the old National Wrestling Alliance. The card was staged in honor of former NWA heavyweight champion Pat O'Connor, who died four months earlier.

Bruiser was the special referee in the main event of the night, a cage match between Sting and The Black Scorpion. On that date, Bruiser was 61 years old and had put on some noticeable weight since his full-time wrestling career ended. Bruiser walked down the ramp to the ring wearing black wrestling boots, white sweatpants, and a sleeveless sweatshirt with large white and blue horizontal stripes. The fans gave him a warm, respectful welcome, but heel TV commentator Paul E. Dangerously gave him everything but. After Bruiser made his ring entrance, Dangerously made fun of him, saying, "He looks like Popeye the Sailor, doesn't he?" Dangerously continued by saying, "*Olive Oil is at home preparing a spinach salad.*"

Play-by-play announcer Jim Ross gave recognition by saying, "*Bruiser was the most dangerous man in wrestling at one time.*" Bruiser embellished his role as referee, shaking his finger at and lecturing the Black Scorpion for some infractions. Paul E. Dangerously kept putting down Bruiser, and at one point, said, "*The referee should never put his hands on wrestlers, even if he does weigh three hundred pounds.*" After Sting won the match by pinfall, the ring was stormed by the allies of the villainous Black Scorpion, including Arn Anderson, who smashed the Bruiser in the back with a folding chair. Later, the Black Scorpion was unmasked as Ric Flair.

It was noticeable to the "smart" fans that Bruiser didn't sell the chair shot, or anything else, for that matter. He didn't sell much during his career, and he wasn't going to begin then.

In all, it was hardly a stellar conclusion to the ring career of Dick the Bruiser, but he did get his hands dirty and put forth a respectable effort.

Scott Romer vividly remembers that night, and his memories were documented in an article by Jim Walker in *NUVO* magazine in 2001:

> "*Bruiser had almost become a carnival act. His body was deteriorating. Muscle had turned into atrophy. Wrinkles started showing. It was very, very sad. No matter what it was worth, he was always my childhood idol. And to see him deteriorate like that, I was very sad. He couldn't get away from the camera.*"

— High School Benefit Card

The Bruiser also took some time to give back to the community of Lafayette, Indiana, where he attended high school and graduated in 1947. He staged a wrestling card at Jefferson High School for the benefit of the school band program, designed to raise money for uniforms. His opponent that night was his son-in-law, the Golden Lion (Tim Replogle), who remembers the gymnasium being packed. It was the biggest turnout for any spot show in the Bruiser's later years. The Golden Lion was the heel that night and taunted the crowd, asking, "*How many of you ladies want to make love to the Golden Lion?*" During the match, the Bruiser told him, "*Don't go out on that side of the ring. They're passing around a knife, deciding whose going to stab you.*" Afterwards, Bruiser allowed himself to be photographed in the ring with high-school classmate Les Wilson, something that may not have happened in previous decades when the Bruiser had a tough reputation to preserve.

Chapter 24
The Final Fall — 1991

— Pays Respects to Dr. Holladay

One of the last known photographs (see below) of Dick the Bruiser was taken at Grand View Cemetery in West Lafayette, Indiana, around April 1991, where the Bruiser paid his respects to the late Dr. L.J. Holladay, a close friend and former commissioner of the Indiana State Athletic Commission. The Bruiser visited the grave site with Dr. Holladay's family, which included two grown sons, Dennis and Tom, and a grandson. When Dr. Holladay passed away in April 1969, the two sons were minors and without an adult guardian. The young teenagers asked that Bruiser be allowed to become their guardian and a lifelong friendship was developed. The boys would go on boating trips with Bruiser at Lake Schaeffer and share seafood feasts at Miller's Catfish Supper, a legendary establishment in Colfax, Indiana. The brothers still cherish memories of their relationship with Bruiser. Tom was quoted saying, *"Dick the Bruiser was as good as gold."*

On June 14, 1991, WCW brought Bruiser into St. Louis as special referee for the Bunkhouse Stampede battle royal in what would be his "last hurrah."

— Events of 1991

In 1991, Bruiser suffered an appendicitis attack while driving home from back-to-back wrestling cards in Northeast Indiana. Son-in-law Tim Replogle remembers, *"When he had his appendectomy, they put him in a wheelchair and he threatened everybody at the hospital. He assumed he would go out as the tough guy he was and never have anybody see him in a wheelchair."* Later that year, Bruiser and his wife traveled to Florida where they had a second home and investment properties. Son-in-law Tim Replogle remembers this time:

"Dick wasn't acting the same as he usually did, more sitting than standing up. Then I found out he was taking Karl's car, a little Toyota or Datsun, down to Florida. Mrs. Afflis took another car down. What I thought was, he was planning that if he had a heart attack or something while he was driving, he wasn't going to have her die. He was thinking of other people and not himself."

Before Bruiser left for Florida, he introduced his son-in-law as his champion to Japanese wrestling promoters for the Golden Lion's first-ever tour of Japan.

During this time, he also was acting as Leon Spinks' intermediary for Atsushi Onita. Onita was promoting a tag-team tournament and had asked Bruiser to supply him with four American pro boxers to form two separate tag teams for the tournament.

— November 9, 1991

On Saturday, November 9, 1991, the Bruiser was paid a visit by Larry Lisowski, the son of Crusher. Lisowski vividly remembers that day:

> "*I was at his Florida Gulf front home. I only live two miles from Dick's house.* [Dick] *was waiting for a package from Tokyo, Japan. Dick was really big that fall when he came down from Indianapolis. I thought he was pumping up for his Japan trip. They like big wrestlers in Japan, even though Dick was already retired. The Japanese were planning a big event for the Crusher's and the Bruiser's return.*"

— November 10, 1991

William Franklin Afflis' life came to an end the following day — Sunday, November 10, 1991, at his beachfront home in Indian Rocks Beach. Bruiser was lifting weights when a blood vessel burst in his esophagus. Replogle reflected: "*He worked out every day and I think it was bound to happen.*" More than likely, Bruiser died almost instantly and there was nothing anybody could do about it. The *Indianapolis Star* reported, "*Dick the Bruiser died while doing what he loved best — pumping iron to continue his reputation as* 'the world's most dangerous wrestler.'" The *St. Louis Post-Dispatch* wrote: "*Mr. Afflis died of internal bleeding according to a spokesman for Sun Coast Hospital in Largo.*"

After his death, the telephone rang in the home of Tim and Michelle Replogle in Fort Wayne and Michelle was told by her mother than her father was dead. Michelle dropped the telephone in shock. Larry Lisowski was called later that day by Bruiser's wife, Louise, who told Larry, "*Dick is gone.*" Larry was confused by her comment and remembered:

> "*I knew he* [Dick] *was a little mad when I left the day before because she might have lost or misplaced the material from Japan. I thought he* [Dick] *maybe left the house and she wanted me to look for him. I said,* 'Where do you think he went?.'
>
> She said, 'No. Dick's dead.'
>
> *I dropped the phone for a second and then asked her where she was, what happened, and how can I help. She needed me to call my father* [The Crusher], *Wilbur Snyder, Bob Luce, and Verne Gagne. I called my dad first. He and everybody else cried on the phone to me. I later went and stayed with Rio* [Louise's nickname] *until her daughter could catch a plane from Fort Wayne. I also called Pretty Boy Bobby.*"

— Congressional Tribute

There was no funeral, memorial, crypt, or gravesite ceremony when William Franklin Afflis was laid to rest in an above-ground crypt at Washington Park

North Cemetery on the northwest side of Indianapolis, a few miles from Dick's long-time home on North Kessler Boulevard. A few days later on the floor of the House of Representatives at the Capitol in Washington, DC, Congressman Andrew Jacobs Jr. paid tribute to Dick the Bruiser proclaiming:

"*Mr. Speaker, most people in Indianapolis were saddened by the death of our friend, Richard Afflis, also known as Dick the Bruiser. The Afflis family is well known in our community for nobility. I suppose it is no secret that professional wrestling involves a lot of professional acting, as well as athletics, and our friend Dick the Bruiser was superb at both.*"

Memorial contributions were requested for some of the Bruiser's favorite charities: The Muscular Dystrophy Association, Wheeler Rescue Ministries, and the Roudebush West 10th Street Veterans Hospital.

— **Distinguished Service to Veterans**

An official of the Veterans Administration in Indianapolis praised the late Bruiser on the television obituary segment on WRTV-TV Channel 6 in Indianapolis, the same station that carried the Bruiser's wrestling program. In one of his last taped interviews for Indianapolis reporter Karen Grau, the Bruiser talked about his not-so-publicized activities for veterans.

"*I love veterans because they served in war and I didn't. I went to the University of Nevada and joined the R.O.T.C. [Reserve Officer Training Corp] and received an Army commission. I went to play for Green Bay and held the Army commission. Several times when I was with Green Bay, I was called to active duty [during the Korean War] and the Green Bay draft board kept me around. I was a low-profile tackle and guard while we had quarterbacks, halfbacks, and linebackers who had to go. But the draft board kept me right in Green Bay in the line and trenches. Everything worked out and I never had to go to active duty and never got hurt, so I always felt I kind'a cheated, so I owe the government something. So my way of repaying what this land has given to me is to go and see all the veterans. I decided to visit the mental hospital of the Veterans Administration. I visit people who have dependency on things or substance abuse. I get in there with them, and boy, they relate to me. I make some of them talk who never blinked an eye or talked for years. I can get to them.*"

Throughout his wrestling career, Dick the Bruiser made time for charities, whether appearing on the local March of Dimes telethon or having proceeds of his t-shirt sales go to a local paraplegic organization. The legion of Midwest wrestling fans will never forget this legendary character and giant of a man. Many of them first became aware of Dick the Bruiser, as was the case of the author, when they were a "little itty-bitty Bruiser buddy."

Chapter 25
Epilogue

— Remarkable 62 Years

Dick the Bruiser was 62 years old when he died, relatively young when compared to the average American male, but more typical of those men who choose professional wrestling as their profession. Bruiser was, without question, a top box-office draw from the 1950s through the 1970s, and even into the '80s. He hit his peak many years before the Hulkamania era and developed a standout reputation in the Midwest states — Illinois, Indiana, Michigan, Missouri, Wisconsin, and Minnesota. However, Bruiser's limited exposure on the Eastern seaboard and the West coast prevented him from developing the optimum national reputation. It is unfortunate that Bruiser's reputation with wrestling fans of the '80s became somewhat diminished as his physical condition and performance had lost much of its luster. However, Dick the Bruiser in his prime was awesome and exceptionally believable.

— Wrestling Magazine Ratings

Bruiser's impact in professional wrestling during the 1960s is illustrated on how the professional wrestling magazines ranked him among his peers.

Issue date	Publication	Bruiser rank	#1 rank
Dec. 1960	Boxing Illustrated & Wrestling News	#8	Pat O'Connor
Fall 1961	Wrestling Revue	#3	Buddy Rogers
Nov. 1962	Wrestling World	#9	Don Leo Jonathan & Buddy Rogers
Oct. 1963	Wrestling World	#7	Lou Thesz
Oct. 1964	Wrestling Revue	#8	Lou Thesz
Jan. 1965	Wrestling Illustrated	#5	Lou Thesz
Feb. 1966	Wrestling World	#4	The Crusher-AWA
April 1967	Wrestling World	#4	Verne Gagne-AWA
Nov. 1968	Sports Revue	#2	Verne Gagne - AWA
Aug. 1969	The Ring Wrestling	#5	Bruno Sammartino

— Associates Speak Out

WWE Hall of Famer Gerry Brisco, as a kid, remembers seeing the Bruiser on the cover of wrestling magazines. Brisco told the author, *"The Bruiser was a legend in the business."* WWE Hall of Famer and former NWA World heavyweight champion Dory Funk, Jr., elaborated on the Bruiser's legacy:

"Dick the Bruiser was a real athlete and really tough guy. In his own way, he created his image in wrestling, and it didn't come because he was a pansy. It came because he was Dick the Bruiser."

When WWE Hall of Famer "Luscious" Johnny Valiant gave his induction speech in 1995, he made a point to specifically thank Dick the Bruiser for giving him his first big break. Madd Maxx, who wrestled for the Bruiser during the leaner 1980s, said about Dick, "*Bruiser was a gentle giant who looked out for everybody.*"

Donna O'Donnell, widow of Chuck O'Donnell, Bruiser's long-time television producer and director, remembered their relationship:

> "*Chuck loved doing the show and had the greatest respect for Dick. Chuck felt Dick was a very generous and kind man. He was a good businessman and showman.*"

Robin Luce, daughter of Chicago wrestling promoter Bob Luce and lady wrestler Sharon Luce, has fond memories on how kindly Bruiser treated young people. Robin was a student athlete who received steady "that a girl" encouragement from the Bruiser.

Besides being a serious businessman, Dick the Bruiser also had a fully developed sense of humor. His co-workers remembered many funny incidents over the years. Promoter and wrestler Johnny Powers saw the Bruiser prancing around outside a dressing room, wearing nothing but a cowboy hat covering his private parts. Wrestler Les Thatcher recalls getting dressed at one of the venues in Indianapolis and gradually hearing the roaring sounds of an approaching motorcycle. Thatcher opened the door to find the Bruiser riding a motorcycle up and down the hallway.

Roger Kirby told a story of making a road trip with Bruiser and Wilbur Snyder. They stopped at a store to buy bread, cheese, and beer for the trip. Later on during the trip, Snyder began coughing and choking while eating a cheese sandwich. It seems the Bruiser, while making the sandwiches, didn't remove the sheets of wax paper between the cheese slices.

Luscious Johnny Valiant remembers a funny TV interview segment that Bruiser produced. The Bruiser called Japanese wrestler, the Great Saki, to step onto the set. The Bruiser asked Saki to remove his shoes and kneel into the shoes. The Bruiser then threw an overcoat across Saki's back and asked him to be a stand-in depicting a Japanese midget wrestler.

Mark Manson, wrestler and manager working for Bruiser and Snyder, remembers, "*Dick the Bruiser was a draw and that's the name of the game.*"

Sonny Rogers added, "*No question about it that Dick the Bruiser played a huge part in the history of professional wrestling around the world and will always be remembered as a true icon.*"

Canadian wrestler and promoter Johnny Powers remembers having constructive conversations with Bruiser in the mid-'60s when Powers was starting out as a young promoter:

> "*I grew to like the Bruiser because he was a forceful person. He was full of pomp and circumstance, but he told it as he thought it was. I had a lot of respect for the Bruiser. He was quite a creative dude with lots of original ideas. The wrestling business is made up of a whole cluster of various egos and circumstances.*"

Jose Martine, a long-time Bruiser loyalist, said, "*When Dick passed away, his wife called me a couple of times and said she had something for me. She was real nice. She gave me his weights.*"

Fellow wrestler Stan Lisowski, who knew Bruiser during the '50s, didn't know about Bruiser's death until decades after it happened during his interview with the author. Stan was really surprised: "*I'll be darned. He was the kind of guy I figured would live forever. He was tough. He wouldn't throw in the towel too easily.*"

— **Farewell**

Dick the Bruiser loved the wrestling business, knew of little else as a livelihood, and never fully retired as did many of his contemporaries. To quote one of young Bruiser's associates from Indianapolis, actor Peter Lupus said, "*If God wanted to create a professional wrestler, it would have been Dick the Bruiser.*"

Dick the Bruiser was survived by his wife Louise, his daughter Michelle, and his son Karl. On the day after his untimely death, Indianapolis anchorman Clyde Lee from WRTV-TV Channel 6 concluded the local newscast with these words: "*We are going to miss him.*"

We all certainly do miss Dick the Bruiser and we will never forget him.

PHOTO SOURCES

All photo rights owned by others but granted to the author for this project.

Actual photos images are not submitted with this copyright application as these original sources reserve ownership rights.

Richard J. Vicek
January 2015

(left) Author Richard Vicek
(right) The dangers authors face when interviewing professional wrestlers. Mad Dog Vachon puts the squeeze on Richard when asked a question he didn't like.

PHOTO GALLERY

210 • BRUISER: The World's Most Dangerous Wrestler

— DICK THE BRUISER —
THE WORLD'S MOST DANGEROUS WRESTLER

> William Franklin Afflis will entertain a group of friends at his birthday party on June 26th from 3 to 5 o'clock.

June 26, 1935

> William Franklin Afflis, former local boy, was graduated at Jefferson high school at Lafayette Thursday evening. He has enrolled at Purdue University for next fall. Among those who attended the commencement were his mother, Mrs. Margaret Afflis of Indianapolis, and Mr. and Mrs. Earl Clawson of Delphi.

June 5, 1947

> A pleasing halftime feature was the wrestling exhibition between huge Dick Afliss, 248, and Buddy Brooks, 218, who grunted, groaned and grimaced in true heavyweight tasslin' style. Affliss, the villain, roughed Broks, hero of the piece, around the mat for 10 minutes of rugged comedy.

January 28, 1951
Bruiser's first exhibition match

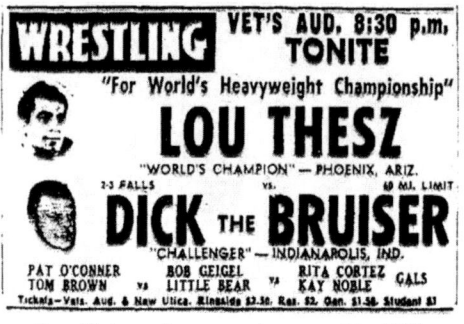

WRESTLING VET'S AUD. 8:30 p.m. **TONITE**
"For World's Heavyweight Championship"
LOU THESZ
"WORLD'S CHAMPION" — PHOENIX, ARIZ.
2-3 FALLS vs. 60 MI. LIMIT
DICK THE BRUISER
"CHALLENGER" — INDIANAPOLIS, IND.
PAT O'CONNER   BOB GEIGEL   RITA CORTEZ GALS
TOM BROWN vs LITTLE BEAR vs KAY NOBLE
Tickets—Vet's. Aud. & New Utica. Ringside $3.50. Res. $2. Gen. $1.50. Student $1

Des Moines, Iowa • January 11, 1965

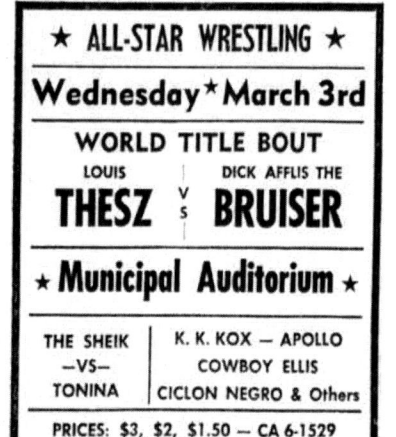

★ ALL-STAR WRESTLING ★
Wednesday ★ March 3rd
WORLD TITLE BOUT
LOUIS   DICK AFFLIS THE
THESZ v s **BRUISER**
★ Municipal Auditorium ★

THE SHEIK	K. K. KOX — APOLLO
—VS—	COWBOY ELLIS
TONINA	CICLON NEGRO & Others

PRICES: $3, $2, $1.50 — CA 6-1529

San Antonio, Texas
March 3, 1965

Photo Gallery • 211

— WILBUR SNYDER —
THE WORLD'S MOST SCIENTIFIC WRESTLER

Wilbur Snyder
University of Utah football
1950

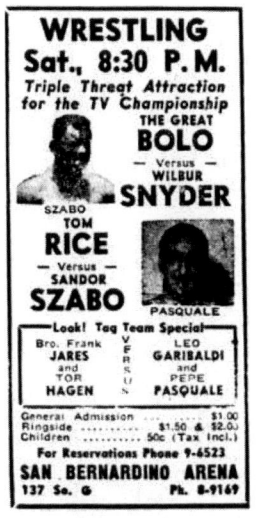

San Bernardino, CA
May 5, 1954

> The first newspaper reference found to Wilbur Snyder as a professional wrestler was in an excerpt from the March 22, 1953 *Independent Press-Telegram*, Long Beach, California
> *In two earlier bouts on the card ... Chris Zaharias will have a try at the darling of the bobby soxers, 240-pound Wilbur Snyder.*

St. Louis, Missouri • April 22, 1955

On the Road with Bruiser

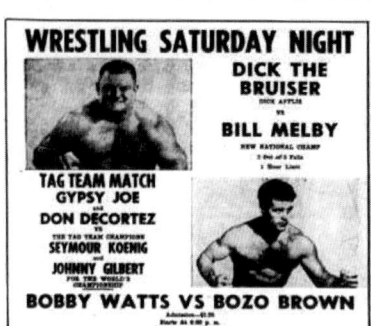

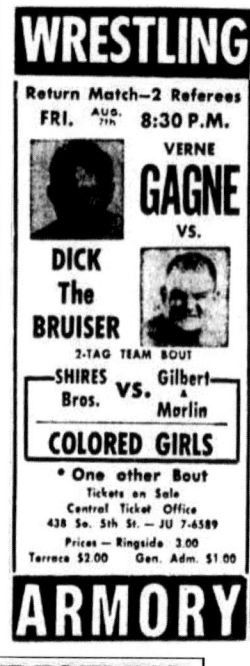

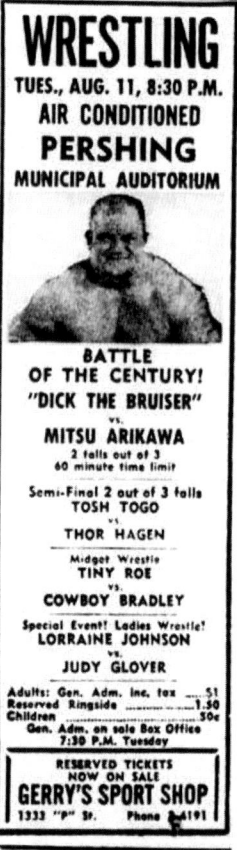

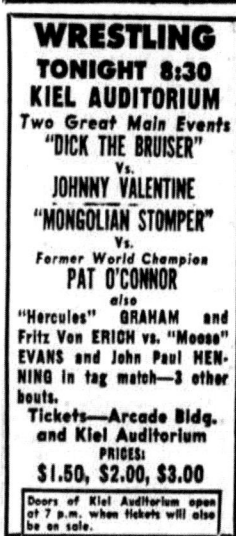

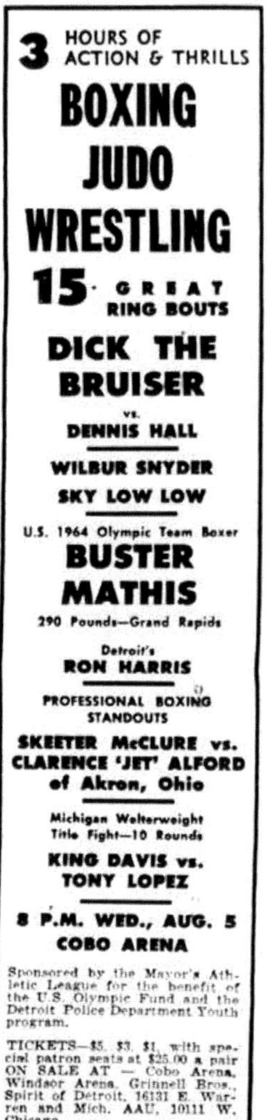

(top left, clockwise) Angola IN, June 9, 1956 • Louisville, Aug. 7, 1959 • Lincoln NE, Aug. 11, 1959 • St. Louis, Oct. 23, 1964 • Kansas City, Sept. 5, 1963 • Detroit, Aug. 5, 1964

Photo Gallery • 213

WRESTLING
TONITE (FRI.) 8:00 P.M.

ARCHIE MOORE
WORLD'S LIGHTHEAVYWEIGHT BOXING CHAMPION
Will Referee the Main Event

Dick the
BRUISER
U.S. CHAMPIONSHIP
VS.
ARGENTINA
ROCCA
OUTSTANDING CHALLENGER

Special Attraction
LEAPING LARRY
CHENE
vs.
BRUTE BERNARD

TAG TEAM BOUT
THE BRUNETTI BROS.
vs.
THE SHIRE BROS.

Yukon Eric vs. Cowboy Rocky Lee
Nick Bock vs. Dr. Bill Miller
Emil Dupre vs. Dan Miller

PRICES: $4, $3, $2 TAX INC.
Choice seats available at Olympia and Grinnell's

OLYMPIA

WRESTLING EXPO CENTER
SAT., OCT. 9TH
8:30 P.M.

BRUISER
VS
THE STRANGLER
(THIS BOUT WILL NOT BE ON TV)

BOUNTY HUNTERS VS SNYDER & MILLER

6 MORE BIG BOUTS

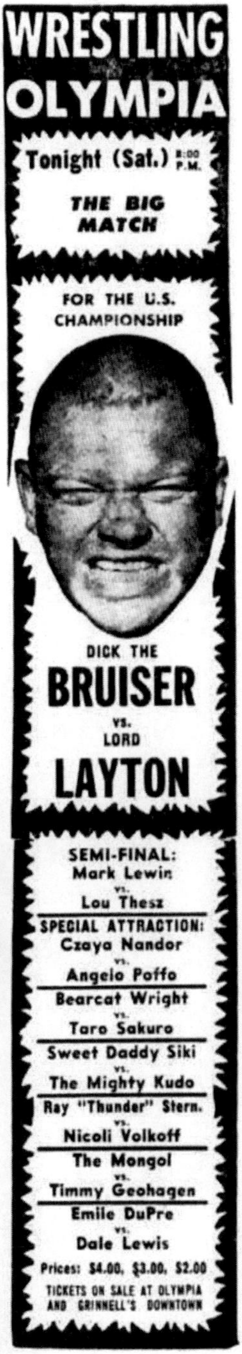

WRESTLING OLYMPIA
Tonight (Sat.) 8:00 P.M.

THE BIG MATCH

FOR THE U.S. CHAMPIONSHIP

DICK THE BRUISER
VS.
LORD
LAYTON

SEMI-FINAL:
Mark Lewin
vs.
Lou Thesz

SPECIAL ATTRACTION:
Czaya Nandor
vs.
Angelo Poffo

Bearcat Wright
vs.
Taro Sakuro

Sweet Daddy Siki
vs.
The Mighty Kudo

Ray "Thunder" Stern.
vs.
Nicoli Volkoff

The Mongol
vs.
Timmy Geohagen

Emile DuPre
vs.
Dale Lewis

Prices: $4.00, $3.00, $2.00

TICKETS ON SALE AT OLYMPIA AND GRINNELL'S DOWNTOWN

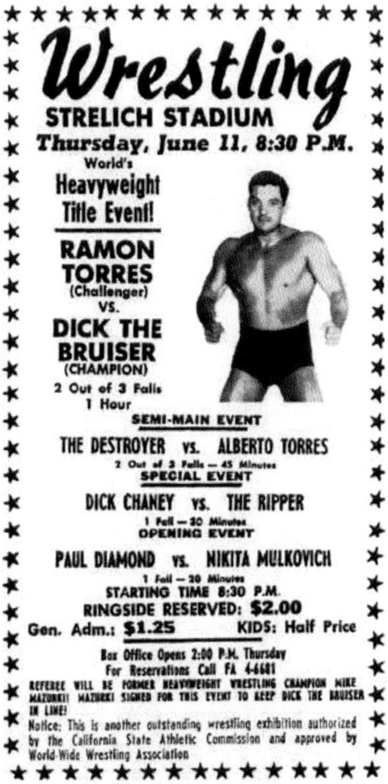

Wrestling
STRELICH STADIUM
Thursday, June 11, 8:30 P.M.

World's Heavyweight Title Event!

RAMON TORRES
(Challenger)
VS.
DICK THE BRUISER
(CHAMPION)
2 Out of 3 Falls
1 Hour

SEMI-MAIN EVENT
THE DESTROYER vs. ALBERTO TORRES
2 Out of 3 Falls — 45 Minutes
SPECIAL EVENT
DICK CHANEY vs. THE RIPPER
1 Fall — 30 Minutes
OPENING EVENT
PAUL DIAMOND vs. NIKITA MULKOVICH
1 Fall — 20 Minutes
STARTING TIME 8:30 P.M.
RINGSIDE RESERVED: $2.00
Gen. Adm.: $1.25   KIDS: Half Price

For Reservations Call FA 4-4681
Box Office Opens 2:00 P.M. Thursday

REFEREE WILL BE FORMER HEAVYWEIGHT WRESTLING CHAMPION MIKE MAZURKI. MAZURKI SIGNED FOR THIS EVENT TO KEEP DICK THE BRUISER IN LINE!

Notice: This is another outstanding wrestling exhibition authorized by the California State Athletic Commission and approved by World-Wide Wrestling Association

WRESTLING
EXPO CENTER
Mon., Oct. 23, 8:00 P.M.

$5000 Non-Interference Bond Posted by Heenan
No Disqualification Title Match

BLACK JACKS
vs.
BRUISER and CRUSHER

WORLD'S HEAVYWEIGHT CHAMPIONSHIP
Baron Von Raschke vs. 7'4"-450-lb. Rosanoff,
The Most Fantastic Wrestler of the Century

FARKAS and BEAST vs CLOUD and EAGLE
POFFO vs SNYDER   CHRISTY vs JARELS
DILLINGER vs LYNCH   HIGO vs ADONIS

SPECIAL
Each paid adult may bring in one child 12 years of age or under at half-price.
Adm. $5.00-$4.00-$3.00
Advance Tickets at Ross and Babcock, 109 S. Illinois
Ross & Young, Glendale
Watch All-Star Championship Wrestling
WRTV Channel 6, Sat. 1:30 p.m.
WTTV Channel 4, Sat. Nite 11:30

SPECIAL! Cowboy Bob Ellis vs. Heenan

Ross & Babcock Ticket Office Open Today 12 Noon-6 P.M.

(top left, clockwise) Detroit, Sept. 30, 1960 • Detroit, Dec. 29, 1962 • Bakersfield CA, June 11, 1964 • Indianapolis, Oct. 23, 1972

214 • BRUISER: The World's Most Dangerous Wrestler

(above) Vigo County Fair
Terre Haute, Indiana
August 16, 1962

(top right) Detroit, Feb. 26, 1972

(right) Indianapolis, Sept. 16, 1972

(below) July 30, 1990 TV listing

7:00 P.M. ⑳ — **Indiana Tonight.** Scheduled: Karen Grau talks with Dick the Bruiser.

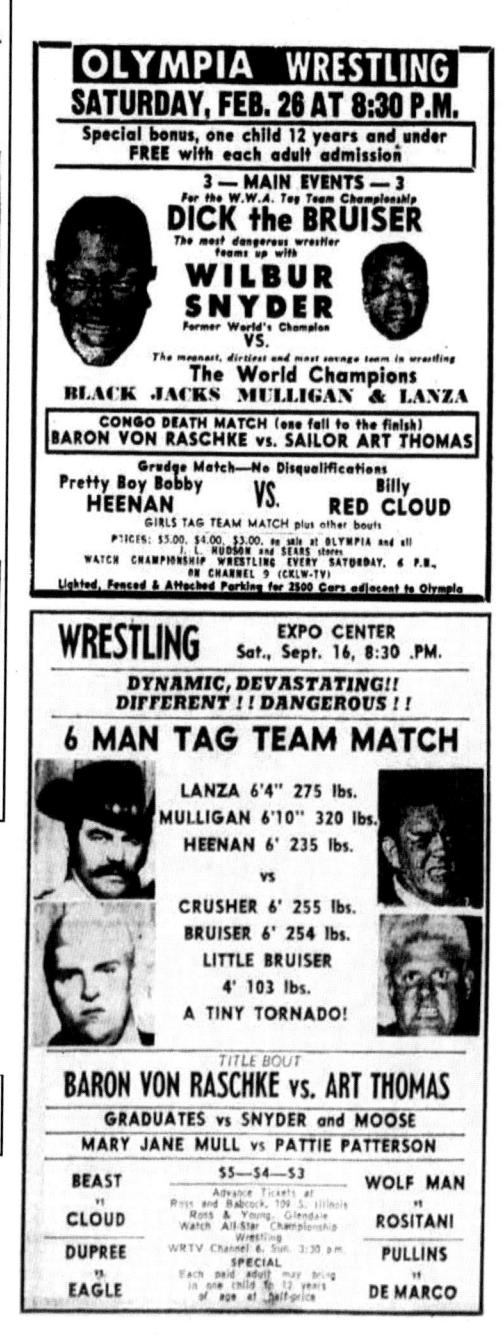

Opposite page --
Bruiser got multiple main event shots in St. Louis against every NWA world champion except Giant Baba, Tommy Rich, and Dusty Rhodes.
(top left, clockwise) April 26, 1963 • March 15, 1968 • Jan. 9, 1970 • March 20, 1981 • April 23, 1976 • Jan. 3, 1975 • (vs. Ric Flair, June 12, 1982, see page 186)

Photo Gallery • 215

Bruiser in St. Louis

WRESTLING TONIGHT 8:30 KIEL AUDITORIUM
Lou **THESZ**
World Champion
Vs.
"THE BRUISER"
Also
Hanning and Valentine
Vs.
Von Erich and Stasiak
in tag match—
4 other bouts
TICKETS—Arcade Bldg. and Kiel Auditorium
PRICES—$1.50, $2.00, $3.00, $4.00
GEneva 6-4400

WRESTLING TONIGHT 8:30
World Champion
GENE KINISKI
Vs.
"DICK THE BRUISER"
PAT O'CONNOR—Referee
also
Tag Match and 5 other bouts
TICKETS—Arcade Bldg. and Kiel Auditorium
PRICES—$1.50—$2.00—$3.00—$4.00
Doors of Auditorium open 7 p.m. tonight when tickets will also be on sale.

WRESTLING TONIGHT 8:30 KIEL AUDITORIUM
World title match
Dory Funk Jr.
(World Champion)
Vs.
"DICK THE BRUISER"
(Challenger)
also
6 other bouts including 6 man tag match
TICKETS—Arcade Bldg. & Kiel Auditorium
PRICES
$1.50 · $2.00 · $3.00 · $4.00

TONIGHT ... 8:30 KIEL AUDITORIUM WRESTLING
World Champion
JACK BRISCO
risks the title, gold belt against
DICK "THE BRUISER"
FUNK JR. & BRAZIL vs. HAYES & RACE ... 4 more bouts, incl. 6-man tag match
TICKETS: Arcade Bldg., Kiel Auditorium
PRICES: $2, $3, $4, $5
Phone: 436-4400, 231-7487

TONIGHT — 8:30 WRESTLING KIEL AUDITORIUM
World Champion
TERRY FUNK
Vs.
DICK THE BRUISER
MISSOURI CHAMPION
RACE vs. BACKLUND
O'CONNOR & TAYLOR
vs.
LANZA & RASCHKE
midget tag bout
3 more matches
Funk
Tickets: Arcade Bldg. Kiel Auditorium
PRICES: $3, $4, $5, $6
436-4400   231-7487

For the Gold Belt WRESTLING TONIGHT — 8:30 KIEL AUDITORIUM
World Champion
HARLEY RACE
Vs.
DICK THE BRUISER
Murdoch & Raschke Vs. O'Connor & David Von Erich ...
Plus 5 more exciting bouts
TICKETS: Arcade Bldg.; Kiel Auditorium
PRICES: $3, $4, $5, $6, $7
Telephones: 436-4400
361-6870

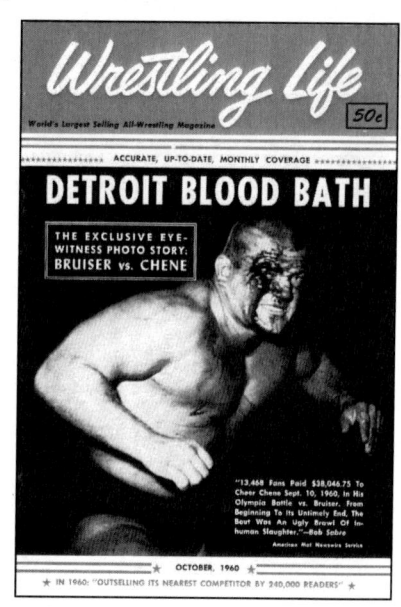

216 • BRUISER: The World's Most Dangerous Wrestler

May 1957

October 1960

DICK, THE BRUISER
Wrestler Afflis Is So Mean He Grosses $100,000 a Year

Headline for a nationally syndicated article
February 11, 1964

Columbus IN, May 1969

Columbus IN, August 11, 1985

Photo Gallery • 217

Vic, Dixie & the Band

Sportsarama Show
(FEATURING TV STARS)
Vic "The Bruiser" and Ada Ash

ADA ASH
the strong lady
SHE WRESTLES ALLIGATORS
She Has Appeared On
"You Asked For It"
"What's My Line"
and "I've Got A Secret"

VIC "THE BRUISER"
the WRESTLING BEAR
(Undefeated)

ALSO FEATURING
AL SZASZ, Professional Wrestler, Chuck Reilly, Professional Boxer & Flamo, the fire eater.

Appearing Nightly—SEPT. 10th thru 15th
on the Midway, at the Kettle River Grounds

Vic the Bruiser
Edwardsville IL, Sept. 11, 1962

Hello Dolly
Detroit's Unique Fun Spot
Presenting The
"DOLLIES FOLLIES"
Continuous 2 P.M. to 2 A.M.
Don't Miss Our LATE SHOW
Featuring
★ ZORO THE UNKNOWN
★ MIGHTY MITE
★ BONES McGINITY
★ DIXIE THE BRUISER
BEHIND THE BAR SUZIE WONG and THE STAR HAIFA

LUNCHEONS DAILY TIL 6 P.M. | OPEN 7 NIGHTS A WEEK
8350 SECOND   Phone 871-2300

Dixie the Bruiser
Detroit MI, Nov. 15, 1965

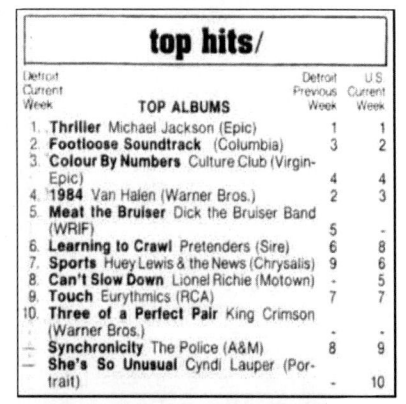

---

top hits/

	Detroit Current Week	TOP ALBUMS	Detroit Previous Week	U.S. Current Week
1.		Thriller Michael Jackson (Epic)	1	1
2.		Footloose Soundtrack (Columbia)	3	2
3.		Colour By Numbers Culture Club (Virgin-Epic)	4	4
4.		1984 Van Halen (Warner Bros.)	2	3
5.		Meat the Bruiser Dick the Bruiser Band (WRIF)	5	-
6.		Learning to Crawl Pretenders (Sire)	6	8
7.		Sports Huey Lewis & the News (Chrysalis)	9	6
8.		Can't Slow Down Lionel Richie (Motown)	-	5
9.		Touch Eurythmics (RCA)	7	7
10.		Three of a Perfect Pair King Crimson (Warner Bros.)	-	-
—		Synchronicity The Police (A&M)	8	9
—		She's So Unusual Cyndi Lauper (Portrait)	-	10

(bottom right) Dick the Bruiser Band
Detroit MI, April 1, 1984

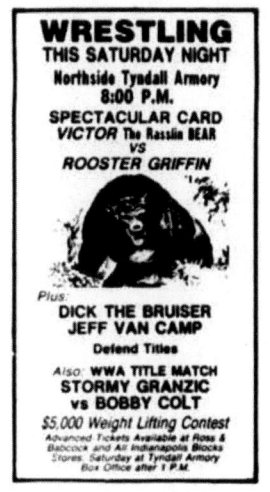

WRESTLING
THIS SATURDAY NIGHT
Northside Tyndall Armory
8:00 P.M.
SPECTACULAR CARD
VICTOR The Russian BEAR
VS
ROOSTER GRIFFIN

Plus:
DICK THE BRUISER
JEFF VAN CAMP
Defend Titles

Also: WWA TITLE MATCH
STORMY GRANZIC
vs BOBBY COLT
$5,000 Weight Lifting Contest

Advanced Tickets Available at Ross & Babcock and All Indianapolis Blocks Stores. Saturday at Tyndall Armory Box Office after 1 P.M.

Indianapolis, Feb. 18, 1984

SPORTS FINAL
with MILT HOPWOOD
MON. - FRI. at 11 p.m.

Milt is no match for Dick the Bruiser in the ring but his ringside interviews plus wide sport coverage make "must" listening for all sports fans.

WATCH LIVE WRESTLING THURS.
9:30 p.m. on ch. 9

CKLW radio 80

Ad for Windsor, Ontario

Indianapolis, Indiana • August 30, 1975
Dick the Bruiser & The Crusher vs The Legionnaires w/mgr. Johnny Starr
(top) Bruiser gets ready to lay one in on Zarinoff Lebeouf
(center) Bruiser controls Rene Goulet
(bottom) Bruiser pulls Starr into the ring

Photos by Scott Teal

Bruiser & Crusher

1977
Source: Scott Romer

Indianapolis, 1967
Source: Rick Johnson

Crusher & Chuck Marlowe • Indianapolis, 1966
Source: Rick Johnson

220 • BRUISER: The World's Most Dangerous Wrestler

The Sheik vs. Dick the Bruiser • Chicago Comiskey Park, 1974
Source: William Ondecko

Detroit, 1973
Source: Brian Bukantis
Copyright Arena Publishing

Comiskey Park, 1974
Source: William Ondecko

Photo Gallery • 221

Winnipeg, Manitoba
Source: Terrance Machalek

**Minneapolis, 1988
Final show at Auditorium**
Source: George Schire

The classic confrontation: Heenan vs. Bruiser • 1973
Source: William Ondecko

222 • BRUISER: The World's Most Dangerous Wrestler

Milwaukee, 1972

Source: David Maciejewski

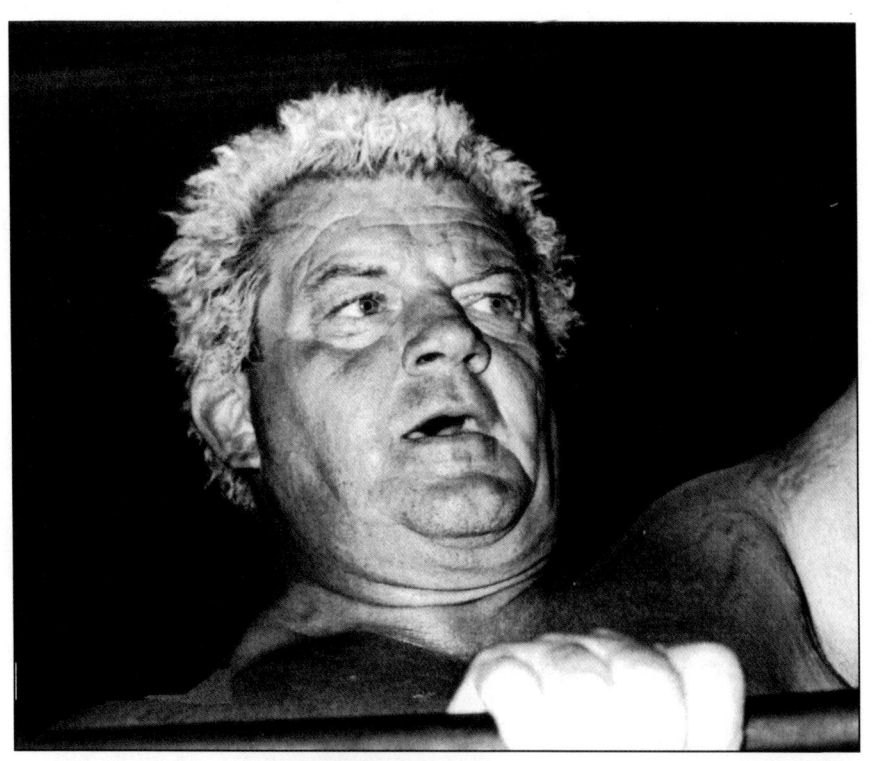

Photo Gallery • 223

Lombard, Illinois spot show, 1979
Source: Glen Rylko

Milwaukee, 1971
Source: David Maciejewski

Bruiser under a mask vs. The Strangler
1977
Source: Scott Romer

224 • BRUISER: The World's Most Dangerous Wrestler

Dick the Bruiser at home
Indianapolis, 1963
Source: Russ Leonard

March of Dimes Telethon
Indianapolis, 1979
Source: Scott Romer

Autograph seekers in Delphi, 1988
Source: Delphi News

Photo Gallery • 225

Quiet dinner at home, 1985
Source: Scott Romer

Bruiser & his pet goat, 1965
Source: Holladay family

Missouri State heavyweight champion 1982
Source: Roger Deem

Dick the Bruiser & Wilbur Snyder, partners inside the ring and out
Source: Scott Romer

Photo Gallery • 227

The scars of battle, 1983
Source: Scott Romer

Weekend bout provided time for reunion

Galionite a former classmate of wrestler

While professional wrestling didn't attract as many fans to Heise Park Stadium Saturday night as organizers had hoped, it did give one Galion resident a chance for a reunion with the show's star attraction.

Jan Shuck, 217 S. Union St., said she remembers Dick the Bruiser from her 1947 graduating class at Jefferson High School in Lafayette, Ind., and asked him to sign her yearbook after the matches. But when he signed her yearbook 40 years ago, rather than scribbling "Bruiser" as he did Saturday night, the wrestler wrote his given name, William Afflis.

Noting that she hadn't seem him since graduation, Shuck said she wasn't surprised that the Bruiser didn't seem to recognize her.

"We didn't run in the same crowds in high school. I was in music and he was in sports," she said, adding, "I always remember him as being friendly."

OLD CLASSMATES, Jan Shuck, 217 S. Union St., gets Dick the Bruiser to autograph her Jefferson High School yearbook from 1947, which is the year the two graduated from the Lafayette, Ind., school. When he first signed the yearbook 40 years ago, he penned the name William Afflis, but this time Shuck said he just scribbled "Bruiser."

INQUIRER PHOTO/MITCH CASEY

Wrestling fair dates in Ohio, 1987
Source: Inquirer, Galion OH

INDEX

AAU Junior Olympics, 16
Albright, Gary, 64, 142-154
Abel, Sid, 83
Aberson, Roy, 16
Afflis, Alma (aunt), 18
Afflis, Elizabeth Darrah (second wife), 36-37
Afflis, Gwendolyn (aunt), 18
Afflis, Judith (daughter with first wife), 32
Afflis, Julius (paternal grandfather), 18
Afflis, Karen (daughter with second wife), 37
Afflis, Karl (son), 113, 183, 196, 208
Afflis, Karl (uncle), 18
Afflis, Louise Iacomo (third wife), 104, 107, 164, 203-204, 208
Afflis, Margaret Louise (mother), 18-20, 22-26, 32, 36-37, 89, 104, 131-132
Afflis, Patricia Ann Cave (first wife), 32
Afflis, Walter William (father), 18-19, 22, 24, 132
Ali, Muhammad, 176-177
Allbright, Steve, 138
Allerdice, James, 23
Ambler, Donald, 27
Amelia, Afflis (paternal grandmother), 18
Anderson, Arn, 202
Andre the Giant, 155, 175-176, 186, 200
Andrews, Tom, 171
Arakawa, Mitsu, 131, 134-136, 165
Assassin #2 (see Hill, John Steele)
Atkins, Fred, 47
Atkison, Ethel (aunt), 18, 131
Atkison, Frank (maternal grandfather), 18
Atkison, Harriet (maternal grandmother), 18
Atkison, Margaret (see Afflis, Margaret Louise)
Austin, Buddy, 140
Axman, Dick, 123, 127
Baer, Barbara Condra, 24
Baier, George, 198
Baker, Ox, 97, 147, 171-173, 187
Barfield, Danny, 63

Barnett, Jim, 16, 49, 52, 68-70, 73-74, 76-77, 79, 81-83, 87, 92, 97, 114-115, 129, 146, 167, 180
Barry, Al, 43
Barth, Benny, 22
Bastien, Red, 141-142
Bauer Rob, 68, 72, 77-78, 199
Bauer, Jack, 52
Baxter, George (Mert), 36
Beauchene, Donna, 77
Berlin, Irving, 168
Bernard, Brute, 68
Beyer, Dick, 51, 74, 100, 113-114, 133-134, 138
Big K, The (see Kowalski, Stan)
Big Whiz, The, 196
Birch, Reginald, 19
Black Gordman, 140
Black Scorpion (see Flair, Ric)
Blackbourn, Lisle, 43
Blackwell, Crusher Jerry, 186, 190
Blanchard, Joe, 73, 112, 115
Blassie, Freddie, 100-101, 107-110, 113, 123, 149, 177
Blazer, Mike, 44
Blears, Lord James, 68
Blickman, Adolph, 22
Bockwinkel, Nick, 174-176
Bold Eagle, Bobby (see Boyer, Bob)
Bowser, Paul, 60
Boyer, Bob, 152, 165, 167
Bradshaw, Joann, 19
Brady, Patrick, 33, 40, 41
Brazil, Bobo, 73, 78-80, 91, 112, 126, 140, 147-148, 164, 183
Brickhouse, Jack, 48
Brisco, Gerry, 139, 173, 206
Brisco, Jack, 173, 176
Brody, Bruiser, 179-182, 193
Brody, King Kong (see Brody, Bruiser)
Brooks, Bob, 157
Brooks, Buddy, 33-35, 42
Brooks, Killer, 158
Brown, Bulldog Bob, 133, 187

Brown, Catherine, 92
Brown, Joe E., 42
Brucato, Angelo, 30
Brunetti, Joe, 73, 74
Bruns, Bobby, 85
Brunzell, Jim, 190, 194
Buck, Gordy, 27
Buck, Jack, 95
Bukantis, Brian, 149, 159
Burnett, Frances Hodgson, 19
Burzynski, Dave, 148-149, 158
Butsicaris, James, 83-84, 86
Cagney, James, 69
Calhoun, Haystacks, 73
Calypso Jim, 199
Campfield, Herbert, 28
Cannon, Crybaby George, 148
Carmichael, Hoagy, 30
Carnera, Primo, 58
Carolan, James, 83, 87, 148
Carpentier, Edouard, 60, 62-64, 100, 133
Carson, Craig, 196
Cernandes, Ramon, 42
Chene, Larry, 73, 77
Chief Big Heart, 63
Chief Lone Eagle, 109
Cholak, Moose, 109, 112, 122-123, 126, 129, 131, 137, 152, 174, 183
Christy, Paul, 106, 152, 183-184
Claw, The (see Andrews, Tom)
Clawson, Herbert, 19-20
Cliff, Buddy Lee, 127
Cobb, Ty, 34
Colt, Bobby, 196
Colt, Chris, 138
Condon, David, 145, 156
Cooke, Jack Kent, 140
Cooper, Allan, 115
Cortez, Hercules, 142
Cortez, Ricky, 73
Cosell, Howard, 176-177
Costas, Bob, 185
Costello, Al, 148, 158
Coulon, Johnny, 58
Craig, Della Herr, 20
Craig, George, 36
Crawley, Marion, 25
Creachman, Eddie, 166, 196
Creechman, Saul (see Romer, Scott)
Crusher, The (see Lisowski, Reggie)
Curry, Bull, 111, 148
Curry, Fred, 148
Daley, Art, 38

Dangerously, Paul E., 201-202
Dark Angel, The, 199
Darrah, C.T., 37
Davis, Russ, 49, 59,
Davis, Wee Willie, 99
DeCero, Sam, 197, 207
Deem, Roger, 147, 185, 186
Delvecchio, Alex, 82
DeMoss, Bob, 29
Dempsey, Jack, 58
DePaolo, Ilio, 47
DeRusha, Al, 126
Destroyer, The (see Beyer, Dick)
DiBiase, Ted, 187, 200
Dickey, Louis, 42
Dillinger, Frank (see McMullen, Kenny)
Dillinger, Jack (see Kalt, Don)
Dillinger, John, 136
Dillinger, Ken (see Russell, Ken)
Dobratz, Ron, 122-123
Dolly, Dennis (see Hall, Dennis)
Dolly, Roger (see Kirby, Roger)
Don the Bruiser (see Manoukian, Don)
Donovan, Art, 34
Douglas, Kirk, 17
Doyle, Johnny, 16, 68-70, 73, 76-77, 79, 81-83, 87, 91
Dr. X (see Beyer, Dick)
Dromo, Bill, 85
Duk, Kim, 165
Duncum, "Bad Boy" Bobby, 175-176
DuPre, Cherie, 64-65
Dupree, Emile, 93
Dupree, Mike (see Parsons, Chris)
Eagle, Don, 73
Eaton, Aileen, 99
Eaton, Cal, 99
El-Kaisee, Sheik Adnan, 200
Ellering, Paul, 194-195
Elliott, Pete, 31
Ellis, Cowboy Bob, 16, 73, 76, 80, 89-92, 94, 107, 112, 114, 140-141, 160, 165, 171-172
Elmore, Dorothy, 132
Elson, Bob, 146
Estes, Balk, 16, 97-99, 114-115, 146, 167-168
Estes, William, 99
Evans, Moose, 95, 124
Fabulous Freebirds, The, 15
Fabulous Kangaroos, The (see Costello, Al)
Fabulous Kangaroos, The (see Kent, Don)
Fabulous Moolah, 140
Fargo, Don (see Kalt, Don)

Fargo, Jackie, 122
Farhat, Ed Jr., 158, 160
Farhat, Ed, 51, 70, 82, 86, 88, 115, 140, 147-149, 151, 158-160, 164-166, 169, 180
Feldkircher, Bill, 30
Field, Bob, 25
Finks, Jim, 43
Flair, Ric, 15, 185-187, 201-202
Frazier, Bill, 107, 110, 115
Fredericks, Jack, 30
Fujara, Allan, 126
Fuller, Buddy, 122, 149
Funk, Dory Jr., 93, 116, 140, 148, 173, 187, 206
Funk, Dory Sr., 52, 115-116
Funk, Terry, 116, 173, 176
Gadaski, George, 140
Gadsby, Bill, 82
Gagne, Greg, 44, 127, 190, 194
Gagne, Mary, 127
Gagne, Verne, 13, 16, 31, 44, 47, 51, 54-56, 58-59, 64, 68, 73, 81, 91, 95, 115, 124, 126-129, 131, 134, 140-141, 145, 155-156, 159, 165, 174-176, 180, 190-191, 193, 195, 204
Garfield, Sir Alan, 47
Garogiola, Joe, 93
Geigel, Bob, 112, 133, 180, 187
George, Bill, 34
Gersh, Ed, 62-63
Giant Baba, 119, 139
Gibron, Abe, 29
Gillis, Joseph A., 84
Giroux, Lee, 42
Glick, Eddie, 55
Gluck, Herb, 83
Goddard, Danny, 91
Golden Lion, The (see Replogle, Tim)
Golden, Bobby, 109
Gomez, Pepper, 73, 147, 165, 180
Gonda, John, 33, 35
Goodish, Barbara, 181
Gordon, Ray, 85, 93
Gorgeous George (see Wagner, George)
Gotch, Karl, 14
Goulet, Rene 165, 170, 174
Goulet, Sgt. Jacques (see Goulet, Rene)
Grable, Betty, 125
Grabmire, Jim, 183
Graham, Dr. Jerry, 62, 63
Graham, Dr. Jerry, Jr. (see Jaffee, Jerry)
Graham, Eddie, 149, 180
Graham, Luke, 141, 149
Graham, Troy, 188
Great Saki, The, 207

Great Wojo, The, 195-197, 199, 201
Greene, Doc, 81, 86
Gudelsky, David, 84
Gulas, George, 180
Gulas, Nick, 145-146, 180
Gunkel, Ray, 27, 91, 171
Gusha, Rosella McCain, 19
Gypsy Joe, 13, 67
Hackenberg, Dick, 123
Hackenschmidt, George, 14
Halcomb, Tim, 96
Hall, Dennis, 107, 110, 116
Halleck, Charles Abraham, 25
Hamilton, Ralph, 113
Hampton, Reverend Tiny, 183
Hankins, Tom, 112
Hansen, Stan, 15
Hard Boiled Haggerty (see Stansauk, Don)
Hargitay, Mickey, 96
Hartley, Chad, 33
Hawk, Rip, 89
Hearn, Chick, 140
Heenan, Bobby, 13, 105, 118-119, 133, 135, 137, 146-147, 150-153, 155, 159-160, 163-168, 173-176, 185, 190, 200, 204
Heenan, Guy (see Hill, John Steele)
Hegstrand, Michael, 194-195
Heim, Johnny, 58
Helfand, Julius, 63
Hennig, Larry, 115, 124-126, 129, 131, 140-141, 155
Henning, Bulldog Lee, 116
Henning, John Paul, 89, 94
Hill, Carolyn, 112
Hill, John Steele, 112, 115, 119, 158, 176, 178, 183, 187
Hogan, Hulk, 13, 190, 200
Hogg, J.R., 196
Holcomb, Stuart, 29-30
Holladay, Dennis, 203
Holladay, Dr. L. J., 116, 203
Holladay, Thomas, 116, 203
Honky Tonk Man, the, 200
Hooded Hangman, The (see Big Whiz, The)
Hoover, Herbert, 18
Hornbaker, Tim, 104
Hornby, Fred, 62
Hornung, Paul, 83
Howe, Gordie, 82
Huber, Michael "Spike", 113, 177, 183, 187-190, 193, 195, 199, 208
Huber, Michelle (daughter with third wife), 177, 195, 204
Hudnutt, William, 89

Hull, J. Dan, 23
Humberto, Juan, 42
Humperdink, Sir Oliver, 125
Hunter, Rock, 85
Husar, John, 174
Hutton, Dick, 76
Inoki, Antonio, 139, 176-177
Irwin, Scott, 171
Jacobs, Andrew Jr., 205
Jacobs, Rudi, 95
Jaffee, Jerry, 70, 183, 196, 198-200
Jarrett, Jerry, 145-146, 188
Jay, Kenny, 176
Jeet Singh, Tiger, 148
Johnson, Kenneth, 91, 191
Johnson, Lyndon B., 131
Johnson, Marvin, 165
Johnson, Rocky, 148
Johnston, Leroy O., 36, 131
Johnston, Margaret A. (see Afflis, Margaret Louise)
Jonathan, Don Leo, 49, 81, 206
Jones, Tom (wrestler), 111
Junkyard Dog, The, 13
Justice, Ben, 158
Kace, Johnny (see Kakacek, John)
Kaess, Fred, 87
Kakacek, Anne, 89
Kakacek, John, 89, 147
Kaline, Al, 82
Kalmikoff, Ivan, 95
Kalmikoff, Karol, 95
Kalt, Don, 50, 103, 111, 136-138, 147, 165, 170, 174
Kamala, 188
Karasak, Al, 93
Karbo, Wally, 45, 142-143, 176
Karlson, Karl, 67
Karras, Alex, 83-84, 86-87, 100
Karras, Gust, 112-113
Karras, Louis, 31
Kass, Denny, 201
Kaufman, Andy, 190
Kelly, Cowboy Bob, 92
Kennedy, Edward M., 43
Kennedy, John F., 89, 131
Kent, Cashbox Jim, 178
Kent, Don, 148, 199
Kenyon, J Michael, 62
Kessler, Gene, 65, 167
Kevorkian, Jack, 198
Khrushchev, Krusher, 14, 198
King, J.B., 22

Kiniski, Gene, 111, 115-116, 128-129, 133, 167, 185-186
Kirby, Roger, 107, 110-111, 116, 183, 207
Kirkpatrick, Charles, 18
Klein, Lou, 68
Knafelc, Gary, 43
Kohler, Fred, 45, 47-49, 52-53, 58, 64, 103, 120-124, 126-127, 143
Koloff, Ivan, 14, 156, 178-179, 181, 198
Koloff, Nikita, 14
Kostas, Johnny, 47
Kowalski, Killer, 13, 47, 57, 73, 80, 91, 131
Kowalski, Stan, 45, 156
Kruskamp, Hardy, 114
Ladd, Ernie, 106, 126, 131, 140, 148, 157, 161-162, 171
Lafleur, Pierre, 171
Lake, Greg, 183
Lambeau, Earl (Curly), 38
Lancaster, Burt, 102
Lancaster, Jim, 158
Lane, Dick (football player), 83
Lane, Dick (TV announcer), 99
Lano, Dr. Mike, 100, 164
Lanza, Black Jack (see Lanzo, John R.)
Lanza, Cowboy Jack (see Lanzo, John R.)
Lanzo, John R, 47, 134-135, 150-151, 153, 156-157, 160, 164, 175-176, 183, 195
LaRose, Guy, 47, 50, 58-59, 66, 68, 73, 86, 123
Lattner, Johnny, 155
Laurinaitis, Joseph, 194
Lawler, Gary, 197
Lawler, Jerry, 197
Lawlor, Glenn (Jake), 33
Layton, Lord Athol, 82, 88, 148
Leader, Harry, 23
Leahy, Frank, 30
LeBell, Gene, 99
LeBell, Mike, 99, 140
LeBeouf, Zarnoff (see Lafleur, Pierre)
Lee, Clyde, 208
Lennon, Jimmy, 99
Lennon, Robert, 23
Lentz, George, 194
Lentz, George, 44
Leonard, Russell, 86, 96
Leone, Baron Michele, 58, 71, 81
Letterman, David, 185
Lewin, Mark, 86
Libby, Bill, 99
Liberace, 17
Light, Harry, 68
Lisowski, Larry, 190-191, 194, 198, 204

Lisowski, Reggie, 14, 51, 58-59, 73, 90, 95, 124-126, 129, 131, 133-134, 136-137, 139, 142-144, 152-153, 156, 157, 161, 164, 175-176, 179, 187, 190, 194-195, 198, 204, 206
Lisowski, Stan, 58-59, 92, 207-208
Little, Major, 86
Logan, Dick, 39
Lombardi, Vincent T., 38, 83
Longson, Wild Bill, 51, 85
Longstreth, Jack, 28
Louis, Joe, 58, 68
Love, Malcomb, 36
Love, Miss Bunny, 106, 183
Lubich, Bronco, 69, 73
Luce, Bob, 52-54, 77, 113, 126-128, 138, 142-143, 145-146, 155-156, 168, 172, 174, 187, 190, 204, 207
Luce, Don, 67
Luce, Robin, 138, 207
Luce, Sharon, 128, 207
Lujack, Johnny, 30
Lupus, Peter, 208
Lynch, Tom, 103, 113
Lyons, Red, 141
Magnum T.A., 15
Man Mountain Mike, 137
Managoff, Bobby, 67, 112
Manis, Gordon, 25
Mann, Bob, 39
Mann, Jack, 88
Manoukian, Don, 34, 40, 93
Mansfield, Jayne, 96
Manson, Mark, 150, 207
Marciano, Rocky, 58
Marino Tony, 158
Marker, Connie, 113
Markoff, Chris, 128, 135, 170
Marlowe, Chuck, 16, 17, 97, 98, 115, 149
Martel, Rick, 15
Martine, Jose, 207
Martinez, Luis, 140, 148
Marudas, Lou, 70
Marxson, Don, 127
Masked Strangler, The (see Hill, John Steele)
Matysik, Larry, 85, 89, 93-95, 133, 159, 177, 181-182, 185-187, 193
Maxymuk, John, 38
Mayslack, Stan, 47
Mazurki, Mike, 100
McClarity, Roy, 49
McClure, Buster, 40-41
McClure, Kelse, 173
McDaniel, Wahoo, 190, 200
McGraw, Rick, 188

McKenzie, Tex, 114
McKigney, Dave, 163
McLane, David, 189-191, 195
McMahon, Vincent K., 13, 177, 183, 191, 193
McMahon, Vincent Sr., 100, 129, 186
McMillan, Jim, 54, 55
McMullen, Kenny, 136-138
Meeker, Robert, 28
Meholic, Andrew Jr., 87
Meholic, Andrew, 84, 87, 148
Melby, Bill, 56-58
Menacker, Sam, 16-17, 69, 75, 91, 149, 155, 161, 165, 171, 181, 189
Mercurio, Mike, 113
Merrell, John, 28
Michalik, Art, 139
Mighty Igor, 148
Mil Mascaras, 140, 149
Miller, Bill, 34, 73, 86, 89, 103, 105, 112, 115
Miller, Dan, 103, 105
Mills, Dorothy Newell, 19
Mitchell, Art, 112
Mitchell, Guy (see Hill, John Steele)
Mitchell, Mad Man (see Hill, John Steele)
Mittman, Dick, 44, 47, 63, 84
Mollenkopf, Jack, 16, 31
Monroe, Sputnik, 160
Monsoon, Gorilla, 148
Moore, Archie, 77, 78
Morales, Pedro, 140
Morehouse, Max, 25, 27
Mosca, Angelo, 179, 181
Moto, Charlie, 99-100, 139
Moto, Dr., 136
Moto, Mr. (see Moto, Charlie)
Muchnick, Helen, 159
Muchnick, Sam, 44, 89, 93-95, 113, 159, 173-174, 177, 182, 185
Mulligan, Blackjack (see Windham, Bob)
Murdoch, Dick, 161, 180
Murray, Emerson, 181
Murray, Jim, 101
Mussolini, Benito, 101
Myers, Don, 66
Nagurski, Bronko, 45, 47, 94
Neilson, Art, 92
Neilson, Stan (see Lisowski, Stan)
Nomellini, Leo, 31, 40-42, 44, 73, 80, 200
North, Jay, 100
North, Mike, 150
Novak, David, 178
Novak, Jerry, 178
Novak, Kim, 65

Index • 233

O'Connor, Chuck (see Studd, Big John)
O'Connor, Pat, 14, 48, 73, 76, 81, 112, 115, 123, 126, 131, 149, 152, 173, 187, 201, 206
O'Donnell, Chuck, 207
O'Donnell, Donna, 207
O'Hara, Michael, 148
O'Neill, Marty, 134, 143
Oliver, Greg, 50, 76
Olofson, Phil (Phil Olaufson), 66, 113
Ondecko, William, 137, 155
Onita, Atsushi, 204
Orlich, Dan, 39-40, 41
Orndorff, Paul, 13
Orton, Bob, 192, 196
Parente, Lorenzo, 85
Parilli, Vito (Babe), 39
Parks, Reggie, 89, 94, 124
Parsons, Chris, 49, 97, 104, 114, 145, 152, 157, 159, 174
Patera, Ken, 185, 186, 190
Patterson, Ethel (see Atkison, Ethel)
Patterson, Pat, 140
Patton, Dick, 52, 67
Pazandak, Joe, 42, 44-45
Peppard, George, 28
Pesek, Jack, 47
Pfefer, Jack, 120-123, 126
Pickering, Carolyn, 87
Piper, "Rowdy" Roddy, 13
Plechas, Danny (Bulldog), 42, 43
Poffo, Angelo, 50, 58, 69, 73, 90, 92, 107, 115, 135, 148, 150-151, 180
Poffo, Lanny, 50, 70, 135, 180
Powers, Johnny, 207
Powers, Roy, 35
Presley, Elvis, 17
Price, Mel, 89
Pronovost, Marcel, 82
Pullins, Prince, 126, 152
Race, Harley, 115, 122, 124-126, 129, 131, 147, 173, 186-187, 196
Ramierez, Ricky, 122
Ramos, Bull, 140
Rasputin, Ivan, 49
Rechsteiner, Scott, 199
Red Cloud, Billy, 105, 152
Redbone, Leroy (see Afflis, Karl)
Regal, Steve, 113, 146, 154, 183, 188, 190, 191
Reidlinger, Dennis, 113
Renesto, Tom, 180
Replogle, Karl, 90

Replogle, Tim, 90, 131, 153, 184, 197, 199, 202-204
Rhodes, Dusty, 55, 161, 185
Rikidozan, 199
Ringo, George (see Sabre, Bob)
Ringo, Jim, 41
Road Warrior Animal (see Laurinaitis, Joseph)
Road Warrior Hawk (see Hegstrand, Michael)
Road Warriors, The, 15, 194-195, 197
Robertson, Dewey, 148
Robinson, Billy, 156, 165
Robustelli, Andy, 34
Rocca, Antonino, 13, 49, 59-60, 62-64, 73, 77-78, 80, 86, 91
Rockne, Andy, 40
Rogers, Buddy, 13-14, 51, 68, 142, 206
Rogers, Sonny, 192, 207
Roman, Rose, 53
Romer, Scott, 183, 189, 195-196, 202
Romero, Raoul, 73
Ronzani, Gene, 38, 41
Roosevelt, Franklin Delano, 22
Ross, Jim, 202
Rossi, Len, 48
Rote, Kyle, 34
Rozelle, Pete, 83
Russell, Ken, 150-151
Russian Brute, The, 199
Rylko, Glen, 162
Sabre, Bob, 124
Sammartino, Bruno, 100, 122, 156, 159, 164, 181, 206
Savage, Dutch, 133
Savage, Randy, 13, 50, 180, 200
Sawchuk, Terry, 83
Schakel, Ray, 23
Schire, George, 45, 95, 124, 200
Schmidt, Hans (see LaRose, Guy)
Schmidt, Joe, 83
Schnabel, Hans, 50
Schnaible, Dick, 23
Schnaible, Gale, 23
Schneider, Kurt, 69
Schricker, Henry, 22, 23
Schumacher, Max, 107-109
Schweitzer, Albert, 101
Sharkey, Eddie, 125, 193
Sheeketski, Joseph, 33, 35
Sheik of Araby, The (see Farhat, Ed)
Sheik, The (see Farhat, Ed)
Shibuya, Kinji, 47
Shire, Ray (see Stevens, Ray)
Shire, Roy, 73-74, 90, 93, 167

Shirk, Bill, 187, 188
Shoren, John, 113
Shortridge, Abraham, 22
Shortridge, Douglass, 191
Sigo, Lanny, 23, 31
Simmes, Charlie, 25
Simmons, Herb, 187
Skaaland, Arnold, 47
Slaughter, Sgt., 15
Smith, Charlie, 91
Smith, Richard, 19-20
Snyder, Cindy, 191
Snyder, Mike, 73, 98, 102, 109, 113, 123, 146, 165-166, 184, 189
Snyder, Shirlee, 104
Snyder, Wilbur, 16-17, 55-56, 58-59, 69, 70, 73, 76, 89, 91-92, 97-99, 101-104, 107-116, 123-124, 126-129, 131, 134-135, 137, 140, 145-146, 150-158, 160, 163, 165-167, 170-171, 173, 176, 180, 183-185, 189, 191, 193, 204, 207
Spinks, Betty, 201
Spinks, Leon, 201
St. Angelo, George, 132
Stansauk, Don, 34, 45, 47, 100, 140, 200
Starr, Handsome Johnny, 137, 165, 173, 184
Stecher, Dennis, 45
Stecher, Tony, 45
Steckler, William, 87
Steinborn, Dick, 73, 74
Steinborn, Milo, 73
Steiner, Scott (see Rechsteiner, Scott)
Stern, Ray, 82
Stevens, Ray, 73, 86, 90-91, 93, 167, 169, 175, 200
Sting, 201
Stomper, The (see Hill, John Steele)
Stram, Henry "Hank", 29
Strode, Woody, 100
Strongbow, Jules, 99, 100
Studd, Big John, 175
Sullivan, John L. (see Valiant, Johnny)
Super Maxx (see DeCero, Sam)
Sweetan, Bruiser Bob, 182
Switzer, Veryl, 39
Szulborski, Harry, 30-31
Teal, Scott, 34, 57, 62, 74, 80, 107, 133, 151, 159, 172, 174
Teetor, Jackson, 28, 32
Thatcher, Les, 105, 107, 207
Thesz, Lou, 13, 16, 44, 48, 51, 54, 56, 58, 81, 84, 86, 89, 91, 95, 128, 140-141, 173-174, 206
Thom, Billy, 51
Thomas, Art, 105, 112, 123, 126, 152

Tito, Richard, 143
Tolos, Chris, 148
Tomasso, Joe, 119
Torres, Alberto, 171
Truman, Harry, 26
Tunney, Gene, 58
Ullman, Norm, 82
Vachon, Butcher, 140-144, 155
Vachon, Mad Dog, 129-131, 140-144, 170
Valentine, Greg, 186
Valentine, Johnny, 114, 116, 122-123, 128, 130, 148
Valiant, Jerry (see Hill, John Steele)
Valiant, Jimmy, 160, 163-164, 176, 183
Valiant, Johnny, 102, 163-164, 183, 206
Vallee, Rudy, 40
Van, George E., 80
Vann, Bobby, 183
Venture, Jesse, 190
Volkoff, Boris, 110
Volkoff, Igor (see Lafleur, Pierre)
Volkoff, Ivan (see Frazier, Bill)
Volkoff, Nicoli, 107, 110
Von Brauner, Karl, 92
Von Brauner, Kurt, 92
Von Erich, Fritz, 73, 81, 86, 88-89, 95, 187
Von Raschke, Baron, 14, 105, 145, 148, 151, 157, 163, 169, 176, 198
Vonnegutt, Kurt, 22,
Wagner, George, 13, 16, 47, 64-65, 67, 73
Walcott, Joe, 122, 156
Walker, Jim, 202
Walton, Jeff, 97, 100, 140-141
Ward, Charles, 69
Watts, Cowboy Bill, 140-141
Wayne, Buddy, 80
Wayne, John, 186
Weingeroff, Saul, 147, 196
Wenzel, Harry, 95
Wepner, Chuck, 176
West, H.E. (Duke), 87, 102, 109
Westbrook, Dan, 141
White, Gordon S. Jr., 62
Wicks, Billy, 57
Willey, Norman, 25, 50
Wilson, Jack, 123
Wilson, Les, 202
Windham, Bob, 150-151, 153, 156-157, 160, 164
Wingo, Bob, 113
Witter, Tom, 28
Wolfe, Buddy, 176-177
Wooden, John, 28

Index • 235

Woolery, Agnew, 132
World Warriors, The, 197
Wright, Bearcat, 82
Wyness, Jerry, 33, 35-36

Yanetti, Paul, 60
Yohe, Steve, 100, 113
Yukon Eric, 13, 49, 69, 70, 72, 80-81, 92
Zatkoff, Roger, 41

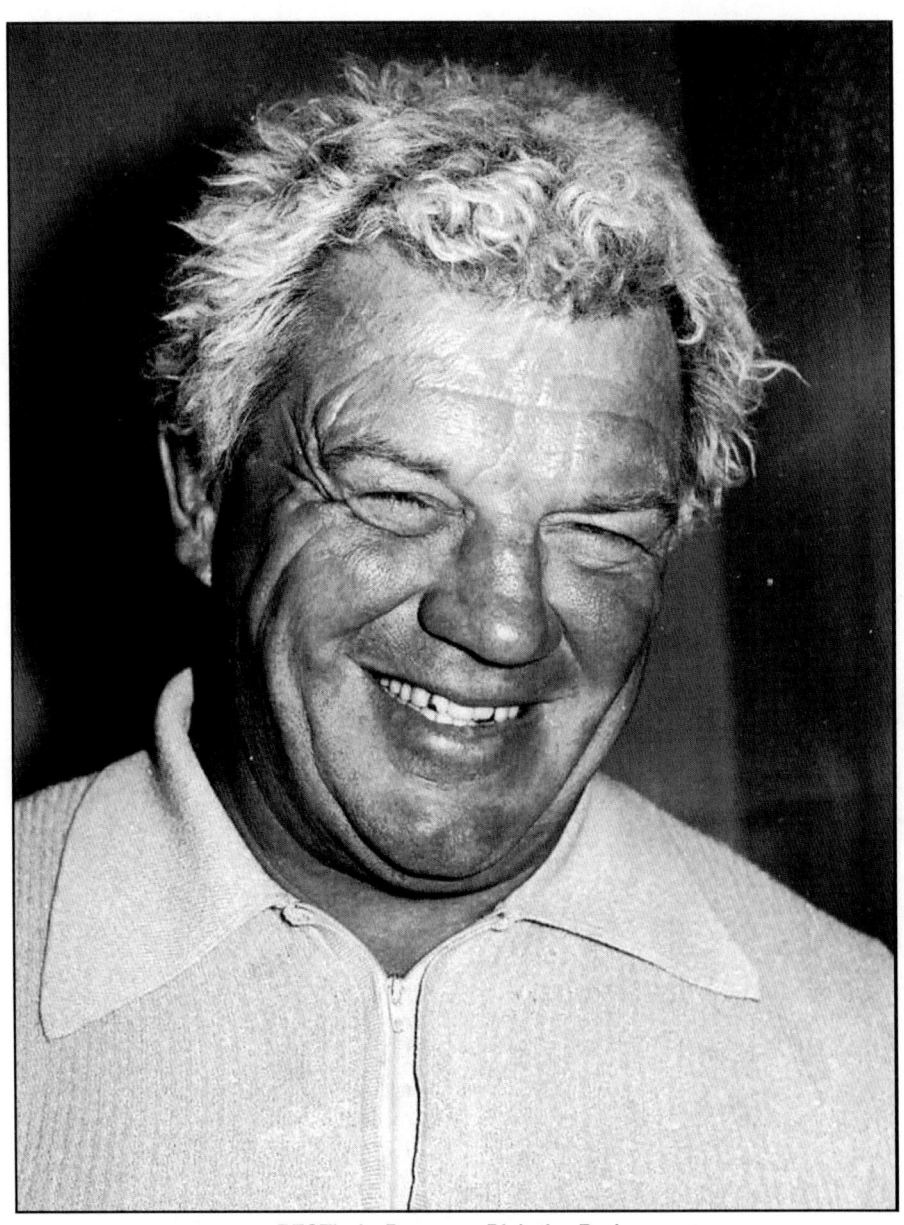

wRESTle in Peace • Dick the Bruiser

Source: Scott Romer

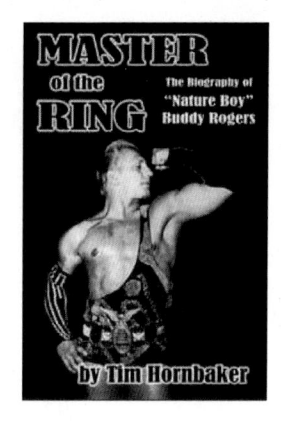

Also available from www.crowbarpress.com

— MASTER OF THE RING —
The Biography of "Nature Boy" Buddy Rogers
by Tim Hornbaker

In 1948, years before the "sports entertainers" like Hulk Hogan, Steve Austin, or "The Rock" were even born, a young man named Buddy Rogers went to the ring in Hollywood Legion Stadium and transformed pro wrestling forever. Billed as the "Nature Boy", Rogers, with his flambouyant personality and underhanded tactics, became an immediate box-office sensation. He was center stage everywhere he appeared, not only in fast-paced matches, but in backstage power plays.

By the late 1950s, he was an unparalleled superstar, but he had one honor yet to achieve ... the National Wrestling Alliance world heavyweight championship. To that point, the contentious environment of wrestling politics stalled his push to the ultimate throne, and only through experience did Rogers overcome the obstacles in his path until, finally, with friends in high places, he was given a title match against champion Pat O'Connor at Chicago's Comiskey Park before a record crowd of 38,000 spectators. By the end of the night, Rogers was the new heavyweight champion of the world! After the match, he strapped on the title belt and stood in the center of the ring, and in his typically arrogant fashion, announced: *"To a nicer guy, it couldn't happen!"*

Backstage assaults, injuries, and other events almost derailed his title reign, and in the midst of his historic run, Rogers suffered serious health problems, which as a cloud over his future on the mat. Since then, wrestling fans have asked countless questions about what really happened on that fabled evening. Author Hornbaker dissects the incident and answers those questions and clear up some of the misconceptions and lies told about Buddy.

— FLORIDA MAT WARS: 1977 —
by Robert D. VanKavelaar, with Scott Teal

"Florida Mat Wars: 1977" will take you back in time to a day when professional wrestling was king. Many of us remember waiting with anticipation for the newspaper to be delivered so we could check the sports page for the upcoming wrestling card or the results from the night before.

This volume contains all the known ads and results for 1977 that were published in the Florida territory, as well as feature articles, letters to the editor, and photo features that appeared in the newspapers in the days before professional wrestling became sports entertainment and no longer deemed worthy of being reported as a legitimate contest. Relive the memories through more than 900 newspaper clippings in "Florida Mat Wars: 1977."

TONIGHT! TONIGHT! TONIGHT!
by Bert Prentice & Scott Teal

Bert Prentice had a view of this business from a perspective that very few have ever had an opportunity to see. There is simply nothing he hasn't done in the business ... sold programs, set up rings, chairs and bleachers, sold tickets, ring announced, cooked hot dogs, cleaned the buildings, refereed, put out posters, produced countless hours of studio wrestling, managed, and on many occasions, wrestled midgets, women, and myself. Bert lived his life with absolutely no filter. Not many people get to do that. One of his favorite sayings was, "What other people think about me is none of my business," and he truly lived that mantra. In fact, his haters energized him to another level. It was an amazing thing to watch.

Bert was a master of promoting pro wrestling the old-school way. In fact, he could have taught the old-school promoters a thing or two about the nuts and bolts of getting butts into the seats.

If you're a fan of pro wrestling, you won't want to put this book down until you read it in its entirety.

— Jerry "The King" Lawler

Also available from www.crowbarpress.com

— RAISING CAIN: From Jimmy Ault to Kid McCoy —
by Frankie Cain & Scott Teal

"Antone Leone got John Swenski on the floor between the lockers and the bench and pounded on his head. Antone wasn't any kind of an outstanding wrestler, but he was on top, and Swenski couldn't move because he was wedged between the lockers and the bench. Of course, that's the way it always was. Anytime one of the wrestlers got into a scrap, it always wound up in a street-fight."

— **Frankie Cain**

If you ask any pro wrestler who plied their trade during the '50s and '60s who they consider to be the top minds in the wrestling business, invariably the name Frankie Cain will appear at the top of the list. Frankie has a keen recollection of things that took place in the wrestling business from the 1940s until wrestling evolved into what we know today as "sports entertainment."

But Frankie's story isn't only about his life as a wrestler. It's a fascinating journey that began when he was just plain Jimmy Ault, living on Depression-era streets of downtown Columbus, Ohio – learning hustles and cons from Gypsies, sleeping on rooftops, and selling anything he could – all simply to keep from starving. He came into his own and finally began to earn a decent living when prostitutes in Cherry Alley convinced him to work as their protector against the dangers they faced on the streets. Frankie, having fought on the streets almost every day of his young life, was born for the job.

Frankie tells about his discovery of pro wrestling and how he helped form the Toehold club, where young boys could mimic and learn the pro style. But it was his introduction to and training by tough shooter Frank Wolfe that set him on a path that would have him fighting in smoker clubs, athletic shows on carnivals, and eventually, pro wrestling. However, the majority of Frankie's early years were spent fighting on the road ... going into towns under assumed names and fighting ranked boxers. What his opponents didn't realize, though, was that he was there to "put them over," i.e. make them look good and give them a win to enhance their record. While they were trying to knock Frankie out, he was fighting back, but only enough to make it look like a real contest before he did what the promoters brought him there to do.

Frankie's story — presented in his voice just as he shared it with Scott Teal — will transport you back to a time of the true legends of both boxing and wrestling. Brutal, honest, and often hilarious, Raising Cain is an amazing look at the life and career of a self-made man who lived his life as none other.

— HOOKER —
by Lou Thesz, with Kit Bauman

Who was the greatest pro wrestler of the 20th century?

The debate is a real one among serious students of the sport. Like the arguments over any effort to crown "the greatest," "the best," or "the worst," that answer is unlikely to ever be resolved to everyone's satisfaction. One fact is indisputable, though. For those who watched wrestling before it became "sports entertainment," there is only one answer — Lou Thesz.

In the late 1940s and '50s, Lou Thesz was world heavyweight champion of the National Wrestling Alliance, and he carried those colors with dignity and class. "My gimmick was wrestling," he said, and it was evident to anyone who ever bought a ticket to see Lou Thesz that he was the real deal. Lou's book was one of the first published by a major wrestling star that discussed the business with candor from the inside.

This book contains pages and pages of new material — stories, anecdotes, and 215 classic photos — none of which has been published in any previous edition and all in the voice of one of the legendary figures of the game. Every sentence has been thoroughly combed over and vetted in order to answer any questions previously asked by readers, or to correct and/or re-order the "facts" as Lou recalled them, and each chapter now has detailed endnotes to supplement the text.

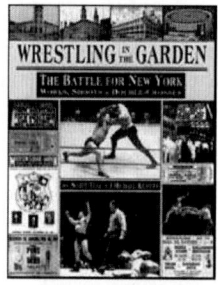

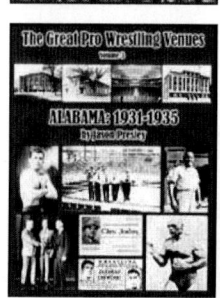

Also available from www.crowbarpress.com

This series, created by Scott Teal, features the most detailed books ever published on the history of specific wrestling cities and territories. Each volume contains a definite listing of every wrestling match we could find for each venue, illustrated with hundreds of images of program covers, advertisements, newspaper ads and headlines, and memorabilia. Also included, when available, are gate and attendance figures, match stipulations, and much more. These volumes represent an incredible amount of research that will be referred to over and over by both everyone.

v1 – Wrestling in the Garden, The Battle for New York
by Scott Teal & J Michael Kenyon

v2 – Nashville, Tennessee, volume 1: 1907-1960
by Scott Teal & Don Luce

v3 – Alabama: 1931-1935
by Jason Presley

v4 – Japan: The Rikidozan Years
by Haruo Yamaguchi, with Koji Miyamoto & Scott Teal

v5 – Knoxville, Tennessee, v1: 1905-1960
by Tim Dills & Scott Teal

6 – Amarillo, Texas, v1: 1911-1960
by Kriss Knights & Scott Teal

— **Fall Guys: The Barnums of Bounce** —
by Marcus Griffin, Annotated by Steve Yohe & Scott Teal

If you're like most people, who think professional wrestling was strictly "kayfabe" in the days before it morphed into "sports entertainment," then think again. In 1937, a book titled Falls Guys: The Barnums of Bounce was published. In the 215 pages written by sportwriter Marcus Griffin, the sport was exposed to the general public and the behind-the-scenes wheeling and dealing by promoters and wrestlers alike were brought to light. It was the first credible book ever published on the subject.

Fall Guys was, and still is, fascinating reading ... with one caveat. A great deal of the book was written by Griffin with an extreme bias for Toots Mondt ... his boss ... and against those whom Toots didn't like. It is filled with inconsistencies, contradiction, and ... yes, downright lies. Nevertheless, the book is the best resource of events that took place during that era, and wrestling scholars have used much of Griffin's writing as a launchpad for their own research.

That being the case, why would anyone want to read this book?

This is the annotated version, in which Yohe & Teal challenge Griffin's statements about events and correct errors that have been repeated through the years in other books and writings. They also add additional detail to the stories and the lives of the book's personalities.

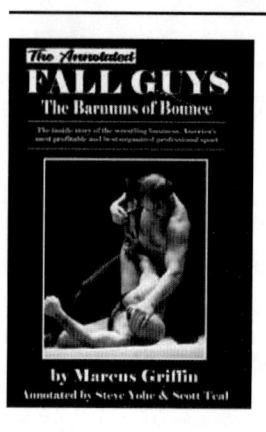